CHRIS JOHNSON &
JOLYON LESLIE

Afghanistan
The mirage of peace

Zed Books
LONDON · NEW YORK

Afghanistan: The mirage of peace was first published by Zed Books Ltd, 7 Cynthia Street, London N1 9JF, UK and Room 400, 175 Fifth Avenue, New York, NY 10010, USA in 2004.

www.zedbooks.co.uk

Cover designed by Andrew Corbett
Set in Monotype Dante and Gill Sans Heavy by Ewan Smith, London
Printed and bound in Malta by Gutenberg Press Ltd

Distributed in the USA exclusively by Palgrave Macmillan, a division of St Martin's Press, LLC, 175 Fifth Avenue, New York, NY 10010

A catalogue record for this book is available from the British Library. US CIP data are available from the Library of Congress.

ISBN 1 84277 376 3 cased
ISBN 1 84277 377 1 limp

Contents

Illustrations

Abbreviations

AIA	Afghan Interim Authority
ATA	Afghan Transitional Authority / Administration
ATTA	Afghanistan Transit Trade Agreement
CLJ	Constitutional Loya Jirga
ELJ	Emergency Loya Jirga
ISI	Inter-Services Intelligence (Pakistan intelligence service)
KhAD	State Intelligence Service (the Afghan equivalent of the Soviet KGB)
NGO	Non-governmental organization
PDPA	People's Democratic Party of Afghanistan
SFA	Strategic Framework for Afghanistan
SRSG	Special Representative of the Secretary General
UNAMA	United Nations Assistance Mission to Afghanistan
UNDCP	United Nations Drugs Control Programme (superseded by UNODCCP–UN Office of Drugs Control and Crime Prevention)
UNDP	United Nations Development Programme
UNHCR	United Nations High Commission for Refugees
UNOCHA	United Nations Office for Coordination of Humanitarian Assistance to Afghanistan
UNSMA	United Nations Special Mission to Afghanistan
UNTAET	United Nations Transitional Administration in East Timor
WFP	World Food Programme
WHO	World Health Organization

Glossary

arbab	local chief
burqa	loose garment with gauze patch over eyes, completely covering woman's body
charahi	road junction
haj	Muslim pilgrimage
hawala	customary system of money transfers
jerib	a measurement of land (about 0.195 hectares)
jihad	holy war
jirga	a tribal council (Pashtun) – see also *shura*
jui	water channel
karachi	handcart
karez	hand-dug underground water channel
khan	originally a title, customarily used for landed elite
kuchi	nomad
loya jirga	grand assembly or council
madrasa	Koranic school
mahram	male relative, as a companion to females
malik	local leader
muezzin	one who calls the faithful to prayer
mujahid	(pl. *mujahideen*) one who leads the faithful in holy war, or takes part in holy war
mullah	Islamic religious leader
pashtunwali	Pashtun tribal code
qawm	a kinship group, can be used at level of family, extended family, tribe, sub-tribe, etc.
sayyid	descendant of the Prophet
shabnama	night letter
shari'a	Islamic law
shura	village council (similar, though often not as formal in its constitution, to the *jirga*)
Shura e Nazar	Supervisory Council of the North
talib	(pl. *taliban*) a religious student
ulema	religious scholars or leaders
uluswal	district administrator
uluswali	district, as subdivision of province
usher	Islamic tax, one-tenth of crop

Preface

The idea for this book first emerged in August 2001 when we realized that between us we had lived in Afghanistan and witnessed the history of international engagement here since 1989 – an experience that seemed worth reflecting upon. Events since September 2001 have served to make the subject matter even more important, and of more global relevance.

During the fifteen years that we have known the country, Afghanistan has gone from being an occupied state to one ripped apart by factional fighting, and variously seen by the outside world as 'fragmented' or 'failed'. Then, under the Taliban, it was characterized as a 'rogue' state, a country beyond the pale. Finally, it became the state that the outside world wished to recast as the first success of American interventionism and the 'war on terror'.

The way in which both diplomacy was conducted and assistance given shifted with each stage of these changing characterizations of the country. The lives of Afghans changed dramatically during this period. Those who had always been poor, war pushed them to the edge of survival. Many of the urban middle classes were reduced to poverty, while others went into exile. There were also, of course, those who got rich on the spoils of war. This book tries to track some of these changes and what they have meant to people.

The West has often seen Afghans as a war-like and exotic people, sifting their perceptions through the lens of its own world-view. At times this bears little relation to how Afghans see themselves and their country. Historically this has always been so, but over the last quarter of a century global politics has further shaped the way in which Afghanistan has been seen, and how in turn assistance has been given and people's rights defended, or not. This book does not, however, set out to provide a detailed social and political history of the country, for others have already done that very ably. Instead, we have sketched enough of the historical outlines for the reader to make sense of the story, and provided references in the text and a select bibliography at the end for those who wish to explore further.

The book is not the result of any research project. Some of the ideas are certainly informed by research one or the other of us has done for other purposes, but mainly these come out of a reflection on our experience of living here as managers of aid projects, sometimes as analysts and policy advisers, but most of all as direct observers of history; of working with and watching the UN, donors and other agencies struggle with issues. Our ideas also come from having many Afghan friends, from endless journeys and of evenings discussing, debating and sharing the experience of war and the struggle for peace. We've tried to deepen that understanding by reading; about Afghanistan but also about other parts of the world with experiences different, and yet similar. If the book raises for the reader more questions than answers we will not be unhappy.

This book is the result of a shared process of writing in the course of which it has become impossible in many places to say which of us wrote what. Yet latterly there were periods when we worked together, most of our earlier experiences were separate, in time and place. Most of our first-hand experiences recounted, therefore, are those of one or the other of us, not both. Often it will be obvious to the reader which of us it was; for the rest we decided it didn't much matter.

The book would never have come into being without the many Afghan friends who have so generously shared their lives and their wisdom with us. Too many of them are no longer alive. We shall not even try to name them, not only because the list would be too long – and even then we would fear missing someone out – but also because the future of the country is still far from certain, and we do not wish to endanger anyone as a result of confidences and opinions that they have shared. For the same reason we have changed some names in the text. We will, however, remain for ever grateful for the way in which they have continues to enrich our lives. The failures of understanding, the omissions and the mistakes are, of course, entirely ours.

Kabul, 2004

Foreword

Afghanistan is not a well-understood country. This is something of a paradox, for a great deal of impressive scholarly work has been devoted to the analysis of its politics, economy and society, and events such as the Soviet invasion of December 1979 and the US overthrow of the Taliban in October–November 2001 earned it a prominent place in the headlines. Yet, all too often, Afghanistan is popularly depicted in terms of crude stereotypes – hirsute warriors, wild-eyed religious extremists, women consigned to the margins of social life. The complex realities of this exceptionally diverse territory have somehow not connected with its wider image. The course of events since September 11, 2001 has not greatly improved the situation. Now a different set of misleading images has been injected into the public realm, images which paint Afghanistan as an American success story, a threshold democracy, and a model of what the Bush administration's approach to 'nation-building' can achieve. Ordinary people comparing these images have every reason to feel thoroughly confused.

There are, of course, good reasons that help to explain the prevalence of simplistic impressions of Afghanistan. Fathoming the politics of remote countries is always a challenge. Many commentaries have been authored by transient media visitors whose brief has been to capture a little local colour rather than shed light on complexity. And some Afghan political leaders in their own interests have sought to exploit stereotypical images to win support. But perhaps the most important is that the course of events in Afghanistan over the last quarter of a century has given rise to a situation that cannot readily be analysed through the casual deployment of concepts or categories appropriate to less disrupted lands.

The most salient feature of this situation is the break-up of the state. After the communist coup of April 1978, the Afghan authorities lost much of their capacity to raise revenues from domestic sources; and after the Soviet invasion, the Afghan state was substantially dependent on resources supplied by the USSR, amounting to an artificial life-support system. With the disintegration of the Soviet state, this aid-flow ceased, and the Afghan communist regime collapsed less than four months later. Its successors inherited only the shadow of a state, with compromised legitimacy and limited administrative capacity. Thus, Afghanistan's challenge has been far greater than that of shaping a government. It is that of rebuilding the state, and establishing its position as the dominant power within Afghanistan's boundaries. There are few precedents on which one can draw to map out a path that Afghanistan should take, and certainly no magic solutions to its problems.

When the state breaks up, other authority centres typically emerge to discharge some of the functions that the state would normally perform. Some win significant local support; others claim symbolic legitimacy on the basis of the roles they undertake, defending communities and interests from external threats. To posit 'democracy' as the only conceivable source of legitimacy in such circumstances is to overlook the intensification of local bonds and the erosion of the willingness to trust strangers, both features of social interaction that one can expect to find when confidence in the state has been severely weakened. But as well as legitimate local authority centres, state break-up also fosters the entrenchment of a range of distinctly unappetising forces: predatory, extractive 'warlords'; drug traffickers; even terrorists. All have some interest in acting as 'spoilers', in blocking the re-establishment of an effective state, and some may flourish with support from state and non-state actors in neighbouring countries, highlighting the transnational character of the problems with which disrupted states can be confronted.

Afghanistan also runs the risk of being forgotten. The sad tale of its efforts to secure reconstruction assistance highlights the problem. In Tokyo in January 2002, it received substantial pledges of assistance, but as of November 2003, only US$112 million of reconstruction projects had actually been completed. It was in the light of this failure that a further meeting took place in Berlin on 31 March and 1 April 2004. In preparation, the Afghan government provided a detailed programme entitled Securing Afghanistan's Future which pointed to some key areas of need. The central conclusion of the report was that 'Afghanistan will require total external assistance in the range of US$27.6 billion over 7 years on commitment basis. A minimum of US$6.3 billion of external financing will be required in the form of direct support to the national budget – preferably more, since budget support helps build the State and its legitimacy.' At the conclusion of the meeting, a 'Berlin Declaration' was published, welcoming the commitments made at the conference. Unfortunately, these amounted to only $8.2 billion for the period March 2004–March 2007, and $4.4 billion for March 2004–March 2005. The Afghan government had little option but to welcome this result, but given the compelling case it had constructed for greater assistance, the outcome was deeply disappointing. In the light of Iraq, Afghanistan is yesterday's conflict. As I wrote in early 2002, the 'War on Terrorism and the hunt for Bin Laden put Afghanistan on the front pages. It will soon be off them.' Yet a powerful lesson of September 11 is that it rarely pays to neglect Afghanistan. If we do, we should not send to know for whom the bell tolls.

These issues are vital to the future of Afghanistan. They are also the central concern of this book.

Chris Johnson and Jolyon Leslie are superbly placed to reflect on these issues. I first met Jolyon Leslie at Bagram airbase, north of Kabul, in the mid-1990s. Khwaja Rawash airport in Kabul was closed for security reasons, and he had driven the then head of the United Nations Special Mission to Afghanistan, Mahmoud Mestiri, to Bagram so that he could leave the country. I managed to hitch a ride back to Kabul with him, and that hour's conversation established just how effectively he had managed to develop a sense of Afghanistan's complexities. Subsequent encounters in Afghanistan, and in cities as remote as Amman and Paris, confirmed this original impression. Chris Johnson was working for Oxfam when I first met her, and her experience with numerous aid projects in Afghanistan has made her one of the best-informed and most informative observers of Afghan reconstruction. The power of their analysis, however, derives from a shared characteristic which social scientists can easily overlook, namely an ability to grasp what one might call the 'smell and feel' of a situation. This book is a brilliant example of the illumination that such an ability can offer. Weaving instructive and moving anecdotes together with the fruits of scholarly research, they convey to their readers a sense of daily life in Afghanistan with a vividness that few observers in the past have ever managed to achieve. Some will find their analysis pessimistic, while for others it may appear unduly optimistic. But no one can fail to benefit from reading their thoughtful and moving book.

William Maley
Asia-Pacific College of Diplomacy,
Australian National University

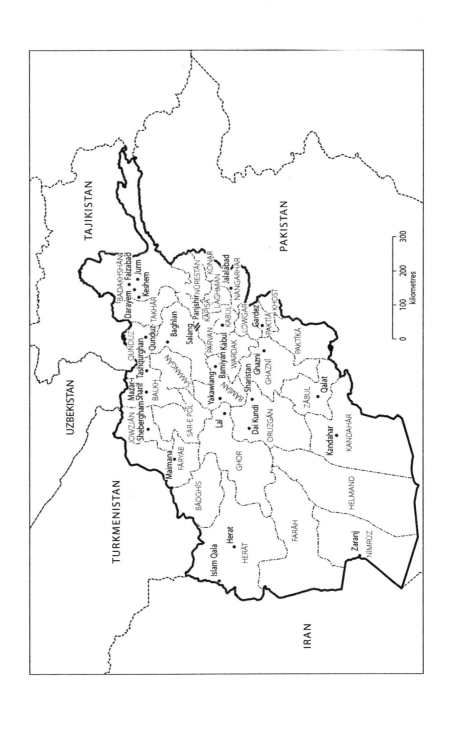

1 *Members of pro-government volunteer youth brigade poised to 'defend the homeland', 1980. (Afghanistan Today)*

1 | The mirage of peace

'Kaka, what are they afraid of?' (Small boy watching heavily armed US soldiers in Kabul, 2003)

The nights in Kabul during the war were eerily quiet. Curfew ensured that the streets became largely the preserve of the city's dogs after 11 p.m. unless you had the official password or could bribe your way past the soldiers with a packet of cigarettes. You could hear a child crying blocks away. The days, however, were punctured by random rocket attacks, launched by the *mujahideen* from the outskirts of the government-controlled city. The crude rockets supplied by the West for use against the Soviets and their allies usually missed their intended targets and smashed into the simple mud homes dotting the low hills of the city.

In the lulls between the rockets or the occasional skirmishes along the distant frontlines, life went on. But not as normal, for the inhabitants of the city lived in fear of the senseless, random attacks, and did what little they could to protect themselves. The doors of our nearby shop served as something of a barometer of what to expect of the day's conflict. The back doors of a powder-blue Citroën van, they were set into a traditional mud wall as though a parked vehicle had simply been assimilated into the street-front. Doors wide open for business, and piles of dusty fruit and vegetables laid out under the shade of the mulberry trees, signified an 'all clear'. When these goods were packed up inside the shop, with doors partly open, there was a need for caution, and passers-by quickened their step while mothers shepherded children inside the walled compounds. When the shop doors were drawn shut but not locked, the signal was one of high alert, and only the intrepid – or desperate – ventured out into the streets. Doors padlocked in the hours of daylight were a sure sign of trouble, and you stayed on the streets at your peril. Then came the eerie silence before an attack, when those lucky enough to have any glass left ensured that no one was near the windows.

Word of which areas were under attack and should be avoided spread like wildfire along the dusty alleys, as did the imminent threats to targets identified by the resistance in *shabnama*, notes pushed under the doors of homes during cover of darkness. Young children knew the 'song' that presaged the impact of a rocket which, if you could clearly hear it, meant

2 *Teenage fighters loyal to Hezbe Wahdat man a checkpost in southern Kabul, 1993. (Jolyon Leslie)*

that you were almost certainly too close for safety. Then came the crack of impact, the dust thrown up by the explosion, out of which rose the screams of the injured and shocked. Lined up for launching in clusters on the barren slopes outside the city, the US-supplied Sakr rockets would usually wreak a pattern of havoc, so people learned not to emerge until the salvo seemed to be over. Survivors would scramble through the dust to dig victims out of the rubble, while passers-by would commandeer taxis, or even bring wheelbarrows, to get the injured to hospital.

Illusions of peace

This was just another day in the life of Afghans caught in a sideshow of the Cold War that, with the withdrawal of Soviet troops in 1989, had slipped out of sight for much of the rest of the world. It was, as Felix Ermacora, UN Special Rapporteur on Afghanistan, put it in his report to the General Assembly in October 1990, a 'forgotten war' (Ermacora 1990). Talk of peace continued to screen acts of war, as *matériel* continued to be supplied to both sides. The few UN observers deployed to monitor the Peshawar Accords could do little but bear witness to violations such as rocket attacks on Kabul and occasional government forays against the resistance. The Kabul government lodged hundreds of complaints about alleged violations, but the UN seemed unwilling to draw attention to continued US support to the resistance (Gossman 1990). Ordinary Kabulis could no more comprehend this form of international 'engagement' in their country than they could the motivation for their countrymen to fire rockets at them.

While the West caricatures Afghans as a war-loving people, recent conflict has been largely fuelled by others. Just as the Russian and British empires during the nineteenth century had described their competition for influence in primarily defensive terms, so too did those who embarked on the twentieth-century Cold War arms race that cost at least a million Afghan lives. On the one hand, the Soviets provided on average $5 billion per year in economic and military support after 1979, while, on the other, the annual military aid allocations of the US administration for the *mujahideen* between 1980 and 1989 were of the order of $2.8 billion (Asia Watch 1991). The deadly symmetry of arms supplies was maintained beyond the withdrawal of Soviet troops, who handed over the bulk of their military supplies to the Kabul government, while the USA – which agreed to exercise 'restraint' only if the Soviets were seen to do the same – Saudi Arabia and Iran continued military support to their respective clients within the resistance. For Afghans, this offered a guarantee of further conflict rather than a hope of peace.

The departure of Soviet troops allowed factionalism to come to the surface within government ranks, as President Najibullah had to rely on deals with local militias to retain control over the major cities and access to key highways. The most important of these were the Uzbek Jozjanis under Abdul Rashid Dostum, who protected the road between Kabul and the north, and the Ismaili Hazaras, under Sayed Jafer Naderi, who kept the Salang pass and tunnel open. In time, both came to exercise as much independence as the *mujahideen*, whom they came to resemble in structure and tactics as well as in their opportunism.

Differences between the resistance groups, once they no longer needed to respond to the Soviet presence, rendered their military activities less and less effective and reduced their ability to confront the government in Kabul. As the control that their sponsors had been able to exercise over the *mujahideen* disintegrated, they increasingly pursued individual and group interests, often with an ethnic dimension, while benefiting from an economic revival through the growing drugs trade. The hard-line factions who, as the most militarily effective opposition to the Soviets, had received the bulk of military support, dominated the political landscape, excluding the moderates who might have been more willing to negotiate.

The dividing-lines between government and resistance began to break down. Gulbuddin Hekmatyar, who had received considerable US assistance throughout the *jihad*, attempted to form an alliance with fellow Pashtuns in the hard-line Khalq clique within the government, resulting in an attempted coup in March 1990. Defence Minister Tanai, an erstwhile Khalqi, attempted to bomb the presidential palace and broach the security cordon south of Kabul to allow Hekmatyar's troops into the city. For those of us who lived in the city at the time, this was a sign that things were beginning to unravel.

As Soviet support for the Kabul government dwindled, the scene was set for a new set of power-brokers. President Najibullah announced in early April 1992 that he would resign as part of a UN-brokered transition of power. A day later, the militia under Dostum (deputy Minister of Defence in the Transitional Administration) seized control of Mazar i Sharif, cutting off Kabul's line of supply from the north. Others also moved quickly to take advantage of the situation, with Naderi's militia seizing the strategic Salang tunnel, while Baba Jan, whose militias had defended the Soviet-built Bagram airbase, changed sides to the *mujahideen*. (This same Baba Jan was rewarded handsomely by the USA for his contribution to the campaign against the Taliban, and by 2003 was head of the Kabul police.) Elsewhere, the Qandahar and Herat garrisons struck deals with local *mujahideen* groups. Najibullah – curiously being driven to the airport in an armour-plated presidential vehicle which had been hastily fitted with UN plates – was stopped while attempting to fly out to join his family in India, and had little option but to take refuge with the UN which, it seems, had offered him safe passage out of the country (Cordovez and Harrison 1994).

'Liberation'

For those of us waiting expectantly on a key intersection in central Kabul one April morning in 1992, the line of Saudi-supplied battle-grey pickups that raced in from the east represented a hope for an end to the rocket attacks and the growing shortages in the city. The convoy carried an assortment of resistance leaders coming to claim the government that had eluded them for so long. Under the terms of the Peshawar Accords, Sibghatullah Mojaddedi would serve as president for two months, to be succeeded by Professor Burhanuddin Rabbani for four months; at this point a *shura* would be convened to select a government for the following eighteen months, to be followed by elections. But the members of this 'alliance' had as much reason to mistrust each other as they did to join forces to ensure peace for their country.

No sooner was the announcement made of the formation of the new Islamic State of Afghanistan than the alliance fell apart. Kabul now became the scene for a power struggle between four main armed groups, Dostum's Junbish-e-Milli militia, Rabbani and Massoud's Jamiat e Islami, Hekmatyar's Hizbe Islami and the largely Shi'a Hizbe Wahdat. While each had different ethnic compositions, all had overlapping areas of influence and, in some instances, shared sources of foreign support, which they supplemented with income from local taxes, customs or drugs. By the summer of 1992, the forces of Jamiat, Junbish and Hizbe Wahdat had repulsed an attack from the combined forces of Hizbe Islami and the Khalqis who had formed the military backbone of Najibullah's previous government. The groups soon staked out parts of the city along ethnic or party political lines. In the face of intimidation and rampant looting, tens of thousands of civilians fled their homes, braving the checkpoints set up by predatory factional fighters as they tried to reach areas where they hoped to find some degree of protection. Government buildings and property were looted, and the public services that the Najibullah regime had maintained were soon a thing of the past. Burnt-out buses were stacked on top of each other to form defensive barricades. Within months, not only was the social geography of the city redrawn but its proud landmarks lay in ruins.

An attempt in December 1992 by Jamiat to take control of the Shi'a neighbourhoods in south-western Kabul prompted Hizbe Wahdat to align themselves with Hizbe Islami, with whom they signed an agreement early in 1993. For similar reasons, Dostum broke ranks with Massoud and attacked Jamiat positions in the north in 1993, after which he was openly allied with Hizbe Islami. The signing in March 1993 between Sunni and Shi'a leaders of the Riyadh Agreement, under pressure from the Saudis, was an attempt to reconcile the groups, and was followed by a joint pilgrimage to Mecca where a collective oath was sworn by the signatories. The agreement, however, was clearly unworkable as it left Rabbani as President with his arch-foe Hekmatyar as Prime Minister. Using his new-found authority, Hekmatyar promptly dismissed Massoud as Defence Minister, a move which President Rabbani rejected, but which prompted Massoud's resignation, even though he continued to command Jamiat forces. On New Year's Day 1994, having been resupplied by Pakistan and Uzbekistan respectively, Hizbe Islami and Junbish joined forces to launch an assault on Jamiat positions in central Kabul.

Prompted by a series of *shabnama* warning of the impending attack, the inhabitants of the Soviet-built MacroRayon blocks in the centre of the city packed what they could and trudged, under the cover of darkness, through the icy streets towards the relative safety of the western part of the city. Well after curfew, those of us who lived along the route were woken by the muffled sounds of the exodus and looked out to see a line of flickering kerosene lamps lighting the way for a huge column of families, clutching their possessions, walking or pushing wheelbarrows or bicycles. The only sounds above the fearful shuffle of thousands of frozen feet were the occasional cry of a baby, or bleating of a sheep. Doors soon began to open along the route, inviting those who were exhausted to rest, drink tea and tell their stories before heading on their way.

Few of those who witnessed scenes such as this can forget that such episodes were caused by men who, less than a decade later, have been rewarded with ministerial posts in an internationally-backed administration, on the basis of sacrifices they allege to have made in liberating their people. About 20,000 people died in the fighting between April 1992 and December 1994 that followed the 'liberation' of Kabul.[1] Almost three-quarters of those who survived were forced to leave their homes and move across the city, or flee to squalid camps for the displaced in Jalalabad. The millions of Afghan refugees who had sought sanctuary in Pakistan from the Soviets were now joined by tens of thousands of families from urban centres, many of who had lost everything. The exodus of those who had kept the government going through the long conflict represented a new stage in the dismemberment of the state, which was reduced to a series of administrative fiefdoms that increasingly came to serve factional interests. Meanwhile, the looting continued. Travelling across the border at Torkham in 1994, trucks piled high with bullet-shredded traffic signs from Kabul were waiting to cross, destined for recycling in Pakistan.

Raising the stakes

Stripped and laid waste, with most of its remaining population reduced to subsisting among the ruins, Kabul continued to be the focus for rocket attacks from the outskirts until 1995. It then came under threat from a new phenomenon, the Taliban, who had pushed back the patchwork of commanders as they moved north from their base in Qandahar. Though led by people who themselves had often been *mujahideen*, the core of the Taliban were young Pashtuns from the south of Afghanistan who had been students in religious *madrasas* in Pakistan. They vowed to return Afghanistan to Islam and to law and order. While most commanders initially fled in the face of threats from the Taliban to deal with those who had created the situation of lawlessness, many fighters simply changed sides. One of the dividends of their control became evident as early as 1995, when those of us running aid programmes in the city began to receive turbaned visitors bearing lists of looted goods that had been abandoned by the *mujahideen*, and which the Taliban had come across during their advance towards the capital. This seemed to back up stories in the bazaar of how law and order had been re-established in areas from which the *mujahideen* had fled as the Taliban advanced. Their arrival on the outskirts of Kabul, however, plunged the residents of the city back into a sense of siege, reinforced by the Taliban's resumption of rocketing, a tactic of those they claimed to despise. It was not until September 1996, however, that the Taliban were in a position to take the capital and, in the face of an ultimatum, the Jamiat fighters defending Kabul vanished into the night.

The key image of the Taliban occupation of Kabul that registered in the international press was the mutilated body of Najibullah, banknotes stuffed into his mouth, strung from a lamp-post on one of the central intersections of the city. The ruthless way in which he was hauled out of the UN premises where he had been given refuge for three years, and then butchered, seemed to epitomize all that was brutal about the Afghans and all that we did not understand about the Taliban. Even those Afghans who had suffered under Najibullah's cruel regime seemed shocked by his murder, and apprehensive about what lay ahead.

While serious concerns had been raised about their policies since their occupation of Herat in 1995, the international reaction to the occupation of Kabul by the Taliban was guarded. The mesmerized fascination with which the outside world had watched a raggle-taggle bunch of religious zealots from Qandahar take over more and more territory by eliminating or co-opting their adversaries gave way to a realization that they also had political ambitions. Having dislodged the fractious government of the Islamic State of Afghanistan from the capital, they now presumed to assert complete political control over what they chose to call the Islamic Emirate of Afghanistan.

By May 1997 they were able to capture the northern city of Mazar i Sharif, aided by the defection of General Abdul Malik, one of Dostum's allies. As soon as the Taliban started to disarm fighters in the city, however, they encountered resistance, especially from the Hazara groups. Taking advantage of this, Malik turned the tables on the Taliban, who were routed. In the course of their retreat, some 2,000 Taliban captives were herded into containers and driven out to the desert of Dashte Leili. With summer temperatures in Mazar topping 50 degrees, many suffocated. Those who did not were shot and their bodies dumped in shallow graves. It was the first in what was to become a series of atrocities in the north, perpetrated by all parties to the conflict (Human Rights Watch 1998).

Arriving in Mazar i Sharif at the end of August 1997, we encountered palpable tension on every street corner; armed men staked out territory as factions vied for supremacy. Gone was the ruthless control of Dostum; now no one ruled, which is always bad news in Afghanistan. A week later, driving east out of the city towards Pul i Khumri, we were turned back by fighting at Tashqurghan, about a hour from Mazar. But Tashqurghan was often a problem and we assumed that it would blow over, and that we could return the next day. Back in Mazar i Sharif, people were equally casual, and even the UN suggested that it was simply a local skirmish. We were all wrong. The Taliban had advanced from the east as far as the airport, from where piles of casualties on the frontlines were pictured in graphic close-up every night on Balkh TV. Other commanders took advantage of the situation to move on the city from the west, or to prey on civilians trying to flee south through the mountains. It was more than two weeks before the Taliban advance was turned back, during which time armed gangs took advantage of the insecurity to loot with alacrity. Worst hit was the UN, whose visibility and perceived failure to bring any tangible benefit to the people of the region prompted a wave of animosity. Offices were ransacked and vehicles driven off, while the stockpile of wheat in the World Food Programme warehouses was cleared out entirely.

Despite the looting, some degree of self-control seemed to remain as Chris remembers:

> One of the young fighters who came over the wall for our vehicles, surprised, perhaps, that the only foreigner on the premises was a woman, insisted that I should not be afraid. 'We will not hurt you,' he said, as his colleagues rifled through the office for the car-keys. Another colleague was saved from having her house looted when Afghan neighbours intervened to face down the gunmen, saying, 'These are good people, they have done a lot to help Afghans – leave them alone.' Shamed, the fighters slunk off.

War, as so often here, threw up contradictions; the new predators were challenged by an older code of behaviour. This did not prevent some agencies exploiting the events for publicity back home. MSF Australia, for example, grandstanded with a lurid story of their (conveniently blonde and defenceless) female volunteer, allegedly hiding in the bathroom while plucky male colleagues protected her from a horde of ravaging *mujahideen*. It certainly got them publicity but, as ever, things were not that simple.

While the Taliban chose conventional military approaches in their attempts to control Mazar i Sharif, they tried to blockade food supplies to the central mountain region of Hazarajat in order to starve the inhabitants into submission. The tactic brought huge suffering, but did not succeed in breaking the will of the people in the area, who showed a great sense of mutual solidarity. Pashtuns and Hazaras have long shared the southern edges of Hazarajat and although in places there has been enmity, in others there has been friendship. In the district of Jaghori, Pashtuns refused to see their Hazara neighbours starve and, at risk to their own lives, smuggled food to them under cover of darkness. Afghans have always been traders, and north of Ghazni a new market sprang up where Pashtun traders organized shipments up to central Hazarajat, taking the wheat by donkey over the mountain trails, but at a price: in 1998 a sack of flour leaving Ghazni at a price of $20 was worth $49 by the time it arrived at Malistan; eighteen months earlier the same sack would have cost $8 (ACF 1999). Hazaras have always been dependent on the sale of livestock and with the roads closed no one could get their flocks to market. Livestock prices collapsed, resulting in mass impoverishment. While assistance came in through cash-for-work programmes, it was never enough to meet the needs of those affected by the blockade. Oxfam found that in some remote villages one cow was being exchanged for as little as one sack of wheat (Johnson 2000).

In the meantime, as concern about the Taliban's policies turned to condemnation, there were mixed political messages from the international community. In April 1998, the then US Ambassador to the UN, Bill Richardson, visited Kabul (and, subsequently, the anti-Taliban north) to discuss demands for the renunciation of terrorism and handing over of Osama bin Laden. It was therefore a surprise for those of us assembled on the steps of the long-neglected US embassy in Kabul to hear him make a statement in which he talked of a 'breakthrough' on the issue of Taliban restrictions on health and education for women. This turned out to be a hollow claim, presumably intended for his domestic audience, as the Taliban proved to be as unmoved by his requests for relaxation of the edicts as they were by demands to hand over their guest. Within four months, the US tune had changed dramatically; Tomahawk missiles launched from warships in the Indian Ocean struck targets in Khost that were allegedly related to the training of terrorists linked to the bombing of US embassies in Nairobi and Dar-es-Salaam.

Apart from sending the Taliban a clear message about the risks of continuing to harbour their foreign 'guest', the unprecedented direct attack by the USA made the country much more dangerous for those of us who continued to work there. The shock and anger after the attacks were palpable, and the Taliban were quick to provide additional security for the handful of aid workers and journalists who remained. After the death of a UN military adviser (see Chapter 3) as a result of an ambush on a UN vehicle, they too were evacuated.

The imposition by the UN of an arms embargo in 1999 increased political pressure on the Taliban regime but did little to affect the military situation on the ground. While official support from Saudi Arabia was withdrawn, there was little evidence of a reduction of cross-border military support from Pakistan and other sponsors. Nor was there any let-up in military supplies to the Northern Alliance, who were not covered by the UN embargo and who continued to resist Taliban attempts to take control of the remaining 15 per cent of the country. The advances made by the Taliban towards Taloqan late in 2000 prompted talk from Russia of the possibility of pre-emptive strikes to protect its southern allies, while the bombing of the USS *Cole* in Yemen raised the chances of further *monicas* (as Afghans now called the long-range Tomahawk missiles) being launched against their guests in the lead-up to the US presidential election.

Bombing-in a peace

It was events in New York and Washington in September 2001 rather than developments inside Afghanistan, however, that finally sealed the fate of the Taliban and ushered in a new phase of the war. Desperate for peace, many Afghans hoped that in this new war they might find the end to their long nightmare, and many spoke of watching in awe from their rooftops as the 'smart' bombs fell. When asked if she was afraid, one woman replied, 'No, we knew they were not for us.' Yet despite America's attempts to portray the war in Afghanistan as a humanitarian endeavour, entered into as much to release the Afghan people from oppression as to avenge the wrong done to the homeland, its pursuit of its 'war on terror' was to become the major impediment to peace in Afghanistan.

Operation Enduring Freedom, which was launched days after the attacks in the USA, was justified as an operation of self-defence in response to terrorist acts against citizens and property, and authorized both by the Senate and a series of presidential orders. Although efforts were made to build a case for the campaign against the Taliban, and to portray this as a joint endeavour, there was no explicit agreement under international law for the USA to go to war. The UN Security Council recognized the inherent right to act in self-defence in accordance with the UN Charter,[2] and required states 'to act against states, organizations and institutions that support terrorism',[3] but this fell far short of an explicit authorization for the use of force. The USA had, however, made its intentions clear and – unlike the case of Iraq in 2003 – few member-states wanted to be seen to stand in the way of a campaign in a far-away land against al-Qa'eda and their protectors, the Taliban.

The US air attack on Afghanistan began on 7 October 2001, with an initial focus on targets in the major cities and what little infrastructure had survived the long war. The initial objective seems to have been to inflict heavy casualties as a means of splitting the leadership. Some 400 civilians were killed in the first week of bombing, and this toll increased tenfold over the following three months of the campaign (*Guardian*, 8 August 2002). Despite this, the USA continued to portray the air war as a humane endeavour, in which collateral casualties could be put down to the movement by the Taliban of military assets to populated areas. For the image of a just war to be maintained, it seemed, the actual human cost of the conflict had to be hidden from international scrutiny.

By the end of October 2001, when the Taliban remained defiant and in control of many areas of the country, and troops of the US-sponsored Northern Alliance seemed unwilling to engage on the ground, there was a switch in strategy to carpet-bombing of frontlines. When this did not immediately produce the desired effect, sub-atomic bombs were dropped on Taliban frontlines in the Shamali plains north of Kabul. Thus the countryside that had been laid waste by both the Soviets and the Taliban was further pounded to dust – from the safe altitude of 30,000 feet. In addition, a quarter of a million deadly bomblets were scattered from the cluster bombs that the USA dropped throughout the country. Given that at least 5 per cent of these bomblets usually fail to explode, the USA added to the deadly legacy of mines and other unexploded ordnance that has caused such suffering to Afghan civilians (Human Rights Watch 2002). On the ground, the fear of casualties meant that those armed groups who were useful to the US campaign received arms and cash, with an estimated $70 million paid out in 'inducements' to selected commanders during 2002 alone (Woodward 2003)

The preoccupation with war resulted in the military onslaught against the Taliban moving ahead of the political process. By the time that the Taliban fled Kabul, there was no agreement as to what would happen next. This left the way open for the forces of the Northern Alliance to take over the city, whereas what Afghans wanted – and needed – was a demilitarized city secured by international forces. At this stage, the coalition was too concerned about the threat from al-Qa'eda to risk alienating its allies by attempting to dislodge Northern Alliance fighters. Stipulation in the Bonn Agreement that militia troops should leave the city upon the arrival of international forces was never enforced, the consequences of which undermined progress on all aspects of the security transition thereafter.

While the Geneva Accords signed thirteen years earlier had focused on military disengagement, the Bonn Agreement set out primarily to define the steps towards a political transition, and had remarkably little to say on military issues. There is, curiously, no mention in the agreement of the US military invasion, nor of the status of those troops who would continue to pursue the 'war on terror'.[4] Apart from a commitment on the part of the UN to deploy an international security force to Kabul, provisions for the security transition were limited to a mention of the fact that 'some time will be required for a new Afghan security force to be fully constituted'. While perhaps realistic, this wording confirmed that the sponsors of the Bonn process did not want anything to stand in the way of their war against the Taliban; any more than the Afghan military factions involved in the negotiations wanted the details of a security transition to stand in the way of their plans to reassert themselves militarily on the ground. The fact that a meaningful political transition could not take place without disarmament seemed lost in the pressure for an agreement. Indeed, some argued that very mention of disarmament in the agreement would dishonour the memory of those *mujahideen* who had given their lives in the struggle (Rubin 2003a). While perhaps the best that could have been salvaged from the situation created by the early stages of Operation Enduring Freedom, the outcome of the Bonn negotiations was far from being a 'peace' agreement. Not only did it provide an opportunity for factional interests to hold the political process hostage but, by largely avoiding the difficult issue of demilitarization, it allowed them to re-establish a stranglehold over the country.

Losing hearts and minds

The last Taliban stronghold to hold out against the combined might of the USA and its proxies was Qandahar, which was finally overrun by anti-Taliban forces in mid-December 2001. In a scenario that had disturbing resonances of the Soviet occupation, the ongoing military campaign then moved to the pursuit of remnants of these forces into rural areas, particularly in the south and east of the country. The hubris of American military policy led to the unrealistic goal of eradicating the remnants of the Taliban and al-Qa'eda over a vast and mountainous territory, with highly porous borders into the adjoining tribal areas in north and western Pakistan.

Even if it had proved possible to hunt down elements of al-Qa'eda, it would have been impossible to root out the surviving leaders of the Taliban in their heartland, where they could simply change their turbans and become something else. The notion that the Taliban movement could be swept away by US military might proved to be yet another case of wishful thinking. High-profile campaigns such as Operation Anaconda in 2003 were portrayed as mopping-up exercises against a shadowy and elusive foe who would be flushed out of the rugged terrain by dint of overwhelming force and superior technology. But unlike al-Qa'eda, the Taliban belong to Afghanistan and will always have tribal connections which they can call upon, invoking age-old traditions of honour to ensure that sanctuary is given. When asked how much support the Taliban have in the southern provinces, an aid worker who has long worked with Pashtun tribes responded: 'Not really a lot. But they turn up in the villages of the tribesmen and ask for shelter, and what can they do? Custom decrees they cannot refuse. The Americans interpret it as support and punish people, but it is not real support. But the people in the villages are also so frustrated with the lack of progress, the new government has brought them little, so why should they risk their lives?'

Conversations with Afghans who travelled in Uruzgan and Helmand during 2003 indicate that there is deep resentment building about the manner in which the US forces and the armed Afghan groups that they have hired are operating. Not only have aerial raids on villages and civilian convoys taken their toll but intrusive house-to-house searches – often based on false information – are losing the coalition the support of the very people they need. 'Not even the Soviets kicked down the doors of our homes and searched like this,' said one village elder. Some of the arms that were distributed to various factions in the early push to defeat the Taliban have, not surprisingly, found their way into the hands of those who now feel the need to defend themselves from US troops or their militias. But not all activity has been defensive, and the extent of attacks against coalition interests has grown over time to well beyond the conservative heartland of the Taliban. So too have targets broadened to include, in some areas, the infrastructure of central government, its personnel and those associated with it, including aid workers. It is, according to an old Afghan friend who went on *haj* in 2003, a very clear strategy. Pretending he had been at Tora Bora and had escaped the Americans there, he spent time talking to al-Qa'eda supporters who were at Mecca. They told him of their plan to infiltrate the country, as returning refugees, as traders, or simply to slip across the border from Pakistan, and to fight the occupying forces and the American puppet government and its allies. The events of the last year suggest these were not just idle words.

The USA was at first reluctant to recognize the growing problem, and in May 2003, the US Defense Secretary indicated with confidence that the military operation was moving from what he characterized as 'stabilization' to 'transition'.[5] The fact that by then more than a third of the country was considered too insecure for UN staff points to a different reality. By the end of 2003, the Special Representative of the UN Secretary General acknowledged that 'Afghanistan has experienced a deterioration in security at precisely the point where the peace process demands the opposite ... In the last 90 days, the number of reported incidents targeting civilians exceeded the total of those that occurred in the first 20 months following the signing of the Bonn agreement ... attacks on the humanitarian community escalated from a rate of one per month to one almost every two days' (UN 2003a). Even where the UN is present, its personnel have retreated behind barricades of razor wire and sandbags, which hardly inspires confidence among ordinary Afghans.

The enemy within While the USA was busy trying to pursue – somewhat unsuccessfully – its elusive enemy, attempts to win the peace were floundering. The two were not unconnected. By ascribing almost everything that stood in the way of the transition to 'terrorists', the USA and its allies seemed to be blind to the fact that the interests its allies represented might in fact be equally as formidable an obstacle to peace and security. With the demise of the Taliban, factional politics returned to dominate many parts of Afghanistan. In the south, the east and the north different groups jockeyed for power, leading to inherently unstable situations. But it was not only a desire for power that drove the conflict; for many commanders war was an economically profitable state of affairs, providing an environment in which they could pillage the country's resources or deal in illegal goods. Peace offered nowhere near such good rewards.

So the low-level war dragged on, bringing misery for ordinary people. Nowhere was this more apparent than in the north of the country:

> What characterizes the situation in the north is ongoing factional tensions, local but which periodically and repeatedly erupt into conflict. The five factions use the north to extend their political base, each will ally and re-ally between and amongst each other for political expediency. There are huge amounts of weapons. Central government is weak and its reach does not extend up here. Administrators at a district or provincial level are either too weak to ensure security or ally with their factional backers. Problems are made worse by the fact that commanders do not follow their own lines of command but beat to their own drum. (UN worker, interview, Mazar i Sharif, September 2003)

In many cases, those who remained useful for the war on terror escaped censure for their continuing aggression, while others became easy targets for blame. The case of Padshah Khan Zadran illustrates just how easily a 'good' Afghan could become a 'bad' Afghan. A participant at the Bonn talks and key ally of the USA during the war, Zadran used US-supplied weapons to lay siege to the provincial capital of Gardez after being replaced at the end of 2001 as governor of Paktia province, a position that he felt was his due reward for assisting in the overthrow of the Taliban. Finally arrested in December 2003 by Pakistani forces in the semi-autonomous tribal belt of Waziristan, he was handed over to the authorities in Kabul, only to be pardoned by President Karzai.[6] The issue, it seems, is not whether you have guns, not whether you use them against the people, and certainly not that you use them for personal gain, but whether or not you challenge US plans.

New beginnings?

For almost all Afghans, by far the most important issue is security. 'Get rid of the guns' is a constant plea. A lot of time and energy, both Afghan and international, has gone into trying to do just that – so far with very little success. At its root, the problem goes back to the fact that the Bonn Agreement never was a peace agreement, and without a peace agreement factions were unwilling to give up their arms. But because this was never properly recognized, a disarmament programme was initiated as if it was the implementation phase of a peace agreement, whereas the very design of the programme became the focus of negotiations about the terms on which the peace process could move forwards.

Fundamentally, disarmament requires two things: that Afghans lay down their arms; and that there is an international force both to act as a deterrent and to give confidence that handing over weapons will not leave people open to attack from someone else. Many Afghans believe that deployments of peacekeepers, to establish security, should precede any attempts at disarmament; otherwise this risks undermining what little security exists.

Given the lack of a peace agreement between the factions, disarmament was always going to be difficult; it was impossible as long as armed groups continued to be paid and supplied by those pursuing the 'war on terror': 'These soldiers are standing up to terrorism like the coalition forces. I asked Karzai to take my soldiers and pay them and make them part of the Afghan National Army. Why train new ones when we have a lot of soldiers, generals and commanders?'[7] Marshal Fahim's words above illustrate all too well how the very commanders who proved useful to the immediate military goals of the US-led coalition now stand in the way of effective disarmament and demobilization.

Officially launched in September 2003, the Japanese- and US-funded disarmament programme followed months of negotiation about reform of the Ministry of Defence, where all the top jobs were held by men from Fahim's faction. In these circumstances, commanders from other groups were unlikely to instruct their fighters to hand in their arms to someone whom they considered a rival. For as long as Fahim insisted that his 50,000 fighters from the Panjshir form the core of the new Afghan National Army, calls for enlistment under the slogan of 'One nation, one army' rang rather hollow for non-Panjshiris.

Four months earlier, President Karzai had summoned provincial governors and regional commanders to Kabul to demand compliance with a thirteen-point resolution that had been adopted by the National

Security Council. This banned the recruitment of private military personnel and unauthorized military action, and reaffirmed the requirement that no individual hold both a military and civilian post, while dissolving extra-governmental bodies and the titles that went with them. Yet the participants at the meeting controlled tens of thousands of fighters whom, being the principal basis for their authority, they were unlikely to disband.

Finally, under intense US pressure, President Karzai forced through the replacement of Fahim's chief of staff and four deputy ministers, which paved the way for the initiation of the flagship UN programme.

The process of disarmament and demobilization in Afghanistan reminds one of the failed family planning programmes that scar the history of many developing countries. People will want to stop having big families only once social and economic conditions make this a good decision for them; yet in poor countries the world over, policy-makers spend large amounts of time and money constructing elaborate family planning policies in an attempt to persuade people to have fewer children. Except in coercive states that have the means to impose policies against the will of their population, they fail. So in Afghanistan, until people no longer feel they need guns for their own protection, disarmament will not happen, no matter how many plans are laid. There is no force that has the means and will forcibly to disarm people. The writ of the Transitional Administration does not run far beyond Kabul, and the international community cannot do it, even if it had the will.

Plans for disarmament, however, continue to be made. Friends who have been involved in similar processes elsewhere in the world have suggested that important lessons have not been learned, and that the formula being applied to Afghanistan simply does not add up. Incentives for mid-level commanders to disarm, for example, include appointments in government, the military or the police, support in establishing private enterprises, or inducements in the form of cash payoffs or property. But the prospect of an ill-paid sinecure in government is unlikely to appeal to commanders who have enjoyed relative autonomy, and hardly need advice on how to start a business. As others have pointed out, commanders 'who own twelve houses in Kabul and several businesses will not be bought off with agricultural land' (Rubin 2003a). The incentives that may be made available through official disarmament programmes are likely to be only a fraction of those being offered by those commanders who will continue to need fighters to defend their stake in the drugs trade.

If there is one thing in favour of disarmament it is that Afghans are so thoroughly tired of war. Yet this potential has never really been drawn upon. As was to be with case with the political aspects of the transition, there was a complete failure to engage local communities in the process.

The first disarmament initiative under the UN-implemented New Beginnings programme took place in Qunduz in October 2003, when 1,000 factional fighters were disarmed as part of a pilot phase of the scheme in six regions. From the start, commitment to the exercise was half-hearted, with no army unit decommissioned in its entirety, and half of those disarmed in fact being part-time fighters. Three months later, an additional 3,000 fighters were identified as eligible for demobilization in Gardez, Kabul and Mazar i Sharif. In Gardez, however, the sizeable US-supported tribal militias were left out of the disarmament process, despite the fact that they represent the principal armed force in the area (Stapleton 2003). While generous support from the international community should allow an acceleration of the rate of disarmament, it is difficult to see how the programme can hope to reach its intended target of 100,000 men during its three-year life. The growing insecurity in southern and eastern parts of the country will clearly act as a disincentive for fighters to disarm in these areas, risking a geographic imbalance in numbers – which could have serious implications for a process that depends on mutual reductions.

The viability of the disarmament process will also hinge on progress in the formation of the Afghan National Army, whose deployment should ensure stability and security as the factions disband and the political transition takes place. The failure to commit signatories to the Bonn Agreement to support for a de-factionalized national army has, however, hampered efforts to replace the multiple centres of military power that exist. As a result, the building of the new army is running well behind schedule, with half of those trained having deserted, and less than a third of the planned 60,000 men likely to be deployed by mid-2004 (Durch 2003). Many of those 'volunteering' for the new army are in fact forced to join by their commanders, who stand to benefit from fulfilling informal quotas. At the current pace of enlistment, the Chief of Operations of the National Army, Major General Sher Karimi, has estimated that it might take until 2010 for the target figure of 70,000 soldiers to be deployed. In the meantime, attempts are being made to have a 10,000-strong Central Corps in three brigades ready before the elections in mid-2004.[8]

International failure If the Afghan side of the disarmament process was struggling, the international community was doing no better. There had been requests from the beginning, including from President (then Chairman) Karzai and from the UN Special Representative Lakhdar Brahimi for ISAF to be extended outside Kabul, but the Americans refused, fearing that it would get in the way of their hunt for al-Qa'eda. When in summer 2003 they did finally agree, it became very clear that their stance had been useful for other nations, who weren't prepared to commit troops anyway.

In the place of ISAF peacekeepers, however, the provinces were given Provisional Reconstruction Teams (PRTs). Nowhere is the confusion as to political, military and assistance agendas – each of which has been invoked as an objective of international engagement – better illustrated than here. Launched by the USA in early 2003, these units had an array of objectives that were impossible to achieve. The underlying concept assumes that a strategic international military presence might help to address the causes of local instability, while strengthening the influence of the Transitional Administration by improving the lives of civilians in the area of deployment.

Neither element of this concept, however, seems to be grounded in reality. Given the limited impact that a 10,000-strong coalition force, with significant air support, has had on the causes of local instability since early 2002, the notion that small contingents of civil affairs soldiers scattered through the country might be more effective in addressing this seems to be a case of wishful thinking. On the other hand, the notion that Afghan hearts and minds will be won simply through an international presence and the disbursement of funds for rehabilitation is questionable, especially in areas where the US-led coalition continues to pursue its war on terror.

A member of the first reconstruction team in Gardez during mid-2003 described how they spent the first three months after deployment establishing themselves in secure quarters, which were the target for twenty-seven rockets during this period alone. Travel was highly restricted, and undertaken only in heavily armed convoys, which precluded much contact with the local tribal leadership. There were few opportunities for extending the influence of the Kabul administration, as the governor at this time was from outside, knew very little about the area, and was never able to travel outside the town.[9]

The British team based in Mazar i Sharif in northern Afghanistan since mid-2003 has been more focused and has stated clearly that its objective is to improve security. Its command has recognized that it cannot do this by force – for to do this effectively across the northern provinces would require more troops than the 5,000 of ISAF, let alone the small PRT contingent – but can only act in support of local initiatives for peace. Acting in liaison with UNAMA and the Security Council of the North,[10] it has attempted to bring stability by mediating between factional rivals in the region, and by undertaking joint patrols with local police contingents in support of locally negotiated peace agreements. They have also indicated that they might guarantee the ongoing disarmament process in the region. Being under coalition command, they have the benefit of a significant deterrent, in the form of US military 'reach back', which can be called upon to enforce the peace, if needed.

While this experience has certainly been more positive, there is real risk that, just as with ISAF's relative success in Kabul, it becomes the entity on which all international hopes for progress on the security front are pinned. The situation in Ghazni, for example, is not the same as that in Mazar, and one cannot simply cut and paste. Moreover, continuing outbreaks of fighting in the north suggest that lasting stability requires national as well as regional political action to resolve long-standing disputes.[11] Yet in the apparent absence of a coherent political strategy, the 'PRT-effect' seems to remain the single big idea for regional stabilization.

While there is little doubt that the presence of international peacekeepers elsewhere in the country could help to build confidence, there is an urgent need to clarify the mandate of the NATO-led PRTs. Their greatest potential clearly lies in improving security, both through acting as a deterrent to the factions, which implies credible threats of force, and as a support to Afghan negotiated peace agreements and disarmament. Yet the political goal of using the teams to extend the remit of central government is dragging them into ever more spheres of activity. It seems that every time an intractable problem emerges, the PRTs are now deemed to be the solution. For example, there have been suggestions that peacekeepers should monitor customs revenue collection in one region, while training the police in another. Whatever the mandate, the question remains: does the international community have the will to be more assertive in efforts to bring peace to Afghanistan?

The early indications are that it does not. Those countries contributing troops to ISAF, which has been under NATO command since August 2003, seem wary of deploying them elsewhere for the time being. The response to the UN resolution authorizing peacekeepers to deploy outside the capital has been cautious.[12] By the end of 2003, only 200 soldiers had been committed by Germany to replace a coalition team that had set up in Qunduz. By early February 2004, the British indicated that they would establish a network of smaller contingents through the north, from their existing base in Mazar i Sharif,[13] although it is not clear whether this would be under NATO command. The reduction of NATO forces in the Balkans seems to offer the chance of eventual deployment of the 18,000 troops that is estimated to be the minimum number required, outside the coalition, to fill the current security gap in Afghanistan (Durch 2003). While NATO has indicated that it will field an additional five teams over the next six months, in the run-up to the election, however, there is a very real risk that this will be too little too late.

'Failure is not an option'

Given what they have seen and suffered at the hands of outside forces and their allies, the fact that Afghans still look to the international community to bring stability and peace to their country seems to illustrate their desperation, rather than trust. Judging by the experience of the past two years, they have good reason to be anxious about the intentions of the international community. The short-term objectives of the US 'war on terror' have in many places let the factional genie out of the bottle, and thereby deepened the domestic dimension of the conflict. Confidence in the wider political project has been eroded in some areas by US military impunity and the loss of civilian lives, which has created animosity towards the coalition and, by association, the Kabul administration. Progress with disarmament has been limited, due to a lack of political will and unrealistic planning. Failure to ensure the deployment of international peacekeepers to oversee the security transition means that whatever stability that may exist in many parts of the country remains fragile.

The USA has long insisted that failure in the 'war on terror' in Afghanistan is not an option. But despite repeated assertions that the remaining pockets of resistance are being stamped out, their military grip on the country appears to be slipping, even as the investments being made in military bases at Bagram and Qandahar suggest they are digging in for the long term. Pronouncements of military victory are risky, and serve only to distract the international community from a task that is far from complete – if it ever will be. The cost to the US of containment through Operation Enduring Freedom is running at some $11 billion a year, yet it has failed to bring them complete military control of the country.

The continuing war in Afghanistan has two main facets: the ongoing factional struggle between groups who are in theory part of the present government; and a growing armed resistance from those who have declared themselves opposed to it. The latter includes both those who never accepted their defeat at the hands of the coalition (al-Qa'eda and the Taliban) and those who have become enemies either because of their exclusion from the political settlement (Hizbe Islami) or because of their treatment at the hands of American forces (as in some tribal areas). Of these only al-Qa'eda are not Afghan; the others belong to the country and will always be able to draw support from some elements of its population. The long history of warfare in Afghanistan suggests that it will never be possible to defeat them militarily, and attempts to do so will simply ensure that the war runs on and on. In their recent attempts to initiate talks with 'moderate' Taliban, the USA seems to have belatedly recognized this. One can only hope that it is not too late. The two years of conflict since Bonn have only served to deepen divisions, and to marginalize those who might have been useful interlocutors. Just as in Iraq, the arrogance that the USA showed in thinking it could bomb its way to a military victory has made peace a more distant prospect. Failure might not be an option, but success remains a mirage.

Notes

1 ICRC News 44, 6 November 1996.

2 UNSC Resolution 1368 (2001), 12 September 2001.

3 UNSC Resolution 1373 (2001), 28 September 2001.

4 At the end of 2003, the USA had still not entered into a Status of Forces Agreement with the Transitional Administration, defining the legal status of the 11,000 US military personnel in the country.

5 Donald Rumsfeld, US Department of Defense statement, May 2003.

6 'Karzai pardons warlord handed over by Pakistan', Daily Times, 6 February 2004.

7 Marshal Fahim quoted in 'Brewing power struggle in Kabul', Christian Science Monitor, 12 October 2003.

8 'Desertions deplete Afghan army', Christian Science Monitor, 17 December 2003.

9 Personal communication, November 2003.

10 Comprising representatives of the key factions, supported by UNAMA.

11 'Rival warlords fighting in Afghanistan', Associated Press, 9 October 2003.

12 UNSC Resolution 1510 (2003), August 2003.

13 Associated Press, 2 October 2004.

2 | Identity and society

New values and old

'I wanna fuck you,' leers a young man, as a foreign woman old enough to be his mother walks along a Kabul street. Such petty harassment has become everyday stuff here and, strangely in this culture, it has no respect for age. No wonder so many Afghan women still chose to stay under their burqas. On one level such sexual aggression is almost the inevitable product of the Taliban years, the taking away of a woman's autonomy to such an extent that she could not even go out on her own but had to have a male relative with her, even if it was her young son. The message about who had power and who did not was not lost on the young men who grew up at that time. On another level it is clearly a statement of what many Afghans think about the takeover of their capital by foreigners – the large four-wheel-drive vehicles that choke the city's streets, the late-night parties with copious quantities of alcohol in what is still a conservative Islamic country, the spiralling rents. Coupled with the lack of any improvement in their own lives, it is not surprising that there is, as so often, a displacement of the anger people feel over something they have no power to control, on to the place where they feel they have dominance – their relations with women.

There can be little doubt that this attitude is also a product of the imported pornography that is everywhere. Afghan house-staff watch it on the television while the foreigners are out at work. Those who have TVs at home watch it there too. Staff in the friendly NGO-run internet café struggle to keep 'teenage sex' and 'hot latinos' off their screens. International organizations have problems with staff downloading porn from their work computers. The women at the Foreign Office let slip that the British government picks up four-figure bills for the porn channels on the hotel TV every time a delegation of ministers pays an official visit. It's as if Kabul has gone into teenage-hood on fast forward. The years of repression under the Taliban, and the *mujahideen* before them, have been released into sudden licence.

'There is', said a friend, 'a clash of cultures: the TV at home and the burqa on the streets.' Everyone wants access to this world outside – even many conservatives, who condemn in public but often watch in

3   Man displaced from central highlands due to drought and fighting, Shai-
    dayee camp, Herat, 2003. (Chris Johnson)

private. The friend continues: 'One of our drivers used to be Sayyaf's driver, he too had his sat. TV at home, Hekmatyar also.'

The new world even finds its way to the countryside. In a tiny district centre in the highlands of Hazarajat, the US-based 'Iran TV' broadcasts an American Iranian woman in a tight-fitting, low-cut black top conducting a flirtatious interview with a besuited man. The interview is cut with music and gyrating young bodies that would not have looked out of place in a Hindi movie. Everyone was glued to it. The next week a district official was watching porn on the same TV, and struggled in vain to find the off button on the remote as visitors entered the room. Staying the night in a village house in Badakhshan, we watched as a colleague idly flicked through the TV channels. Up came a rear shot of a blonde woman wearing nothing but a pair of knee-high red leather boots, bum provocatively towards the viewer's face. This is a place where people rarely even visit the provincial capital, many hours away by dirt road, and most have never been to Kabul. Until the recent surge in poppy profits, almost nobody had a TV set. It's a land where men and women cover their bodies and live their lives according to fixed codes. If you drink alcohol or have illicit sex then you don't do it in public. There is an old Afghan saying, 'A shame that is not seen is not a shame'. But the new foreign world knows nothing of discretion and places no value on the form of things. It is not only the blonde woman's bottom that is in your face.

This clash of cultures is part of a wider onslaught on Afghan values. Radios Bagram and ISAF churn out coalition propaganda woven in with pop music and 'public service' announcements. They compete with a growing number of private broadcasters, whose mix of pop and risqué chat is held up as evidence of the new-found freedom of the Afghans. It is difficult to imagine the impact of the new cocktail of psychops and pop on a population that previously relied on radio for critical information and education. Many a long night during the 1990s was spent with groups of villagers huddled around a crackling shortwave radio keeping track of the turbulent political changes under way in Kabul, or listening rapt to the latest instalment of the BBC series 'New Home New Life'. The newly deregulated media focus on western values at the expense of the sense of collective identity that has enabled many Afghans to cope with the long conflict. It seems to be an attempt at the colonization of the mind; sell them your culture, your values, and they willingly buy in to your political and economic system. The lessons of previous attempts to fast-track social change in Afghanistan seem to have been forgotten. In this lies a danger, for it is the continuity of some form of social order that has held people together during the terrible upheavals of the last decades. The danger of a conservative backlash is evident. The mullahs preach from the mosques: 'See where your democracy gets you; they want to kill our values.'

Many Afghans are extraordinarily adept at dealing with this onslaught on their culture, balancing competing world-views within their daily lives. They negotiate the new world, taking from it what they want, rejecting that which they find of no value. They may explore the previously forbidden porn but they also come back from abroad horrified at the values they have seen. People may be poor here but, despite almost a quarter of a century of war, they still have certain standards below which even in the hardest of times they do not fall.

Asking a friend what he thought was crucial to Afghan identity, brought the reply:

> Honesty, unity, honour, pride, that we help each other, do not care about money. Language and behaviour, our hospitality. The importance of family, how we will eat together, how the young will always respect the old. Traditions, like taking tea ... I'll tell you a story. An Afghan came back from abroad and he went to his uncle's house:
> 'Will you have tea?'
> 'No, I don't take tea. Do you have boiled water?'
> 'No, I do not have boiled water.'
> [He smiled.] He wanted to show him: you are an Afghan, we still have our traditions, do not forget them, do not think you are above them.

Yet the long-term impact of the onslaught of the new world on Afghan values and culture is uncertain. 'People have become money oriented,' says Samadi, the director of ADA, one of the most respected Afghan NGOs. 'They are ignoring the old authority and going for new economic opportunities. Now people have got involved with the mafia, through drugs and politics, and they cannot get out. One end of the chain reaches the community, the other ... who knows where it ends?' Drugs money eats away at the old values, it builds the village mosque, pays previously unthinkable bride-prices.

'The drug lord', says another friend, 'wants to marry a woman. He goes to the father. The father refuses. "How much do you want?" "Twenty thousand dollars," says the father, sure that this is an impossible sum. "I will give you one hundred thousand."'

Whether all the stories are completely accurate is not the point; what is important is that a new narrative begins to be created: money can buy everything. Respect for the elders starts to be replaced by respect for money. The international community plays its own part in contributing to the seeping corruption. In the run-up to the Emergency Loya Jirga, the UN gave out hundreds of expensive satellite phones. No one ever asked for them back. In Kabul, ISAF has a contract for ten tankers of fuel a day from, as it happens, a very close associate of a very important minister. Often it takes only three tankers to refill their tanks, the other seven get sold on the city streets. Stories like this abound, the message is, it does not matter, money is there to be wasted, accountability is just a word.

As always, and as everywhere, it is those who have the least power in society who suffer from the collapse of values. ADA has long worked in the south of Afghanistan, in some of the most conservative areas of the country. Samadi was visibly shocked at the impact of some of the changes. 'In Zabul,' he says, 'newborn babies are found in the bushes, kids without a father. Their mother hides them at home, sometimes even the girl's father does not know. Then after she has given birth it is left in the bushes, and so no one has to know.' In some ways it is not new; women have always been used, and it has always been hidden. Sharifa was interviewed in Kabul in 1996, just before the arrival of the Taliban.[1] It was a hot summer and flies buzzed in the air of her single room, landing on the sick child who lay curled in the corner. In better times her husband earned good money and their house, she said, was beautiful. Then a rocket attack destroyed it, killing her husband and two of her children. She and her remaining children were living in its ruins. She limped from a shrapnel wound and her eldest daughter still screamed in her sleep. Asked how she managed for food, her answer was so veiled that it took some time to be sure of the meaning. 'A soldier gives her food, brings rice for lunch and she keeps some for tea,' a female colleague translated. 'Don't ask how she pays: it is a shame to our women.' What is different about a remote place like Zabul is that, unlike Kabul, traditional society is still so strong; if it is happening there, it is surely worse elsewhere.

For many Afghan women and men, the new order has meant little more than exposure to renewed abuse at the hands of those who feel that they can act with impunity again in their 'free' country. The presence of international troops was meant to bring an end to this but, as a member of a US patrol in Bamiyan in early 2003 put it, 'Gee, we don't do rights'. Meanwhile the boys and girls in uniform flaunt their own form of military pornography. Driving by a crowded bus stop on the wide avenue leading down to Darulaman Palace one bright morning, we saw all heads turned towards an open-topped ISAF jeep in the traffic. Attracting the stares was a blonde German woman sprawled over the front seat, with wraparound sunglasses and a tight T-shirt, feet wide apart on the dashboard. The men were no better, perched Rambo-style in skimpy singlets on armoured personnel carriers, cruising around town. Men simply do not show themselves off like this unless, as many Kabulis quietly conclude, they are trying to attract other men. Food for thought, perhaps, for the macho boys from ISAF.

The question of how to retain what is positive in the old values, to ensure that they are transmitted to a younger generation, is one of the big issues facing Afghan parents. A friend recently brought his family back from Islamabad. They live in MacroRayon, the Soviet-built four-storey walk-up flats on the way to the city's airport. People like to live here because it is safe, though from the outside it looks like the worst kind of UK housing estate and the piped water flows only for a few hours a day. But even here, in a sought-after location, he will not let his kids out to play because of the language they come back with. 'Yet', he asks, 'what can I do? You can't keep them in for twenty-four hours, I try to get back in time from work to take them somewhere each day, but it is not always possible.'

Rooted in Islam

Integral to Afghan values is Islam. Though its interpretation is often contested, it remains vital both to the way society functions and how most individuals see themselves. Almost all Afghans are Muslims and of these some 80 per cent are Sunnis belonging to the Hanafi school, the most tolerant of the four schools of Sunni Islam. Of the other 20 per cent of Afghanistan's Muslims, most are Shi'a. Despite the image given by both Taliban rule and today's conservatives, tolerance underlies the practice of Islam in Afghanistan. Devoutly religious Afghans may be, but in general they see religion as a private affair, ideally conducted within a community of fellow-believers but not something dictated by the state. You worship as you feel right and you make your own peace with God. While there is undoubtedly peer pressure from within the community to be a good Muslim, the notion that the state might lay down rules about how you pray, or what constitutes proper Islamic dress, is alien and has little resonance with popular notions of piety.

Religious belonging works outwards from the individual through those who worship together, to the *ulema* (the religious scholars), to those who undertake the *haj* (the pilgrimage to Mecca), and thereby to the worldwide community of believers. People will save for years to go on *haj*, and their pilgrimage will not only be an individual act but something that is shared by the community, that brings it status and knits it into the wider Muslim world. Arrive at Kabul airport when a *haj* plane has come in and the approach roads are completely blocked with the cars of those come to greet the returning pilgrims, who will spend several days visiting friends and family before they can even consider a return to work. Go to the villages and the bunting will be hung out and an endless stream of visitors will come through the *haji*'s door to pay respects and hear the stories.

Notions of religion and community go together. The village mullah is not part of a clergy appointed from outside but part of the village, chosen by the people, one of their own. In the space between the locality and the state sit the *ulema*, an important part of Afghanistan's 'civic society', yet largely ignored by western agencies, which operate in an almost entirely secular framework. The Herat *shura* of the *ulema* is one of the oldest in Afghanistan and is much respected, so much so that when the Taliban left they were able to keep security in the city until the arrival, some forty-eight hours later, of Ismael Khan. The *shura*'s head, Mullah Khuda Dad, explains how: '*Ulema* have a very important place in Afghan society; he is the first to call in the ear of the newborn and the last to speak to a person as he goes to the grave. The people understand the importance of the *ulema* in society and they will follow.'

Islam threads its way through daily life. Walk through the fields at prayer time and those you are with will stop, take off their shawls, lay them towards Mecca, and pray. Sit in a house and before long someone will roll out a prayer mat in the corner. This is the essence of religion, not rules and regulations; it does not interrupt the rhythms of life, it forms them. The five daily prayers, the fasting of the month of Ramadan, structure time. The *muezzin* call from the city mosques, men leave their shoes at the door, enter and pray. In the countryside, flags flutter over shrines, or the simple graves of fallen *mujahideen*. Trees or stones close to significant graves become sites of importance on which scraps of cloth will be fixed as a token of respect or to signify a special request. Passers-by will raise both their hands in respect and brush their beards in deference to the site. Stories tell of *barakat*, the holiness that some men possess. On the road out from Faizabad to Baharak there is a huge boulder perched just above a house. It came down the mountain, but Allah stopped it or everyone would have been killed. A miracle. A thousand such stories abound. Drive further along the road, stop at the village of Hazrat i Sayyed and walk up the hill to the shrine of Nasir Khusraw, a renowned poet and thinker whose missionary activity in the cause of the Ismaili faith forced him to flee his home in Balkh and pursue his work in exile under the protection of an intellectual Ismaili prince in Yamgan in the remote mountains of Badakhshan. In exile, he turned his energies to contemplation and writing for the next thirty-five years of his life. Local legend has it that after his death the Seljuks sent someone to bring his body to their capital, but the people dug deep and buried his body and the Seljuks could not find him. So then the minister of the Seljuk king sent instructions that a shrine should be constructed of very expensive stone. But the shrine collapsed, and then, in a dream, the minister was told not to construct it of expensive stone but of local materials, and thus it was done. The local people have looked after it ever since.

Have you heard? A squash vine grew beneath a towering tree.
In only twenty days it grew and spread and put forth fruit.
Of the tree it asked: 'How old are you? How many years?'
Replied the tree: 'Two hundred it would be, and surely more.'
The squash laughed and said: 'Look, in twenty days,
I've done more than you;
tell me, why are you so slow?'
The tree responded: 'O little squash, today is
not the day of reckoning between the two of us.
Tomorrow, when winds of autumn howl down on you and me,
then shall it be known for sure which one of us is the real man!'

(Nasir Khusraw, Divan, 20)

In the wonderful old city of Herat is the Masjid i Jami, the main mosque, one of the few of Afghanistan's architectural treasures to have survived the war intact. Here you feel how Islam has travelled down the centuries, part of a rich civilization that war can never totally erase. It is reflected in the building itself, fragments of thirteenth-century Ghorid work still surviving alongside the lavish Timurid decoration. Even more, it lies in age-old ritual, the sense that these spaces have been used in essentially the same way, and have invoked the same feelings, for generations. As the early-morning sunshine slants down into this sacred space, children come to read their schoolbooks and adults to pray, to give or receive alms, to talk or just to be. It is impossible to imagine an Afghanistan without Islam.

Identity and others

Key to understanding the Afghan notion of identity is that it is formed in relation to others: to family, to community, to tribe or ethnic group. A person's sense of self and place in the world works from the family outwards through ties of kinship and other networks. An individual is never alone; that would be terrible, and the solitude that westerners often seek remains a mystery to Afghans.

The family, wrote Nancy Dupree in 1984, is 'the single most important institution in Afghan society'. 'It is', said a woman in Kabul, 'like a strong chain, every member linked to each other' (de Berry et al. 2003). Starting from this point helps outsiders to understand not only how men see the world but also how many women see it, and how they define their priorities. The private home is an inviolable sanctuary, a place of security and protection. Access to the home by visitors is carefully controlled by spatial and social means, and respect for these limits is a sign of respect for the family itself. We often found ourselves stalled by hospitality in the room set aside from the family quarters, before a member of the household emerged to discuss the reason for the visit. In most of the countryside, men who are not part of the immediate family will never get to meet the women. Even in more liberal areas it is only older and very respected men who, under controlled circumstances with a male relative present, can talk to the women.

To violate the home is to violate an Afghan's honour, and the honour of his family. Writing about the early days of the *jihad*, Oliver Roy (1986) noted how 'members of the resistance never carry out a house search'. Even groups carrying out military missions would ask permission before entering a private home. Despite hopes that their presence will win hearts and minds, coalition soldiers conducting 'search and destroy' missions have clearly failed to do their homework. Even liberal urban Afghans are scandalized by stories of US marines and their proxies kicking down the doors of rural homes in the south and east of the country, and conducting body searches on men and women. Little do they seem to realize that such intrusions alienate all members of the community, and make it easier for forces opposed to the government to gain ground in these areas.

It is hard for a westerner to understand how deeply the idea of honour is embedded in the Afghan world-view. It seems to come from another age and to lead people to do things that appear incomprehensible: a brother might kill his own sister because she was believed to have brought dishonour on the family, or a father his son. It is a system that operates largely around the spoken word rather than the written. Just as Afghans are bemused by foreigners' insistence on bits of paper, they find it difficult to understand why foreigners break verbal agreements. Here a person's word is still his bond. Nowhere is this more evident than in the large amounts of money transferred through the *hawala* system which, after the collapse of the formal banking system, has not only been the mainstay of the economy, but also a life-line for many families receiving remittances from relatives working abroad. Aid agencies used it too – to the consternation of their accountants and auditors who struggled to believe that it was possible to deposit hundreds of thousands of dollars with an offshore trader and receive, after a phone confirmation, the corresponding amount from a designated person within the country, without anything ever going missing.

Visitors are often bemused by how they are able to walk away from the stalls of Afghan carpet-sellers with valuable goods for which they have not yet paid. Not only is this an astute way to close a deal, but it also places the potential buyer under an obligation to reciprocate the trust that has been shown. 'Anyway – we always know where to find them,' chuckled a carpet-seller friend who traced to Moscow an errant journalist whose promised payment had not come through after two years of waiting. He flew to Moscow, where he confronted the morti-fied journalist whose bank had failed to make the original transfer. The journalist did not hesitate to invite his unexpected visitor to stay with him for a week, and he paid for his flights.

Ironically, the very sophistication of this verbal culture is often per-ceived as 'primitive'. To believe that undertakings can be guaranteed by basic trust is confusing in the modern world, even more so in a society that is often caricatured as being riven by deceit and betrayal. During the darkest hours of international opprobrium, many a long hour was spent discussing with Taliban representatives the expectations of the outside world as to their responsibilities. For the UN, this came down to written undertakings from the administration on a series of contentious issues around the delivery of aid. In the incongruous neo-rococo setting of the Ministry of Foreign Affairs, carefully worded drafts – in English, of course – of agreements that had been pored over by legal advisers in New York, were handed over to the minister by a group of diplomats who had come on one of the many one-day *démarches* to Kabul. Impeccably mannered as ever, the minister accepted these drafts graciously and, barely glancing at them, offered green tea while elaborating on the need for trust and understanding with the international community. When asked for his reaction to the draft agreement, he responded, 'We shall look at these papers and get back to you tomorrow'. The expectations of the assembled diplomats and UN officials of a definitive agreement on the issue of the week were politely rebuffed, and plane schedules were hastily adjusted. By the next day, the minister had a detailed list of unfulfilled UN promises which he raised before referring back to the agreement that was on the table. The draft agreement, still unsigned, sat between the empty teacups, a symbol of the gulf that lay between the culture of paper and that of the word. Given the mutual atmosphere of mistrust, it was perhaps little wonder that the international community craved to pin down the latest 'bottom-line' in black and white, but this rarely achieved the results that they so badly needed. It remains to be seen if the successors to the Taliban are as adept in dealing with their international interlocutors.

Women and the family 'Family attitudes, not government guarantees, decided the future of girls', wrote Nancy Dupree (1984), reflecting on the 1970s. In many ways little has changed, and those who focused on the Taliban's restrictions forgot the all-powerful depth of tradition in some places. Women carry the honour of the family and their behaviour reflects on the men of that family; change for women is thus impossible unless there is a change in the attitudes of men. These attitudes do not just exist in rural areas, nor do they solely belong to uneducated people, but they are engrained in the most educated and seemingly worldly of families, those who have jobs with embassies and the UN, who travel abroad and dine with foreign friends. Explaining how foreign agencies wanting to run programmes with women should talk first to their husbands, one professional Afghan working with a foreign agency put it quite simply: 'If you talk to my wife first, I will kill her.'

Afghans are not all the same. A good Afghan friend has a wonderful husband who has suffered death threats for his wife's uncompromising work with women. Another young woman's struggle started at the age of six, when she pulled out her first teeth because the teacher said she could not go to school with baby teeth. She has been fighting ever since: to stay in Peshawar and go to school rather than accompanying her parents to a distant rural village with no schools for girls; to go to university; to take a job with an international organization. She attended her first international conference by saving up enough money to take her younger brother with her, so she could have a *mahram*, otherwise the family would refuse permission for her to go. At every turn on her way, the most difficult challenge was not achieving what she wanted, but convincing her family of the worth of it. Then she was engaged, without her knowledge or consent. Even men in the family had not been able to resist arranged marriages, so how could she? How could she bring so much hurt and humiliation to her parents? How confirm all the warnings of relations who prophesied that allowing her to have education and to go to work would only bring trouble?

There are, of course, families where parents would always discuss the question of marriage with their children and would never force anything upon them, but for those still held within the bounds of conservative tradition it is often impossible to go against parental wishes. Not only do the demands of honour exact a fearful price – and people have been killed or locked away for the rest of their days for such transgressions – but in a culture where family means so much, how do you countenance being cut off from all your kin? For women it is hardest. Married or not, men have a freedom to move as they please and can build a life outside the home; but to educated women it is like being allowed to look through the open door but not go through it. That even a strong young woman could not push that door fully open gives some indication of just how long the process of change will take, how it will need generations. We should not be surprised; and yet often the international community has talked of women's rights as if someone could just flick a switch and bring them into being.

Discrimination is most often thought of in connection with Pashtun tribal traditions, yet many other parts of the country are also deeply conservative with respect to women. Working in the district of Shar i Buzurg in Badakhshan in the aftermath of the 1998 earthquake, it proved almost impossible to find women able to work as community health workers; they were simply not allowed to travel from village to village, even if accompanied by a husband or brother. Nor is the problem confined to rural areas. In urban Qunduz the female head of the girls' secondary school is a wonderful strong woman, full of warmth and wisdom. Her daughter went for, and was offered, a job with the UN. Her brother would not let her take it. 'If it were Kabul,' he said, 'I would agree. But here people will talk.' The Afghan Independent Human Rights Commission office in Mazar finds the worst cases of women being married very young, or being married against their wishes, occur in Uzbek, rather than Pashtun, communities. According to the commission only two women in Sar i Pul do not wear the burqa; not because women want to wear it but because they get endless problems if they do not, including repeated 'requests' to marry commanders. One commander asked a twelve-year-old to marry him; when her parents refused, she was taken by force. In another incident, the commander of Sar i Pul reportedly asked a beautiful thirty-year-old widow to 'work' in his office. She was a *loya jirga* (grand council) representative and said to him, 'You already have seven wives, why do you want me?'

Yet although the demands of family can bring many strictures to women's lives, few would chose to define themselves outside it. In part this is because children are immensely important – Afghan women, and indeed men, find it strange that people should chose to live without children. But Afghans are also realistic, they know things cannot change quickly. When the Taliban brought out edict no. 8, banning women's employment, the UN commissioned a report into the situation of women. Its authors noted: 'Numerous Afghan women interviewed for this paper emphasised that the way forward was through creating a future for their children – both male and female. Afghan women interviewed for this paper seemed mostly concerned for the rights of their children as mothers and then concerned for their own rights as women' (Fielden and Azerbaijani-Moghadam 2001).

Circles beyond Beyond the confines of the family is a web of complex relationships, and from these spring the nitty-gritty of politics, the making of decisions and the allocation of resources. In Afghanistan, you know a person first by where they come from and to whom they are related, not by their work or claim to a particular social class. In his work on the impact of the *jihad* on Afghan society, Oliver Roy (2003) suggests: 'Afghan identity is based on a common political culture which could be summarised as follows. "Real" political life is played out at the local level and primary loyalty lies with the "solidarity group", whatever its sociological basis. Ethnic identities are important but they never prevail over this primordial identity, nor do they undermine a common Afghan identity.'

The basic solidarity group in rural areas is often, but not always, the village, which in small settlements is usually no more than an extended family. Beyond this, the patterns of power and influence are complex. According to Roy, 'Power in Afghan peasant society resides neither in a specific location nor in a person, but in an elusive network, which needs constant maintenance and reconstruction.' Quite what constitutes these networks varies from place to place, depending on how tribal an area is and on the nature of inter-group relations. In areas where relations are good, people will liken this network to a set of concentric circles: first the village; then the nearby villages; then the valley and so on, with the nature of the relationship changing – and the degree of obligation decreasing – as one moves out from the centre.

The concentric circles evoke more than physical proximity, given the extent to which many communities have been dispersed well beyond their area of origin. You may have moved to Kabul, or even abroad, but you still have obligations to your family, and through them to the village. It is part of an Afghan's sense of honour to meet such obligations. So keenly is it felt that in the drought of 2000 and 2001 there were villages in the south where *khans* left their homes because they could no longer meet their obligation to provide a meal for those in need. Similarly, it is part of a person's honour to protect from harm those with whom he has relations of solidarity. Thus a friend from the province of Logar, where relationships between the different tribal groups are generally very good, spoke of how no one, even across tribes, would tell anyone from outside who had joined the Taliban, for fear that they might fall prey to the witch-hunt that followed their overthrow. Many people had been Taliban then, just as in previous eras people had been *mujahideen* or communists. They were not bad people and did no harm to others, therefore they were to be protected; it would be dishonourable not to do so.

The relations that affirm a sense of solidarity within a group, however, are not immutable, and the protection that they might offer needs to be earned, generation after generation. Failure to live up to one's obligations can result in censure that, if considered serious, is inherited from father to son, until one of the offspring is deemed to have earned his family's place back within the group. Conflicts or disputes can rupture relations even within a family. A friend who was a senior civil servant disappeared from his post in Kabul overnight in 1990. The word was that he had committed adultery, and had failed to answer for his behaviour to the elders of his family, or the relatives of the woman concerned. He was ostracized to such an extent that he felt obliged to flee the country. His sons, who still live in Kabul with their mother, under the shadow of this shame, last heard of their father in a mental asylum in Ukraine, which was presumably as far from Afghanistan as he could get at the time.

The communists, with their ideas of reform, failed to understand that it was the intricate set of relations between landowner and the rest of the village that, exploitative though it might have been, ensured poor people's survival. Without the landlord there was no credit, no access to seed, no safety-net at times of shortages. They also failed to appreciate how deeply rooted was the Afghan sense of the order of things. In many areas people did not even take up the land allocated to them under land reform initiatives because they believed it was wrong. 'God', it was said, 'gives land'. Reflecting on how the communists killed a large landowner in Keshem, Badakhshan, but still failed to redistribute his lands, a local leader spoke of how: 'A person's holding a lot of land is not necessarily seen as illegitimate or wrong, it depends on how he obtained it and how he behaves. Those who took land by force, or bought it with money that was obtained illegally, are resented, but not others.'

The assistance community has understood this little more than the communists. Unlike the Afghan state, which dealt with the village as an entity, leaving its inhabitants to sort out between themselves how they would meet their dues, assistance workers have tended to deal with it as a collection of individual families. They arrive with their survey forms or their participatory methods for ranking the wealth of families, and they decide who will benefit from their largesse. And then they go away. The village takes over. The assistance that has been provided is often redistributed according to power and custom. Sometimes it does not matter. As an elder in the central highlands of Hazarajat noted: 'We have to look after the poor anyway.'

Other villages are not so generous: the poor are deprived of what should be theirs and the rich get richer. Asking why the poorest had not worked on a food for work scheme brought the reply: 'The land-lord wouldn't let them, he said he needed their labour.' There is little an agency can do. The poor have to live there long after aid work-ers have gone. The problem does not just affect food distribution or other emergency programmes; the realities of village power dominate decision-making at all levels. The *shura*, or other village committees, may be set up according to all manner of carefully devised criteria but such attempts at social engineering do not necessarily alter things, they just ensure that the real decisions get made somewhere else. Not that this is unique to Afghanistan. In East Timor, the World Bank's Community Empowerment programme carefully excluded the old elites from the new community structures in order to foster more egalitarian decision-making. The evaluation of the programme showed how the decisions were simply made outside the formal structures that had been established (Ospina and Hohe 2001). Change, if it is to come, will come only slowly. Changes to structures might, if handled well, contribute to this but they will not suddenly bring greater democracy or equality.

For those who have moved beyond the confines of their village to the urban context, there is a range of different reference-points that complement those that link them back to their rural roots. While educa-tion in general bestows status, attendance at a particular school adds a further dimension of belonging – and influence. 'He was my classmate at Habibia', for example, becomes an assurance of getting all manner of things done, from sorting out visas to fixing the electricity supply. The imprint that is made by higher education is, not surprisingly, one that affects the rest of students' lives. The seeds of some of the major political factions in the country were sown at Kabul University during the 1970s, based on the ideas or charisma of one professor or another. The sense of solidarity or enmity that developed on campus is carried into later life. Even middle-aged students will continue to locate themselves in relation to their lecturers at that time, as much as the years during which they attended the faculty.

Being a government employee has long been a source of status and pride, which in part explains why many carried on even when the direct material rewards had become totally insignificant. A government job was a job for life, you did not get sacked and you did not resign. Remembering the time after the fall of the Najibullah regime, one friend recalled: 'I was still going to work, but the salary was very low and we had no coupons. But a government job is a permanent job and if we resign it is a very bad thing.' The sense of pride that many Afghan civil servants once felt has now become tarnished by the corruption that is perceived to have penetrated all levels of the government system. While association with the government has long brought status, official employment offered little more than a modest sinecure for the families of civil servants, but one that was felt to be secure. Once, they say, 'Government staff were happy to have a salary, even though it was very low. The misuse of public property was dishonourable.' 'In the communist days', says Shah Wali, picking up his tea glass, 'there was an inventory even for these. Things had to be accounted for. If something was broken you had to show it.'

The fact that those days are long gone is, for many, a source of shame. The pride that once went with a foothold in government has been devalued, to the extent that many official jobs are now viewed simply as opportunities for personal enrichment. All groups are complicit in this process, but none is more discredited than the Panjshiris who, since early 2002, are believed to have reverted to the behaviour that characterized the *mujahideen* government between 1992 and 1996. The actions of those who are using their current dominance in key institutions in Kabul for their own benefit has discredited the group as a whole. As an elder of a village at the mouth of the Panjshir valley put it: 'They are raping Kabul in the name of the *jihad*, but it will bring dishonour on all of us.'

Afghans survive because people do not operate only as individuals; they also operate as members of networks. You look after those in your network: a salary does not just feed your immediate family, it supports an entire group of people to whom you have obligations. Those in work share with those without, remittances from those lucky enough to have gone overseas keep entire villages from starvation. Although networks are more diffuse in urban areas, there remains a high degree of interdependence between country and town, and beyond. A family from a village near Qarabagh, whose home survived the worst of the fighting centred around the strategically important road to the north, provided refuge for their relatives who were forced to flee Kabul during the worst of the inter-factional conflict in 1993. Once re-established back in Kabul, the urban relatives provided a home for the younger cousins from the village during the mid-1990s, so that they could take advantage of what education was then on offer in the city. By 2000, however, the family from the village were in turn forced from their homes by the Taliban during fighting in the area, and were taken in by their urban relatives. They have spent the last two summers moving between the city and the village, where their home was reduced to rubble in October 2001 by a 'smart' coalition bomb directed at the nearby Taliban frontlines. The pace of its reconstruction is set by remittances sent by relatives abroad.

Few are the Afghans who consciously cut their ties with their roots, usually as a result of exposure to radical leftist politics. Most of the students who fell under the spell of Trotskyist ideologues during the 1970s subsequently left the country, but those who stayed – and in some cases their families – still bear the association, despite efforts by some firebrands to reinvent themselves. Even abroad, people's past can catch up with them. A number of those who had used their communist past to claim asylum in the Netherlands when the Taliban were in power found themselves the objects of inquiries by the Dutch immigration service investigating human rights abuses during the Soviet occupation.

Radical past or not, the system of obligations extends to the settling of scores as a result of your ties. You may be living somewhere else but you can still be targeted because of the political views or the controversial past of your brother, father or son. A bemused British radio journalist who had attended an Afghan community meeting in a church hall in north London during the late 1990s simply couldn't understand why the session ended with people hurling abuse and chairs at each other. Even opposition to the Taliban was, it seems, not enough to keep the differences of this disparate group under control.

Civil society?

The nature of these networks raises questions about the usefulness of the notion of civil society. Often used but rarely defined in the Afghan context, the concept implies a secular entity that is distinct from, and yet is expected to act as some kind of counter-balance to, the influence of the bureaucratic state. In Afghanistan, as other authors have observed for African states (e.g. Chabal and Daloz 1999), this separation does not really exist; for as long as there has been a state, *qawm* has penetrated it. But are social networks such as *qawm* civil society? Classical definitions would suggest not, civil society is seen as transcending family, kin or even communal ties. But in the rural areas a village and a *qawm* are often one and the same, and thus any form of organization, be it a *shura*, a village health committee, or the new committees for the National Solidarity Programme, is essentially a *qawm* organization. Yet if *qawm* organizations are not civil society, then what is left?

In emphasizing the secular nature of civil society, there is a risk of ignoring the significance of the *ulema* in acting as a counter-balance to government by providing independent guidance on a variety of levels. Through this work, *shuras* of the *ulema* have retained the respect of many Afghans, who continue to look to them for arbitration on issues that for any reason cannot be handled using traditional methods of resolution, or for interpretation.

If, on the other hand, civil society does include *qawm*, then what does this say about its relationship with the state? As Oliver Roy notes: 'the existence of group solidarity does not mean that there is an alternative centre of power in opposition to the state, since such groupings are easily absorbed within the state structure' (Roy 1986: 26). The power of the clan stands both within and outside of the state. For example, the current Minister of Defence, Fahim, 'controls a huge and largely invisible network that extends throughout the government and economy … run by his own "clan" of Panjshiris' (Starr 2003). The experience of other leaders, such as Rashid Dostum's role in exacting benefits for members of his clan from the Najibullah regime in the early 1990s, has served as a useful precedent.

The hastily convened civil society consultation that took place in Bad Honnef in Germany in late November 2001, in parallel with the Bonn negotiations, seemed to represent an attempt to mark out a political space for a group of Afghans who were representative of a wider cross-section of society than the factional and other interests that were party to the UN-brokered political talks. Discussions with some of the group before they left for the meeting, however, revealed confusion as to what they were expected to do, and deep unease as to how their views might be por-trayed as representative of Afghan society, when in fact they represented little but themselves. In many ways, the consultation itself illustrated the weakness of the political negotiations before they had even started – for had the group negotiating the political transition been more representa-tive, the civil society sideshow would not have been needed.

The Bad Honnef civil society initiative was perhaps the most formal recent effort to identify a discernible non-factional Afghan constituency, following the mixed experiences of aid agencies in working with Afghan communities as part of attempts to find alternatives to working with the Taliban. While the prime focus of international organizations in tapping into Afghan civil society has been on NGOs, professional or business associations, these are almost entirely urban phenomena which, being largely comprised of the educated elite, are hardly representative of Afghan society as a whole. The importance of such associations is secondary to the vertically structured links of family, tribe and ethnic group. Even as an individual professional or businessman you do not leave your position within your social group outside the door of a meeting of such an association. Indeed, like the state itself, such associations are penetrated by, and often undermined by, ties of family and tribe.

Making decisions, being represented

Traditionally, decisions are made in Afghanistan by a time-honoured process of discussion and consensus. Sometimes this is a myth; but even as a myth it has value, for it carries the message: this is how things should be. The key decision-making body is the institution of the *jirga* (Pashtu) or *shura* (Dari). Both words are probably best translated as 'council', and thinking of it in this way, rather than as some unique Afghan institution, helps understand its variability. There is not just one way of doing things in this country but a complex array of alternatives, and the contradictory accounts given by different people reflect the different dimensions of that reality.

In theory, a *jirga* can be convened at any level of tribal organization, from the smallest lineage to an entire confederation. Called in order to make collective decisions about important issues or resolve disputes, it would normally include all adult males of the tribe. *Loya jirgas* (grand councils) have been held at national level at key moments of the country's history. Their role has as often been more to legitimize decisions already made than actually to debate them, and by no means all have been considered legitimate by the people. The *jirga* is a deeply rooted part of Pashtun tribal tradition and holds great symbolic value for these communities. The notion that conflicts are resolved or decisions made by this collective mechanism is a core part of Pashtun identity. How far this actually works in practice seems, like much else in Afghanistan's traditions, variable.

Shuras can also exist at different levels (village, district, province) and in relation to different kinds of groupings (for example, professional people or religious scholars). But for all their folkloric status, many Afghans question the extent to which *shuras* really existed prior to the assistance community's need for organizations to engage with. In some places they are a genuine part of how society traditionally functioned; in some places a creation of the *mujahideen* in areas liberated from Soviet control, a genuine attempt at the time (even if subverted later) at community involvement; in some places they have been creations of the assistance community; and in yet others people still do not have anything they refer to as a *jirga* or *shura* but decisions are made by the village elders who, if necessary, will call a village meeting. The *shura* can either be a meeting of representatives or a meeting of all male adults (very occasionally with female participation also) in a village. At levels above the village, it is always representative. Who these representatives are can vary enormously. In some places they have been taken over entirely by commanders, while elsewhere commanders prefer to influence from the outside. 'Otherwise', said a friend, 'they fear they may be bound by collective decisions.' Four viewpoints, from different people and different parts of the country, give some idea of the variation:

'Mullahs, elders, even in some communities women, participated; and they solved all conflicts and never allowed them to leak out, very few were referred to the government. Youths would go also, but to sit and listen and learn, they would never talk. From more than a thousand years back this was the tradition.' (Kabul-based NGO worker speaking of the south)

'In the past it was said that there were *shura*, but they were very weak or not existing. It was the *khan* or the *malik* who influenced people's lives, who made decisions. The *shura* were just there to say they were practising democracy, they would say they had discussed with the *"shura"*.' (Human rights worker, speaking of Jalalabad)

'"The district level *shura* – ten to fifteen people – comes to the district governor and talks through issues. The *shura* members are the powerful people, big landlords, though occasionally poorer people if they are very clever – educated but also with an ability to make good decisions – can be chosen.' (NGO worker in Herat)

'These *shura*, they cannot act, there is no space, they are not independent, all are controlled by the factions, they are a device for commanders to legitimate their activity.' (Local government official in Mazar i Sharif)

Traditionally, in all these gatherings, people would sit round in a circle and decisions would be made by consensus. The outward egalitarianism of form did not, however, mean that all voices were equal; age and socioeconomic standing affected how different voices are heard. The extent to which age is deferred to is often difficult for a westerner to grasp. Chris went to meet a group of elders in Qalat, the capital of Zabul province, one of the most strongly tribal and traditional provinces in the country.

The four men who came into the room include one wonderful old man, who was 108 and had been to four *loya jirgas*. He was known simply as 'the senator', in recognition of his role in the earlier parliament. For more than an hour I sat and listened as he answered my questions and talked of the community's hopes and fears for a new Afghanistan. None of the other three men said anything. At the end I asked if anyone else had anything they wanted to add. One answered: 'Senator speaks for all of us.' It was not that they were not articulate individuals with opinions, far from it, but this, in Afghanistan, is how respect works, and only for us is it strange. After that I would always go and see the senator when I visited Zabul and sit on the roof of his house in the early evening, looking over the orchards to the desert beyond and feeling the heat seep slowly out of the day. 'People', he said, 'do not want the Taliban back, but they are afraid.' Zabul, in those early months after Bonn, was a province that could be won or lost; and the international community lost it. Some four and a half hours on a bone-jarring road from Qandahar, few people bothered to go there and find out what the people felt, far less deliver any of the improvements in services that the people so longed for. By the middle of 2003 the Taliban were back, occupying the outer districts, making raids into Qalat, rendering the road to Qandahar unsafe. I think often of the senator, and of his hopes for a different Afghanistan, one that was secure, where educated men were respected, where there was once again the rule of law. For a few tantalizing months there seemed to be a chance, but now in this, one of the least secure provinces in the country, it is fast receding.

That trip to Qalat was not the only time Zabul taught me things. On another visit I was in one of the districts interviewing an elder on the process around the formation of the new constitution for Afghanistan. We had discussed the issue of selection of delegates to the Constitutional Loya Jirga and I was then trying to ask whether he felt there should be provincial-level consultations on the content of the draft constitution before the *loya jirga* itself. He repeated his answers on how the delegates should be chosen. I clearly wasn't getting my point across and I tried to put the question in a different way, wondering if something was getting lost in translation. The reply was the same. I tried again. Then it dawned on me that the question was not being answered because it made absolutely no sense to him. What I had been missing was that in his frame of reference you chose your representative to represent you, and like the younger elder with the senator, you trusted him to be able to respond on your behalf to whatever was being said. Why else would you have chosen him? And having chosen him, what would be the meaning of an additional local consultation?

A similar confusion often arose when discussing how someone was selected to a position, for example, as the *uluswal* (district administrator). 'He was elected', is usually the answer. Yet closer questioning about the election process reveals it to be very different to what is meant by 'election' in the West. There is no suggestion of one person one vote, let alone a secret ballot; rather, a process of selection of the right person for the job takes place by a kind of osmosis. The decision is gradually made through discussion; sometimes it is simply a foregone conclusion – people just 'know' who the representative of the village should be. Then, if necessary, the decision is confirmed in a meeting. The notion that you should leave such an important decision as choosing your representative to a random process of individual vote-casting is, to many Afghans, irresponsible. Rather, those with wisdom, the elders, people perhaps with some education, maybe the mullah, are expected to exercise these talents on behalf of the community and, through debate, come to a consensus that can then be confirmed. This process is reflected in the language itself. The term commonly translated as election is *intekhabat*, which is found in both Dari and Pashtu. The same word also means 'selection' and it describes a process that does not involve voting, which is covered by a separate term.[2] While such an open process of selection may indeed by subject to hijacking by commanders, or by powerful landlords or drug barons, it can also work well for a community. Where powerful people abuse the system, it is unlikely that this can be stopped simply by changing the system; the prevailing power relations are such that there will always be ways to manipulate or intimidate. Despite the hoped-for opportunity for change, fewer than 120 of the 344 generally elected delegates at the Constitutional Loya Jirga had no affiliation to one of the major armed factions. Commanders dominated the elections in Kabul, Wardak and Nangarhar provinces, while 98 per cent of the delegates from Herat were close to governor Ismail Khan.

War and social change

Solidarity networks may be the strength of Afghanistan but they can also be its weakness, for they can easily be fractured, pitting group against group. *Zan wa zameen*, women and land, have been the cause of conflict for centuries, but more recently the most divisive force has been that of politics. The coming to power of the Communist Party set in motion a whole set of social changes. These came about both as a direct result of communist policies and as a consequence of the armed opposition to these. One friend recalled how:

> When the Communists entered Afghanistan the first thing they did to harm Afghanistan was they replaced traditional leaders with artificial leaders. The old leaders they were gaoled, killed, forced to flee. But the people they never obeyed the new leaders. The Islamists they did the same, they replaced the old leaders by ones without education, without values.

Another friend remembers that:

> During the *mujahideen* time the Russians divided people into tribal groups to fight against each other. There used to be elders and *jirgas*, then they came under the influence of Pakistan and Iran and they brought the *tanzeems* and the elders escaped or died. Those left in the country were just for fighting.

While their sense of identity has, for some educated Afghans, long been influenced by political belief, it was allegiance to a particular party – leftist or *jihadi* – that seems to have had an impact on relations within the solidarity group. In conversations, Afghans tend to perceive this as really affecting them from the 1970s onwards, and they acknowledge that membership was as much a means of survival, through the benefits and protection that the card offered, as an ideological statement.

As the old order collapsed, civilians who feared they might be subject to violence from the various parties to the conflict began to find ways to gain protection within the new systems. A colleague who at that time worked in the Ministry of Planning explained how, as the collapse of Najibullah's regime became obvious, 'People within the government tried to have their own connection with *mujahideen*, for protection. Everyone knew when Najibullah was about to go, information leaked. Even low-level people had a worry as to what would happen when the *mujahideen* came. When Najibullah announced he was going, everything changed, everyone tried to find a card, a connection with the *mujahideen*.' Fears were similar in the countryside. Another friend

4 *In villages to the west of Herat, women tend the silk worms and men spin the raw thread for the city's famous silk industry, 2003. (Chris Johnson)*

who has long worked in the rural areas of Afghanistan remembers how 'The *mujahideen* easily controlled the district centre, they started from the beginning to collect from the people, to beat them to get food. Teachers tried to find a mullah, to form a relationship with him, give him money so they would be safe. Even *arbabs* got beaten, they too sought protection from the mullah.'

As the conflict came to Kabul, and the frontlines shifted across the city, pinning the poster of the incumbent *mujahideen* commander on your front door or taxi windscreen was one way of demonstrating outward solidarity to the faction: whether the fighters paid any attention to these was another matter.

Such systems of protection have been a vital part of survival strategies. As the Taliban made their way through Hazarajat in the autumn of 1998, the people of Jaghori district considered two courses of action: to fight, or to negotiate the best possible terms for surrender. Despite their fears of the Taliban and their pride in their own reputation as *jihadi* fighters, they decided in the end to negotiate, and to do this before the Taliban attacked Jaghori. Their reasons were many but included the fact that, unlike the Taliban, they would get no outside support, that the Taliban had already conquered most other areas, that fighting would be likely to damage communal relations with their Pashtun neighbours for a long time to come, and that they were confident both in their own ability to negotiate and in the fact that there would be few Taliban present in such a remote area – and thus they would have the opportunity to get round many of the restrictions. They sent delegations to the provincial capital of Ghazni, to Kabul, and to the seat of the Taliban leadership in Qandahar. They pointed out their shared values in Islam and the responsibilities leaders have under Islam towards civilian populations. They reminded the Taliban of their promise not to punish those who surrendered. They also pointed out that if the Taliban were not extreme in their behaviour the people would be more easily governed, and they reminded them of how the Russians were hated for their behaviour. They insisted on the importance of education for the girls and women of the district. Their leaders were in constant communication with the people and there was a high degree of solidarity with their actions. The terms of the agreement being offered were clear: the military units in Jaghori would turn in their arms, be reintegrated into their villages and promise not to attack the Taliban, if the Taliban in turn agreed not to commit atrocities and not to interfere in cultural affairs. The Taliban insisted on limiting the agreement on education for girls to primary education, but the Jaghori *shura* continued to insist that this was not acceptable and that they would continue to work towards full education. Their key strategy in this was building an alliance with the Taliban education officer, whom they eventually turned into an ally. He allowed secondary schools for girls to open as long as they closed when a Taliban delegation was visiting, and he allowed women to continue teaching. They continued to teach a full curriculum, reverting to Taliban-approved materials when a delegation visited. They also adopted a variety of other stratagems: in schools with both primary and secondary levels the older girls would suddenly become 'teachers' when Taliban were around; a Talib who seemed to be spying on a school was invited to join the school staff (Suleman and Williams 2000).

Commanders and power The armed struggle brought about a new class of local power-holder: the commander. He was the head of a local armed group, sometimes a traditional leader but more often a younger person, perhaps someone coming from a lesser family but active in a political party. Not all commanders were bad, and there was idealism as well as self-interest in the early days of the struggle. High up a mountain valley in Badakhshan, an ex-Jamiat commander tells the story of how: 'The *mujahideen* did not even eat at people's houses unless invited, to ask was not allowed. They took nothing from the people, not even a pea was going in to their pockets at that time. A *mujahid* once ate one apricot without permission and the others disarmed him, beat him and paid the owner 20 afs.' The story may be apocryphal but it does sum up something of the spirit of the early days – and how people wanted leaders to live up to their expectations.

With time, divisions between commanders seemed to overshadow the sense of purpose of the early *jihad*, as they competed for externally supplied arms and funds that enabled them to consolidate their grip on the countryside. Local strongmen used their access to weapons, links with other more powerful commanders, with smuggling groups and with foreign countries or NGOs or UN agencies to increase their power. A friend who was active on the Hizbe Islami frontlines at the time recounts how he confronted his commander about firing rockets on residential areas of Kabul, where civilians might be at risk. 'We can do as we like, as we have Allah and the US on our side,' he was told. Many shifted allegiance so regularly that the old adage from the time of the British campaign, 'You can't buy an Afghan but if you have enough money you can rent one', gained a new relevance. Commanders in many places came to usurp the role of elders, and the traditional provincial or district *shura* were sometimes entirely controlled by commanders.

The new power is with the commanders, the old power was with the religious people, the *malik* and the *arbab*. Ordinary people expect the big people will defend them. Some people can keep their position regardless of the political changes going on around them, others change with the governor. Sometimes people are taken off the *shura* but still have influence; and sometimes people introduced by governor are not accepted by people. Thirty per cent of the leaders of the *shura* are people who are really there from their heart, who want to do good for the people; from father and grandfather it runs, they have always been the head of the *shura* and they try to keep the reputation of their families. Sometimes commanders become part of the *shura* but often not, because if they were part they would have to accept decisions – so often they don't go but they seek to influence from outside.

A range of comments illustrates how, in deliberately eroding the respect reserved for the elders, the new commander culture perhaps had most impact:

'When people started fighting each other the leadership changed, young people became breadwinners, there was a lack of respect for elders. But these young people could not get the respect of the community.'

'Before income was brought by the father, but with the new system young people with the gun brought bread home, they had the power.'

'Now the *mullah* and the leader have no role in the village, everything is done by the commander, and he knows only money.'

While frontlines were as often maintained by quiet deals as defended by arms, the proliferation of weapons had an undeniable impact on the tradition of debate, as force came increasingly to be used to settle disputes.

As the promise of the *mujahideen* turned to the brutality of the commanders, people looked for a new leadership: 'People want to go back to traditional [pre-revolution] leadership; they believe factions have done nothing for them, but many of the traditional leaders have gone. People feel that no one has heard their voice in the last twenty years.'

At first it seemed to some that the Taliban might represent a new start, but in many places their disregard for local leaders and local processes soon put an end to this. In the case of the tribal areas, it was said that, 'people lost trust in one year – the tribal people they just carried on their own affairs'. A large measure of this disillusionment was the failure to respect old structures.

As the war progressed, some of the big local families managed to re-establish themselves, at times under different patrons. In parts of Hazarajat the Taliban deliberately drew on the old leadership to establish a new and acceptable local government, which drew its support not only from its traditional role but also from the widespread dislike for the way many Hizbe Wahdat commanders had behaved.

Warlords Warlords are essentially commanders who have extended their power beyond their own group to build a wider regional base. Their power rests not primarily on direct control of territory but on influence through networks of commanders. As a result, the boundaries to the area they control can easily shift so that sometimes there are enclaves in a warlord's fiefdom where loyalty is to a rival. A warlord's power base is not necessarily confined to one ethnic group. Ismail Khan, for example, sees himself as the emir of western Afghanistan, an area with a mix of different ethnic groups; history, rather than ethnicity, defines who is currently within his patronage and who lies outside it. Pashtuns are at best treated with circumspection, and at worst discriminated against because of their association with the Taliban. Hazaras are accepted because of their perceived role in the *jihad*.

Warlords in the Pashtun tribal belt are dependent on tribal structures, which also can provide an important check on their potential ambitions. History suggests that in tribal areas it is the intervention of an outside force, be it central government or from another country, that allows one warlord to triumph over another. Tribal support will be given when it is seen to be beneficial to the whole tribe, and will be withdrawn if it is thought likely to lead the opposite way – the winner is the one who succeeds in getting support from dominant players. For example, the grip of the dominant Sherzai clan in Qandahar was lifted by Pakistani intervention in 1994. The returning Sherzais have, however, wasted little time in re-establishing themselves as power-brokers in and around the city. Despite the fact that Gul Agha Sherzai, initially a key US ally, was removed as governor and 'promoted' to the post of Minister in Kabul, his brother continued to enjoy tribal support in his absence. This has proved very effective in undermining the replacement governor, Yusuf Pashtun, who, even though he originally comes from Qandahar, seems not to be able to rely on significant tribal backing.

The interdependence between warlords and the local structures is less pronounced in non-Pashtun areas. Without the need to rely on customary leadership, warlords have tended to try to replace it with their own administration, with varying degrees of effectiveness. The first modern example of such a presumptive administration was perhaps Shura e Nazar, the Supervisory Council of the North, established by Ahmad Shah Massoud, which held partial sway over several provinces in the north during the *jihad*. In the case of Abdul Rashid Dostum, the structure of central government was simply co-opted into a northern regional administration – complete with its own currency and airline – prior to the Taliban capture of Mazar i Sharif.

While the terms 'warlord' and 'commander' are both used in a pejorative sense, the truth is more complex. The two commander brothers who have ruled the Uruzgan district of Sharistan for the last twenty years can certainly be ruthless in ensuring that they remain in power, and have no hesitation in extracting 10 per cent tax from the people on the lucrative poppy harvest. They have also built roads and promoted education. The result is that this remote district has a high proportion of educated women and sent many students to Kabul University in 2003. Democracy it is not, but it is a degree of law and order; and compared to neighbouring Dai Kundi, which has neither security nor services and is pulled apart by the different commanders ruling each valley, it is preferable in the eyes of many Afghans. Just as traditional leaders before them needed to earn the respect of the community and thereby gain legitimacy, so commanders are judged by how they use their power and the benefits that they might bring to their constituents.

Perhaps one of the most vivid current examples of the warlord/governor syndrome is Ismael Khan, presumptive emir of western Afghanistan. To the central authorities who wish to rein in his power, he is a warlord. To the educated of Herat, he is a reactionary. To the human rights movement, he is an abuser of rights. All these are true – as is the fact that, unlike in many other provinces, government employees are paid in Herat, investments are made in public services, and security is taken seriously.

Ismael Khan also illustrates the limits of non-tribal warlord power. Unlike Gul Agha Sherzai, who can take up a position as a minister in Kabul in the knowledge that his tribal networks will make little difference to who actually occupies the governor's mansion in Qandahar, Ismael Khan has resisted attempts by President Karzai to get him to Kabul. He knows too well that his power relies on his presence in Herat, and more specifically on control of the customs revenue at the border post with Iran, at Islam Qala. Dostum, similarly, never leaves the north for long.

Ethnicity

Ethnicity in Afghanistan is both complex and fluid. Categories do not necessarily stay the same; they are social and political constructs which change according to the pressure put upon them. War not only brought about an increased awareness of ethnic identity, it also changed how people categorized themselves. Before the war, Sunni Persian speakers did not use the word 'Tajik', though the label was applied to them by western and Soviet ethnologists (Roy 1986). Today they tend to define themselves as an ethnic group. Some define themselves differently to the way others define them; some Sunni Hazaras, for example, see themselves as Tajik, but are seen by Tajiks as Hazaras.

The central highlands area of Hazarajat is an interesting example of this fluidity. It is the most mono-ethnic area in Afghanistan, but beneath the broad designation Hazara there are complex divisions, and the extent to which members of these groups see themselves as separate has varied over time and is linked to the political movements in the area. Group membership derives from traditional leadership patterns related to religion and to land and family, all of which can overlap. Most confusing is the position of Sayyeds. The traditional religious leadership of the Hazaras, and estimated to form between 4 and 5 per cent of the population of Hazarajat, Sayyeds trace their lineage back to the prophet. While an endogamous group – the status of Sayyed is something you can inherit only through the male line – the title bestows not only a religious but also a social identity.

Although marriage of Hazara men to Sayyed women is rare, marriage of Sayyed men to Hazara women is common. Hence there are many Sayyeds with Hazara features, sometimes known as Hazara Sayyeds. Sometimes they describe themselves as Hazara and are described so by others, sometimes with the person adding, 'he's Sayyed', as a secondary categorization. At other times they describe themselves as a separate group. This sense of separateness increased during the war years. Prior to 1978 it seems that Hazara Sayyeds identified as Hazara and there was much less of a sense that Sayyeds were separate. Over the course of the war this has changed. In the early 1980s, in what was one of the bloodiest times of Hazara history, the Sayyeds allied themselves with the radical parties linked to Iran to drive out the traditional leadership of Hazarajat, the *mirs* and the khans, only to in turn be driven out by the radicals. The story didn't end there. Shi'a parties linked to Iran continued to try to divide Hazara and Sayyed and sow conflict between them, as part of a continuing quest for political influence. For ordinary, non-party, Hazaras the story was one of politics and parties. As one said:

'Before the revolution nationality wasn't an identity card. Only after the Russians did Sayyed start to separate out as a group, not before. They started to talk of themselves as a different race and to form a political party. Since the departure of the Taliban, and the changed political situation, there are indications that this sense of distinction on the part of the Sayyeds is again fading into the background, as this aspect of their identity comes perhaps to be perceived as of no real advantage. Whether elections, and the competition for power that these represent, will change this remains to be seen.

Most Afghans you talk with date the rise of ethnicity as a problem to the communist era:

> The ethnic problem started in the communist times, with clashes and tension within the Party. People used it to try and get individual benefits. After, with the *mujahideen*, it became a big problem. Mazari came to Dashte Barchi and said: 'I don't care about your background, which party, what you have done, if you are Hazara you are OK for me'. It was the same with Massoud. The leaders, people like Sayyaf, were saying, why are Hazaras living in Afghanistan?

As the uprising sparked by the Soviet invasion spread, the mobilization of people over areas bigger than the *qawm* inevitably led to a greater consciousness of ethnicity. The trend was deeper because it had age-old inequalities to feed upon:

> The problem started with the fighting, though you can see the roots of it in earlier inequalities. I remember in my childhood, we always had Uzbek and Hazara people in the house as servants, they could only find the labouring jobs. Pashtuns and Tajiks could compete [with each other], but the others were always below; and the Hazaras the lowest, they could never get jobs in the police force or in government employment. It was the irresponsibility of the authorities. And once Afghanistan turned to war, that was the opportunity for people to use it and make themselves different, and create threats for others. In 1992 and 1993 there were too many killings of Hazaras by Pashtuns and Pashtuns by Hazaras – and Tajiks the same.

Similarly, although the politicization of Sayyeds was seen as recent, it was acknowledged that it tapped into an older social differentiation. Sayyeds were said by non-Sayyed Hazaras to see themselves as 'higher' people and to expect tribute: 'In past Hazaras paid *khoms* to Sayyeds [one-fifth of the crop or of income] but now this is no longer believed in. Sayyeds didn't have land or work, but a poor Hazara would have to give to a rich Sayyed.'

Yet, though it started with the communists, the ethnic issue really gained momentum only when the fighting started: 'Commanders had no other speech but to say, "You are a Tajik minority, if you don't fight now you will be killed". And people with no other way to get a livelihood joined up. How else to feed the family? In their locality they were kings, and they could not go to another place.'

As the war continued, identity came to be fashioned by fear. Recounting a story told to her by her neighbour about her husband's war experience in Kabul, a Tajik friend says:

> One day a Panjshiri Tajik was going to Karte Char and he was stopped by Hazara people. 'Come', they said, 'and see the dance of the dead people.' And they took him to the place where the Hazaras killed Tajiks, and he saw a hole with the bodies stacked upright. 'Come', they said again, 'and you will see something else.' And they brought a captive and with a big knife they cut off his head, and the body it continued to move. And then they said to the man, he was a very old man, 'Do you want lunch?' 'No'. 'Then, OK, but we want to give you something. You should take it back to Panjshir, and you must not look, you must go home.' And he went home and called his wife and told her the story. 'I have something on my shoulder,' he told her, 'and I am afraid to open it.' And the wife said, 'You don't open it. You stay with the children and I will go far from the house and open it.' And she told me, 'I saw all the eyes, hands, noses, ears and...' – she pauses briefly – 'genitals. I found forty-two pieces. And I was thinking, as a Muslim I must bury the pieces as people. So we made forty-two holes in the earth and buried the people.'[3]

'But', reflects our friend, 'Hazaras were also killed by Tajiks and Pashtuns, two, three times; they have great sadness.'

With stories like that to remember, it is not surprising that in Mazar i Sharif, in the summer of 1997, one could watch the fear build as fighting ringed the city. In the tense weeks that followed the Taliban attack there was little fighting in the city itself, but a pervading fear that it could arrive at any time. Tajiks feared Hazaras, and told tales of wild savages from the mountains, of boys forced to use the gun at an early age, of the dreadful things they did to people; they were like townsfolk who were afraid of the barbarians. Hazaras in turn feared Pashtuns; tales of the Taliban mingled with hand-me-down horror stories from the days of Abdur Rahman Khan and the campaign to subdue Hazaras during the consolidation of the Afghan state. Many Kabulis had fled to Mazar in order to escape the fighting of the mid-1990s, and their tales added to the terror. All was amplified. Stories spread. Facts were impossible to prove, so rumour took over. From here it is but a short step to attacking before you are attacked.

At other times, fear was deliberately inculcated in people. In Northern Alliance-controlled Badakhshan in 2000, an Uzbek schoolteacher in the town of Keshem told of how:

> Some government people come to the schools and immediately
> they start saying Pashtuns want to kill all Tajiks. They bring divisions
> between the people of Afghanistan. This kind of thing will have a very
> negative effect on the minds of children. Now it is dangerous for a
> man to say Pashtuns are our brothers and we should live together. I am
> frightened. I have thirty-six years experience in education, and if it is
> impossible for me to say this kind of thing to students – imagine how
> impossible it is for others.

An incident at a dusty road junction in Kabul during the depths of winter in 2000 indicates just how pervasive this fear was. Clutches of bicyclists made their way through the pall of woodsmoke and fine dust. Boys, for whom going to work was now more normal than going to school, clung to the crossbars of their fathers' bikes. At the junction, several aged destitute men squatted, hoping to receive alms from the passing cyclists. The talk was of a grisly murder. The news soon generated a small group of passers-by, curious as to what was happening. They were soon elaborating on the facts of the case.

> 'A corpse was found at dawn on the *charahi* down there.'
> 'Yes, I saw the bloodstain on the tarmac. They tried to cover the
> blood with sand, but we could see it as we passed.'
> 'Someone in the taxi said that it was dumped there as a warning, with
> money stuffed in its mouth, like poor Najib...'
> 'No, it was the body of one of the criminals who had been executed
> in the stadium. I was there.'
> 'That's not true. I've been told that it was someone from the other
> side, who had been caught spying by the Talibs'.
> 'No. it was Abdul Rahman, ex-chief of the military court, who was
> killed on the orders of Mullah Omer.'
> 'But how could they tell – without its head?'
> 'No one knows, but it was a clear warning, you'll see ...'

A traffic policeman, in a frayed uniform that might have been a hand-down from an amateur dramatic musical society, emerged from his tiny post and, with virtuoso shrieks on his whistle, tried to get the growing huddle of people to disperse. The group gathered at the crossroads, however, stood its ground. The word was out and, in no time at all, the corpse had been found without its head, or its hands, or disfigured, depending on which side of town you lived, or which end of the street. Like so many times before, the details of the tale were adapted to the skills or memory of the teller; for there are few people in the city without a cause for fear – and a grievance.

'They say that the Talibs told no one to take the body away.'
'So how did it disappear?'
'I don't know, it's a warning, like those people being driven around on the backs of pickups with their faces tarred, to confess their crimes … '
'But this one was dead!'
'His family was told to come and collect the body.'
'He must have been a serious criminal. They know everything, just like Najib's men did before.'
'They're all the same, communists, *mujahideen*, Taliban.'
'In Najib's time, we never even found the bodies. People just vanished.'
'The Taliban say that there are mass graves in Pul e Charkhi.'
'No, those were the victims of Hekmatyar, when he controlled the area.'
'Does it really matter? They're all the same … '

Rumour was met with refutation, ideas were countered, anecdotes aired, as more passers-by wheeled their bicycles within earshot. As ever, small boys attached themselves to the group of adults, listening rapt to the developing story. Finally, a wizened old man, carrying his broom across his shoulder, like a beacon above the heads of the group, became the focus of attention.

'It is simple. I was here before dawn, when a *karachi* carrying offal shed its load at the *charahi*.'
'But what about the body?'
'There was no body. It was offal, which left blood and guts everywhere on the tarmac. The owner asked us to help him get it all back on to the cart. He was worried about being late with his delivery, and the traffic police were screaming at him.'
'So no one was murdered?'
'Look at my hands, covered in the muck. The *jui* over there is frozen, or I would have cleaned them by now.'

He held out his hands for all to see the evidence: the blood and gore dried by now on his cracked skin. 'I swept sand over the mess that it left on the tarmac.'

The old man shuffled on his way, holding out his incriminating hands, in search of running water in which to remove the marks of his deed. But the *juis* were dry. The men looked at each other and shook their heads, their conjecture stopped in its tracks by his account. Far from showing any obvious sign of relief, they seemed to simply accept this new version as another episode in the history of the cold, dry city. Those who had newly gathered at the junction, attracted by the throng, had the entire story recounted to them in turn. Slowly, they began to move off, singly or in pairs, on foot and on bicycles, into the morning, carrying with them a myriad versions of the incident, which was passed across compound walls, and from rooftop to rooftop, throughout the day.

Closing ranks

For all the ethnic divisions that have been generated, if there is one thing that will unite Afghans, it is the need to drive out invaders. The anniversary of the retreat of British forces from Kabul in the winter of 1842 is one of the few official celebrations that successive Afghan regimes seem to have in common. The ceremony organized by the PDPA in Kabul in 1990 was a sober reassertion of the glorious freedoms of the Afghan people, which rang rather hollow beside the fading statements of internationalist solidarity that still adorned many government offices. The *mujahideen*, on the other hand, used the occasion after 1992 to portray the flight of the imperial British troops as a precursor of the triumph of Islam over the godless Soviets whose empire the Afghans had toppled, thereby ending the Cold War. Perhaps the most colourful celebrations, however, were those of the Taliban, who summoned the few remaining diplomats and aid agency staff in Kabul to the ballroom of the Inter Continental Hotel to listen to their version of history. We were seated under a huge mural, in the best tradition of crude Soviet propaganda art, showing a huge green sabre lacerating a Union Jack boot planted on a map of Afghanistan. As the speeches wore on, the blood that spouted from the wounded ankle of the boot seemed to merge with the deep red carpet of the ballroom, and flow out of the cracked glass doors.

Managing the world beyond

The *qawm* has long made use of kinship to obtain favours and privileges from the state; and where legitimate allocation of resources did not meet the needs of the group, diversion was the accepted norm. On the whole, this was not regarded as serious corruption (which did, of course, exist) as long as it was conducted within well-understood limits and for the collective benefit of the group. The other advantage of having members of your *qawm* in key positions in government meant that you could keep the state at bay, and thereby minimize demands for conscription or taxes. Just as the village protected its information, so it protected its space. Government buildings continue to be set apart, and in some places they are not in a village at all but, like some bazaars, are located at the junction of trading routes.

Control of information was one of the keys to keeping authority where local people wanted it. Speaking of foreign ethnographers who had the misfortune to be mistaken for government officials, Oliver Roy (1986: 22) noted how, 'The foreigner always finds himself confronted by an endless series of evasions, procrastinations and side-stepping of the issue. The person who is responsible is always somewhere else, the horses are in the mountains, and the truth is in the depths of the well.'

One of the reasons why it has been so difficult to undertake a census in the countryside is because of the mistrust that exists of official intrusion. The extent of the actual village, in terms of population and wealth, rarely squares with the official version in the official gazetteer. The same game has been played, to good effect, with assistance agencies. Faced with agencies' questions, villagers quickly work out what is going on. The Afghan head of office of an NGO in the west of Afghanistan recounted how he would no longer trust any research. 'Even us', he said, 'with all our experience, we go and maybe the first day we get some real information. Then at night they all sit together, discussing what we asked, working out what we want ... After that it is useless, you just get what they want you to hear.'

Many were the aid agency workers who at the time of the drought were assured, with much wringing of hands, that the village had no livestock left. Sometimes, for good measure, they were even taken out to see the carcasses. Yet if they stayed the night, as the sun sank beneath the horizon, a cloud of dust moving slowly towards them would herald the arrival of the flocks from the hills. It should be understood, that it's not exactly that they lied, but rather that truth lies somewhere in the essence of the words, not in their literal meaning. A lot of livestock did die. The villagers had suffered. Why squabble about the meaning of 'all'? And why did outsiders need to know? Who owns the right to information about people's lives, and the control that brings?

There is a belief in the aid community, especially in those parts of it whose *raison d'être* is research, that aid workers have a right to be told everything that is going on. As one experienced worker noted: 'Lots of visitors go to villages, they don't introduce themselves properly, they don't explain why they are there, why they are asking these questions. They raise expectations. Often they treat villages as a research site, they have no intention of coming back. The village sees it differently.'

Even with the most thoughtful research, the question remains: what if people don't want to be objects to be studied? Maybe the agency staff are arrogant, wanting to know everything as the price of their help. Maybe villagers prefer to be 'unknown'. And so understanding eludes them, because on some level it was always intended that it should. This should not be read as a reason for doing poor-quality work, for not seeking to understand, not caring if assistance goes straight into the hands of the gunmen; but we have to earn the right to knowledge, and maybe there will be some things that always will remain beyond us.

Dreaming a past

'Change brings amnesias ... out of which springs narrative,' wrote Benedict Anderson (1991). He could have been writing about Afghanistan.

Over the last twenty-five years the country has seen changes that none of its people would have predicted and which have been deeply troubling to them. The tyranny of the communists, the anarchy of the *mujahideen* and the obscurantism of the Taliban were an anathema to most Afghans; as is the violence that still besets much of the country. Faced with all that has happened, it is perhaps not surprising that there is a selective forgetting and a corresponding re-creation. The past is often remembered as a golden age of order and calm. 'Before, the district governor had control even up the remote valleys, with just a few soldiers he could go. No one had a gun. Without a gun the police would go to a villager and would bring the person about whom a complaint had been made and bring him to the district centre.' The system of administration is remembered as free of corruption: 'Before the coup taxes were collected on the land, and an office of tax collection was responsible for this. It was set against budgets, there was a system of reporting. But now it all goes into private pockets.'

The story is told in the same way wherever you go in Afghanistan. And yet, as a friend who had recently returned to Kabul after twenty years away said:

Many of us hark back to the good old days when we had a government, but forgetting the problems. Even from my memories growing up in Kabul as a middle-class child who lacked for little, it was clear that all was not well. There was huge inequality, corruption was rife, and the government was largely reliant on outside support. We too easily forget how fragile everything was – which is why it was so easy for a few officers to topple the regime. And this, in the end, is why so many of us left.

Many of those who stayed also acknowledge that there was poverty. 'In Zahir Shah and Daoud's time,' said a man from Qandahar,

> people were very poor, the living was low. There was one primary school for the whole *uluswali*, and there was no doctor, no medicines, only the mullah – you went to a holy place to pray for a cure. Some people had no bread, they were living by maize or barley, keeping the land of others. Some people were coming for a year to work in Qandahar, and then the money would last for a whole year in the village, some would go for a year to Iran.

In remote areas services are often actually better now, because of the international community's involvement, than they were in the pre-war days. Yet the longing for the golden days of the past does not diminish. Perhaps this is because the one thing Afghans desire more than anything else is security, and the past was at least secure. Perhaps it is because none of the new modes of government that have been on offer over the last twenty-five years has brought anything but trouble. Communism, the *mujahideen*, the Taliban, they have all brought problems, so why stake your future on yet another new import; is it not safer to go back to the past?

The king offered a powerful symbol of this ordered past. In the time after 11 September but before the Bonn agreement, a time when it was clear things would change but not clear what shape the change would take, there was much talk among Afghans of bringing him back as a unifying figure. Even among the educated of Kabul, who largely recognize that he was too old to be a ruler, there was a respect for what he represents, and when at the Emergency Loya Jirga he was pressured into not running for president there was much disquiet. For rural Pashtuns it cut deeper. Not only did he symbolize the days when Pashtuns ran the country, but the fact that he could be pushed aside spelt the end to any belief that the future might be one in which they could have a stake. 'If they stopped the king from being elected,' said an elder in Qandahar, 'how can we believe in free and fair elections?'

While the past continues to be evoked by Afghans as a symbol of their country before the fall, a veil has been drawn over the nightmare of its destruction. The factions responsible for much of this destruction became adept at presenting the *jihad* as a justification of their actions. While sacrifices were made by opposition fighters in the cause of freedom, a devastating power struggle continued between factional groups for more than a decade after the Soviet withdrawal. Despite outside involvement, the destruction and suffering that this caused can in the end be blamed on no one but the Afghan leaders who competed for power; yet, this era has been deftly reinvented as a continuation of the *jihad*. It has become the official version of history, as demonstrated in the Bonn Agreement's reference to 'heroes of the *jihad* and champions of peace, stability and reconstruction of their beloved homeland'.

Alongside the selective remembering of the past is the invention of new tradition, and the use of it to stake one's claim to govern. The assassination of Massoud days before the attacks of 11 September 2001 might have been mourned, but it has also been put to good use since by those who inherited control over Shura e Nazar. There has been no shortage of manipulation of the symbolic value of the fallen dead, the martyr to the cause. From the huge hoardings bearing his picture to the pomp and ceremony of Massoud Day, *jihad* is claimed for the Panjshiris, and history becomes the legitimator of their right to govern Afghanistan. Others, who remember the brutality of Shura e Nazar, are outraged by the triumphalism. The glorification of the armed struggle also sits uncomfortably with another aspect of the new Afghanistan, whose identity is claimed by the technocrats.

Language is part of this battle over who gets to define the nature of the Afghan state, as it always has been. The Taliban had Pashtu, now it is time to settle that score. Language is inclusion, and exclusion. It is not just a case of who can read what: 'Why don't you speak Pashtu?' say Pashtun friends who are not only bilingual in the country's two official languages but are also fluent in English. Language is about whose culture is valued, whose expression becomes the common currency of the land, whose myths become the national myths. But language is not the only battleground.

In the struggle over the shape of Afghanistan's future, the question of who gets to define tradition is being fought out on many levels and over many issues: Pashtuns against Tajik, men against women, progressives against conservatives. Within this lies a danger that Afghanistan's customs, a hallmark of which has been a measure of flexibility, will become codified, hardened into prescription. Custom, at its best, gives the Afghan a sense of belonging, of identity, but it also allows for adaptation. There is little enthusiasm among the country's people for a return to the strictures of the Taliban, not even in the conservative tribal areas.

Notes

1 Interview by Chris Johnson, 1996.

2 Another term, *rai gri*, means 'voting' and was used in communist times, but no one seems ever to use it now.

3 The story is not fictitious but is one of the documented activities of the war; see for example Human Rights Watch (1998).

3 | Ideology and difference

In Afghan history the communists had an ideology and the Taliban
had an ideology, they were fighting for something they believed in.
It is good to believe, to have an aim. You didn't see that with the
mujahideen, or even now. In the communist time the people in key
positions had just a few possessions, they didn't want to misuse government property, or to have bribes. It was the same at the beginning
with the Taliban. Now, the government does not have a strategy, an
ideology, a goal. This is a disaster. Where is the sense of value, the
spirit of building a country, the honour? (Ex-government employee,
now NGO worker, Kabul, 2003)

During the twentieth century the outside world has offered Afghans
a succession of ideological frameworks as models for change. From
the revolutionary to the regressive, however, the transformations that
these ideologies imply have provided a pretext for conflict, rather than a
focus for unity. This experience helps to explain why many Afghans feel
ambivalent towards ideas or values that lie outside of, or are perceived
to intrude on, their collective frame of reference.

Islam and the sense of belonging to a community, group or tribe
have shaped how Afghans relate to their immediate environment and
how they deal (or not) with alien ideology. Until the *jihad* this remained
relatively unchallenged. The impact of the technology-inspired vision
of the 1960s and 1970s that, it was hoped, would catapult the country
into the modern world, was confined primarily to an urban elite. Despite
the push for liberal values by some educated Afghans, the social base of
liberalism was always very narrow. However, by the mid-1970s, the social
foundations of the old order were eroding and both Islamist and communist parties were actively organizing, especially among the students
and the armed forces. When the Afghan communists took power in 1978,
their attempts to move rural communities from feudalism to socialism
sparked a nation-wide *jihad* that had its roots in local reactions to what
were perceived as intrusions on established values and traditions. This
uprising in turn provided a base from which the various parties could
organize and recruit as political and military organizations.

As Soviet support for President Najibullah dried up, he was forced

5 Postcards of Indian filmstars are pinned to the wall of the mausoleum of
   Timur Shah in Kabul, 1991. (Jolyon Leslie)

to buy support through the militias and to make accommodation with a range of Afghan groups that did not subscribe to communist ideals. By the 1990s little was left of the communist policies the regime once fought for. Meanwhile, on the other side of the frontlines, the common cause that had held together the resistance groups for more than a decade evaporated with the departure of the Soviet troops. This lack of unity was already manifest in the deep differences that existed within the interim government that briefly replaced Najibullah's regime. By the time that the full successor administration, the Islamic State of Afghanistan, came into being, disunity had descended into bitter internecine fighting. As old scores were settled and allegiances between groups shifted, it was difficult for Afghans to distinguish between ideology and political expediency; peace remained a mirage.

It was into this landscape that the Taliban first emerged, offering to restore stability and order to those parts of the country beset by anarchy. As with the *mujahideen* who had preceded them, they portrayed themselves as protectors of the faith, and it was with an appeal to a 'true Islam' and a reassertion of Afghan identity and traditions that they staked their claim to govern the country and issued a series of edicts that aimed to codify the terms of their rule. Although their vision of Afghan society was routinely portrayed as an anachronism, their attempts to draw on their past resonated with the values of many conservative rural communities. With time, however, the uncompromising imposition of their interpretation of Islam came to be seen by many as equally intrusive as the depredations of the factions that they had replaced. While most Afghans are deeply conformist in their belief and attach great importance to rituals such as regular prayer, the notion of the state – which, in time, the Taliban claimed to represent – imposing strictures over this belief was seen as an anathema to all but the most conservative Sunni elements of society. In particular the activities of the Department for the Promotion of Virtue and Prohibition of Vice, which was established (allegedly under the influence of Saudi clerics) during the late 1990s, came to be seen by some Afghans as intrusive. Virtue has customarily been protected at the level of the family, community or tribe, not imposed from the outside, and certainly not by the state.

While the Taliban edicts covered issues from law and order to property ownership, it was those that imposed requirements for prayer, dress and social interaction that were the most intrusive, particularly on the urban population. But it was the formal exclusion of women from employment and girls from education that triggered a response from the aid community.

Confronting the Taliban

The first real confrontation occurred in 1995 after the Taliban had taken Herat and banned girls from attending school and women from working. Agencies saw this as a direct attack not only on their values but also on what they believed to be universal rights. Finding it impossible to continue running programmes in keeping with the agency's principles, the British NGO Save the Children suspended its programmes in health and education, while UNICEF took a policy decision not to fund education in parts of the country where girls were barred from going to school. This provoked a debate as to whether withholding resources to try and achieve change was simply a denial of education to boys, or whether it represented a shift of the organizations' resources to parts of the country where they could be better used.

It was not until the Taliban took Kabul a year later that the issue of their restrictions on women and girls hit the headlines. Even then few aid organizations were prepared to speak out. One exception was Oxfam, whose country representative defended women's rights on CNN and went on to announce that Oxfam would close its programme in Afghanistan if the Taliban did not moderate their position. Oxfam formally suspended its Kabul programme on 4 October and issued a press statement saying that Oxfam would 'work with women in Kabul, or not at all'. Despite attempts to rally other agencies to the cause, there was little enthusiasm for following suit.

The Logar water supply project was Oxfam's major programme in the capital. The scheme, originally built in 1970s, had been badly damaged and looted after the *mujahideen* took over the city in 1992, and its repair and recommissioning seemed a logical response to the city's worsening water problems. Its rehabilitation, at a cost of several million dollars, had the potential to restore piped water to 40 per cent of the city's residents. For Oxfam, however, committed as it was to gender equity and with a firm belief that programmes to provide safe drinking water were of little benefit without concomitant programmes of health education with women, proceeding with work on Logar without the involvement of women made no sense.

The Taliban, however, proved impervious to pressure and Oxfam had little idea what to do next. Despite the hard-line stand taken on CNN, the agency was not prepared to pay the price of closing its country office. There were also strong differences of opinion within the organization as to whether Oxfam should in fact be suspending work on Logar. While one side argued the stand on gender, others argued the humanitarian case for supplying safe drinking water to the city's residents. In the end those advocating suspension won the day and the official position became that Oxfam would not undertake programme work in the capital but would maintain its country office there, believing it could have an influence on the Taliban's behaviour through a programme of advocacy and bearing witness, aimed largely at donors and the international community. Its female Afghan staff, meanwhile, remained at home on full pay. By this time a number of other NGOs had found ways of employing their female staff, through redefining them as health workers or letting them work from home. Oxfam's representative in Kabul refused to adopt this strategy, holding that without express permission for Oxfam staff to resume their jobs they would be at risk. She also refused to explore the compromise of having female staff from the Ministry of Public Health undertake the programming with women, insisting that Oxfam had the right to employ its own female staff. Oxfam's male staff, however, were soon back at work – the contradiction of which seemed lost on those who advocated taking a hard line on the gender issue. It was believed that the Taliban would eventually decide they wanted the water project sufficiently to agree to Oxfam's terms; but they refused to relent. In spring of 1998 Oxfam ceased to pay the salaries of its female Afghan staff, who by this time had been at home on full pay for eighteen months. An independent evaluation of the project, which was critical of the organization's actions, was suppressed.

Other organizations fared no better in attempts to confront the Taliban. Neither Save the Children nor UNICEF achieved any change on the position of girls' education, and Save the Children ended up closing its Herat office. It then moved to Mazar i Sharif, thinking it could continue to run programmes for women in a Northern Alliance-controlled part of the country. The programmes were only just up and running when the Taliban attacked Mazar, precipitating a period of fighting and instability that only ended eighteen months later when they finally captured the city.

In the meantime, a number of other aid agencies in Kabul tried to negotiate their way around the stream of regulations issued by the Taliban. It was clear from the way in which some agencies were able to deal with their official counterparts that there was no clear Taliban party-line on the work of external aid agencies. Neither did it seem that the restrictions were deliberately intended to make their presence untenable, so that agencies would leave. Many Afghans who continued to work in the administration negotiated to retain the support of aid agencies in their work and thereby managed to continue employing women, notably in healthcare. Even the hard-line Department for the

Promotion of Virtue and Prevention of Vice, which was the most prolific in issuing edicts, was not immune to arguments about need and allowed emergency programmes such as distributions to widows to continue. The edicts did, however, combine to make it a difficult working environment, especially in Kabul where the lines were most strongly drawn. Even here, there was potential to explore differing interpretations of the restrictions, but the agencies that had the savvy to explore it were few. Outside the cities, where edicts were less keenly observed, it was often easier to continue activities, and a number of agencies focused on places where they felt they could still get something done.

The very diversity of the NGO community made it difficult for them even to agree, much less hold, a common position on issues. Despite intense soul-searching, the respective positions and priorities of the NGOs ruled out a common strategy on how to work (or not) under the watchful gaze of the Taliban. The severest test of their resolve came in the summer of 1998, when in a context of worsening relations the Taliban issued a directive that all NGOs should move their offices in the Kabul Polytechnic. The official reason for this decision was that it would enable NGOs to make better use of available resources by sharing common services and reducing their overheads, while allowing the authorities to ensure effective security – which they had been repeatedly reminded was their responsibility. Most NGOs refused to move and claimed that the proposal infringed on their operational effectiveness. Just as with Oxfam and the Logar project, few aid workers seemed to have thought through what they would do if the Taliban did not back down – which they did not. Instead, they ordered the closure of most NGO offices in Kabul, resulting in an exodus of expatriate staff to Pakistan.

As had been the case earlier, few agencies were prepared to lose their programmes in Afghanistan, especially as the capture of Mazar i Sharif and Hazarajat in the weeks following the NGO retreat from Kabul had limited the options for working in areas outside Taliban control. Most agencies soon started negotiating terms for their return to Kabul and, forming a consortium, they met a demand that they deposit money into an account to cover the costs of the repairs to the polytechnic buildings, where work soon began. As a condition of the agencies' return to Kabul and reopening of their offices and programmes, the Taliban insisted that they all sign statements agreeing to relocate to the polytechnic. Few refused. However, concern for the security of international staff following the death of Lieutenant Calo (see Chapter 4) meant that it was months before most NGOs fully returned to Kabul. By the time they did, the Taliban had moved military personnel into the now partially refurbished polytechnic buildings, leaving the NGOs free to return to their original offices. In the aftermath of this episode, the more seasoned aid workers reflected that a different strategy might have got them to the same place with a lot less trouble. Although lessons were clearly learned within the NGO community, the same was not the case with UN headquarters, which pushed for 'tough' stands in subsequent stand-offs with the Taliban.

The UN and the Strategic Framework for Afghanistan

The many difficulties the assistance community experienced in try-ing to work out how to relate to the Taliban coincided with a growing concern about the evident failure of international political, assistance and human rights strategies to work effectively in the cause of peace in Afghanistan. At the same time the UN was struggling with the wider issue of what role it should play globally in countries with long-running conflicts. This had already prompted the Secretary General to consider proposals for system-wide reform (Macrae and Leader 2000), as part of which a decision was taken to use Afghanistan to test an innovative ap-proach in the form of a Strategic Framework for Afghanistan. In seeking to link the political and assistance efforts, the underlying assumption was that an impartial political strategy could be pursued. The cost of this became clear only later. Acknowledging that the system did not know if assistance was part of the problem or the solution, the Strategic Framework set out a series of objectives, based on common 'rights-based' principles which were endorsed by the UN and donors alike. These principles represented the terms on which international assistance could be provided in the country, and stated that assistance should not be subject to any form of discrimination. In asserting that cooperation would be extended only to authorities that 'fully supported' the principles contained in the UN Charter, the Strategic Framework attempted, on the Afghan stage at least, to transform what had started as ad hoc reactions to discrimination into a coherent system-wide policy (UN 1998b).

Integral to the Strategic Framework from the beginning, and later to be elevated to the status of one of its three pillars (the other two being politics and assistance), the concept of rights was always key to attempts to define a principled stance in negotiating with the Taliban. Rights became the lens through which assistance was viewed, whether it was the question of humanitarian space (the right to assistance) or discrimination against women.

Behind the response to the string of edicts issued by the authorities in Kabul and Qandahar lay a game of game of cat-and-mouse, as aid workers looked into the implications of restrictions, while testing the resolve of the authorities to enforce them. This is perhaps best illustrated by the furore that surrounded the edict issued early in 1998 that required expatriate Muslim women working in Afghanistan to be accompanied by a male relative or *mahram* – as was already the case for their Afghan colleagues. Within the international community, there were those who held that the mere application for a visa for an expatriate Muslim woman was unacceptable (even though all visitors needed a visa) as it risked discrimination because the Taliban might ask for her *mahram* to be identified. Meanwhile, those who were trying to negotiate the revocation of the edict were quietly assured by their Taliban interlocutors that the requirement was unworkable and would not be applied. The issue of a visa in June 1999 to the (Muslim) gender adviser for the UN without any question of a *mahram* suggested that the Taliban had again provided the rope with which the aid community tied itself in knots.

With the spotlight on the behaviour of the Taliban, acts of war came under increasing scrutiny. The issue of scorched-earth tactics in the Shamali plains north of Kabul during 1999 illustrates some of the problems encountered in trying to put this rights focus into practice. The rich, densely populated Shamali plains, which straddle the road north from Kabul, had been devastated in fighting between the Soviets and the resistance after 1979 and had witnessed widespread displacement. While there had been a significant return of refugees during the mid-1990s, the continuing conflict in the area had discouraged extensive reconstruction. As fighting intensified along the frontlines at the end of July 1999, residents of the affected areas fled north to the Panjshir or south to Kabul. Both the Taliban and the Northern Alliance appealed to the international community for support in assisting these displaced people. The numbers involved lent credence to the stories of those displaced of forcible clearances of villages by Taliban fighters. Worse still, there were reports of the systematic burning of homes and vineyards, as well as the felling of fruit trees, apparently to render the area uninhabitable.

As was routine, the UN issued calls for both sides to show restraint; it also added its specific concerns for the protection of civilians. Prompted by the Northern Alliance's claims of 200,000 displaced people in the Panjshir valley, the initial focus of the relief efforts was on the largely Tajik population who had been displaced north. The figures were, however, soon found to be a gross exaggeration – the actual numbers were in the tens of thousands. The Alliance also portrayed the Taliban advance as an act of ethnic cleansing, despite the fact that many Pashtun communities had also been forced out of their villages in the Shamali plains.

Meanwhile, some 30,000 people had made their way either on foot from the southern side of the frontlines in Shamali to Kabul, or had been trucked there by the Taliban. Most found refuge with relatives in the city. The fraught experience of managing camps for the displaced during the inter-factional fighting of the mid-1990s prompted aid agencies in Kabul to refuse requests from the Taliban to establish camps for those fleeing Shamali. Moreover, in setting up camps, they feared being accused of facilitating forced displacement. While UN field staff tried to extract from the Taliban guarantees that the villagers might return to their homes in Shamali as a precondition for providing assistance to those sheltering with families, those with nowhere to go were brought by the Taliban to the compound of the former USSR embassy in southern Kabul. Faced with this, aid agencies could do little but attempt to render the bleak ruins of the embassy blocks habitable for 13,000 of the displaced, most of whom were ethnic Pashtuns. The embassy site, which became a focus in the city for visiting delegations, divided the humanitarian community between those who perceived the relief effort as an uncomplicated response to need and a vindication of core humanitarian principles, and those who felt that as the Taliban had caused the problem they should deal with the consequences. One of the few issues on which the Taliban and those aid agencies who agreed to assist families in the embassy compound agreed was on exclusion of the press, which they feared would run stories of agencies being complicit in forced depopulation. No such concerns, it seems, troubled visitors to the second compound for the displaced, set up by the Northern Alliance in an unused textile factory on the north side of the frontlines.

For the Kabuli families who took in the majority of the displaced there were no such dilemmas. They had themselves sought refuge in Shamali during the turmoil in Kabul after 1992 and it was a straightforward obligation to look after those in need. As one elderly woman arriving in Kabul, having lost the village house that had only five years earlier been a refuge for her relatives from Kabul, said ruefully: 'My house is nothing; we rebuilt it after it was destroyed by the communists and again after the *mujahideen* and shall do the same after the Taliban; what is important is family.'

Trying to engage It was in the midst of this confusion that a UN team was despatched to Kabul in May 1999 to try to reach agreement with the authorities on an operational framework for UN agency activities in the country. The very initiation of negotiations on a Memorandum of Understanding (UN 1998a) with the Taliban was regarded by some as an accommodation with unacceptable values. On the other hand, there were those who genuinely believed that guarantees from the Taliban of appropriate levels of operational independence would allow access to vulnerable populations. In many ways both parties needed some form of agreement. The Taliban needed to maintain what they perceived as an appropriate level of control in order to ensure that assistance activities were carried out without contravening Islamic traditions. The UN, on the other hand, needed to show that 'principled' engagement could result in a relaxation of the more intrusive restrictions, including the ban on female employment and education. Although the gulf between the two positions was clear, the Taliban needed the UN, which in turn needed a written agreement on which to base continued activities in the face of increased political hostility towards the regime. The memorandum, which was negotiated over ten days between the UN and Taliban teams, was distinguished as much by substantive differences in the English and Pashtun versions of the document – the latter intended to mollify the Taliban's hard-line constituency – as by the common ground that it staked out.

Few in the aid community were happy with the memorandum. Certain of its provisions, such as Article 13 that stated that 'women's access to, and participation in health and education, will need to be gradual', were met with righteous indignation. Even though this gradualist approach represented the reality of the situation on the ground – where universal access was clearly not feasible overnight, as much because of shortage of resources as restrictions – the wording was perceived to be a betrayal of international human rights standards (Physicians for Human Rights 2001).

In many ways, the controversy that followed the signing of the memorandum was rather convenient for the Taliban, for whom the very notion of a written agreement with the UN, no matter how vaguely worded, was something of an anathema. In the ensuing discussions, which went on for months, about the implementation of its provisions, they were justifiably able to claim that the international community could not agree on what they wanted for Afghanistan.

The continuing failure of the UN to sort out either its position or its tactics was borne out by yet another long-standing controversy, this time regarding widows' bakeries. Believing that there were a significant proportion of vulnerable female-headed households in need in urban areas – particularly when formal employment was ruled out under the Taliban – the aid community directed a significant amount of assistance to them.

Unfortunately, international workers failed to understand Afghan social relations. The Afghan custom is for a widow to be remarried to a close relative of her late husband, or simply taken in by relatives. They therefore were not in need of food assistance simply because of loss of a husband. But twenty years of war and associated relief efforts have taught Afghans that the way to obtain relief is to define yourself into whatever category is currently receiving the goods. So if the international community were giving food to 'widows', Afghans were quite prepared to define their social categories (though not their practice) accordingly. It was, of course, very difficult to distinguish who was a real widow with no family support and who was a widow in a, quite possibly well-off, family group.

Over and above this, there was evidence of serious corruption within WFP, including widows' bakeries cards being sold by their own staff. The scale of abuse was such that it was picked up by representatives of the Taliban who – even though it was hardly in their interests – urged WFP to undertake a review of beneficiaries, to enable resources to be used more effectively.

Feeding widows had, however, become the UN's symbol of what was possible in the face of Taliban intransigence and was therefore sacrosanct. Although both ICRC and CARE had acknowledged similar problems with their own feeding programmes and had taken action to clean out the corruption, the World Food Programme resisted calls to review the beneficiary lists – a clean-up that risked drastically reducing the scale of a programme that was portrayed as a life-line for Afghans in the city. By the summer of 2000, the issue had become a source of real contention, with WFP finally acknowledging the need for reassessment of beneficiary lists, but arguing that the severity of the drought justified a more liberal attitude to food distribution. In summer 2001, in the face of growing evidence of malpractice, WFP agreed to resurvey on condition that its own female staff would carry out the house-to-house surveys. Pointing out that it was WFP staff who were in fact part of the problem, the Taliban proposed the involvement of surveyors from the Ministry of Public Health, who had undertaken similar joint surveys with, among others, the ICRC. WFP refused, and publicly threatened to close the programme. Despite the likely impact that this might have on legitimate beneficiaries of the urban feeding programme, the Taliban called the UN's bluff and announced that they would attempt to identify alternative sources of food. With their flagship programme in jeopardy, WFP overnight found the ability to compromise.

> So much more do they attend to granting favours than respecting rights (Elphinstone 1815)

In the absence of meaningful political dialogue, aid programmes had by the second half of the 1990s become the lens through which the world viewed the country, and their values were the yardstick against which Afghans – and specifically the Taliban – were to be measured. Nowhere was this more apparent than in the ideology of rights that was at the heart of the first major confrontation between the Taliban regime and the international community, and which remained central throughout.

The claim of the human rights movement is that its values are universal. Yet this is a concept of human rights that stems from a peculiarly western, individualist view of the world. A person is seen as an individual agent and his or her rights are conceived in those terms. In Afghanistan, as in many non-western countries, a person is embedded in his or her social environment, and rights can be constructed only on this basis. At the most fundamental, these relationships constitute the immediate family and a whole network of close kinship relationships; for some they also constitute the wider network of tribe. Any action by an individual to claim his or her rights has to be judged in relation to its effect on these relationships, a balance struck between what is gained and what is lost. Decisions are structured less by what you want as an individual than by what your family needs or expects of you. We have been struck on more than one occasion by Afghan friends describing how, despite good jobs abroad, they had returned to Afghanistan because of changes in family circumstance. No regret was expressed, or any sense of having done something particularly virtuous; it was just how it was. Duty was followed without question. The issue of responsibilities towards others structures the moral universe more than claims to rights for oneself. Any strategy to increase the rights of individual Afghans needs to acknowledge this, to recognize that moral universes can be structured in different ways that are equally legitimate, though not always compatible.

If we didn't understand their world-view, they were certainly perplexed by ours. Returning from a first trip to the West, Afghan friends often spoke of their shock at the fact that homeless people are forced on to the streets, or parents committed to institutions in their old age rather than being cared for at home. You do not sleep on the streets here, even in bombed-out Kabul; nor do old people die alone. There is puzzlement at westerners' claims to the higher moral ground on issues of human rights while behaving in their own countries in ways which are perceived to be deeply immoral.

It was not simply that values differed; it was also how concepts such as 'rights' and 'principles' were presented and negotiated. The Taliban's refusal to moderate their position over the Logar water project was portrayed by some as a callous disregard for human lives, but the problem lay more in the way in which the differences in belief were handled. Oxfam, like other NGOs, worked within an essentially western framework that believed that the way to get decisions changed was to apply pressure on the party whose behaviour they sought to alter. While politicians and corporations in the West might be susceptible to such tactics, it was to prove completely counter-productive with the Taliban. Not only did they perceive it as an attempt to dictate – rather than negotiate – the terms of engagement of a significant international investment in their country, but the confrontational manner in which the issue was handled made it impossible for the Taliban to change their position without loss of face. In Afghanistan, the successful resolution of problems does not come from confrontation but from negotiation, from a recognition that no one must lose face, from the crafting of a solution designed to appear as if everyone has 'won'. A change of position is not acknowledged, because that would be to admit fault. Many Taliban edicts were quietly forgotten like this, as with the kites that always fluttered over Kabul despite having been banned. That is how things are resolved, not through the formal revocation of edicts that were too often demanded by agencies that failed to realize that such action was not possible. Seen from this perspective, Oxfam's demand for formal permission for women to go back to work only ensured that this would never happen.

The aid community's failure to make progress was also in part due to a pervasive tendency to overestimate its own importance and influence. We often saw ourselves as powerful because of the resources we controlled, and which we believed the Taliban needed in order to build their domestic legitimacy. Yet the amount of money involved was not that great, compared, for example, to the smuggling economy, nor did it speak to those issues that were uppermost on the Taliban agenda. As one study at the time put it: 'The aid community, from donors to field workers, often seems to have difficulty in seeing beyond its own relatively limited sphere of influence' (Fielden and Azerbaijani-Moghadam 2001).

Had aid agencies been more able to see themselves as but a small part of a bigger picture, they may have made more progress. They might also have got further had aid workers understood that Afghans saw them as guests in their country; indeed, some aid workers were happier to portray themselves to the outside world as frontline fighters. They were under intense external scrutiny to hold a 'principled' position, while at the same time delivering assistance in an environment with as many mixed signals as there were edicts, and where the rules of engagement, on either side, remained far from clear.

The mutual failure of the Taliban and the international community to understand each other, is also vividly illustrated by the contentious issue of the 'space' that was claimed for humanitarian action in the country. Previously, in the absence of an assertive central authority, there had been few official limits on the activities of humanitarian groups, which had negotiated with the various factions for access to populations in need. The questionable legitimacy of many 'counterpart' commanders was ignored, and their predatory behaviour often perceived simply as the price of working in a warzone. In an effort to reassert Afghan sovereignty in the areas that they controlled, the Taliban were thus faced by aid agencies that believed they had a right to intervene on their own terms, anywhere.

In Afghanistan as elsewhere, aid agencies increasingly used the language of human rights to define their own agenda in other people's countries. The notion that there might in fact be common ground to be explored between the principled approach of the aid community and the values espoused by the Taliban was inconvenient, given how much was by now invested in the differences. Unwittingly in many cases, there was as much energy spent on widening the gaps between 'them' and 'us' as on working towards a common cause.

The nature of the human rights discourse itself also contributed to the problem, particularly around the contentious issue of protection. Human rights activists tended to see only the immediate situation, and to define those affected as individual victims in need of protection. But in the context of the widespread abuse of civilians during the Afghan conflict, the situation was usually more complicated than that. There were certainly many victims, but they, or their fathers, husbands or sons, were often also complicit in the fighting, or they were associated with groups that had committed earlier acts of atrocity, and therefore were targets for revenge. This is not to suggest that revenge does not constitute abuse, but to acknowledge the need to understand that layers of conflict, abuse and dispossession often overlap, and to be even-handed in condemnation.

The second difficulty was that international human rights standards were developed in relation to territorial wars between state armies, where there was a clear distinction between military and civilians. But in Afghanistan, as with other examples of what have been termed 'new' wars or 'network' wars (Duffield 2001b), the conflict had dissolved boundaries between people, army and government. In the context of loose affiliations that made up the armed groups, the customary distinctions between military/civilian and combatant/non-combatant became blurred.

The final, and perhaps most serious, problem was that rights quickly became another item in the toolbox of those who were party to Afghanistan's wars. The Afghans were savvy political actors and it didn't take them long to work out that 'rights' was a button they could press to draw attention to their cause – as was exemplified by the accusations of 'ethnic cleansing' in Shamali. Well-meaning human international rights workers who knew little of the country and spoke even less of its languages were easy to lead by the nose. Rights thus became corrupted into a tool of war, manipulated with considerable success by some parties to the conflict.

Just as the West's morality often puzzled the Afghans, so too did their approach to the restoration of law and order. If there was one basic right that those who had lived through the reign of terror exercised by the *mujahideen* groups between 1992 and 1995 wanted to realize, it was the right to basic security. Public executions in the sports stadium in Kabul, which had frequently been staged to popular acclaim during the *mujahideen* era, suddenly became a symbol to the outside world of Taliban inhumanity. Many Afghans, however, supported the Taliban's hard-line approach towards law and order. While undeniably often carried out without due process, the summary justice that was meted out seemed to represent the only way to halt the predatory violence of the factions. In the absence of functioning courts and legal systems, due process was clearly a distant prospect. A person has, perhaps, to have lived with real fear to comprehend why the denial of rights to a few people was considered a small price to pay for the restoration of law and order. In a country where the judicial system had largely broken down, the question became the very basic one of: their right to a fair trial, or our right to live in safety in our homes? Yet despite the fact that the Taliban's uncompromising approach towards law and order rendered much of the country safe, the absence of due legal process was seized upon as an excuse to characterize them as savage. Their adherence to shari'a law was also held up by some as evidence of their barbarity, although when it was the stated policy of the previous administration it had passed without comment.

The attitude of the international community to the justice issue was also at times simply confused. When a UN military observer was assassinated in Kabul in 1998, the day after the US missile attack on Khost, the Taliban were urged to bring the culprits to justice. Indeed, among other issues, this was one of the preconditions for discussions about the return of UN expatriate staff evacuated from the country in response to the incident. When the alleged culprits were identified and the Taliban leadership offered to hand them over to the UN, they were told that they should be dealt with according to Afghan law. When the death sentence (which had been on the statute book for murder well before the Taliban) was passed on the culprits, the UN were faced with the prospect of an execution in their name. The issue was quietly dropped.

Could it have been different?

For those of us who worked in Afghanistan during the Taliban years, the question remains: could we have played it better? If we had started from a greater understanding of how things worked, rather than determinedly trying to bend a proud people to our version of the world, would we have got further? Often we made it more difficult for the more moderate elements within the Taliban to deliver because we insisted on proclaiming victory. We also placed key Afghan staff who were the translators and interlocutors with the Taliban in an impossible position.

What if, for example, instead of confronting the problem of restrictions on healthcare facilities for women head-on, we had paid more attention to the potential of exploring the notion of female-only spaces? After all, western feminists have clamoured for years for the right to female doctors in their own countries. Similarly, given that western researchers have long argued that females perform better when education is provided in girls-only classes, could we have better explored opportunities for the negotiation of segregated facilities? Shirin Ebadi, the Iranian winner of the 2003 Nobel Peace Prize, credited the strict dress code and segregation of the sexes at university with opening the doors to emancipation, saying that once universities became places where fathers could send their daughters without worrying about 'moral corruption', then society began to change (*Guardian*, 10 November 2003).

In Afghanistan we rushed to defend the right to mixed facilities. The Taliban, it was assumed, were just making a rhetorical commitment to female-only provision, with no intention of actually implementing it, and those donors and agencies who considered such options were condemned as 'accommodationist'. While the Taliban (or at least some of the Taliban, for like any other movement they were rarely all of one voice) may well have just been saying these things, they were hardly unique in this; most people playing a political game have a tendency to massage the truth they present to their constituency. The question remains, could we have achieved more by taking them at face value and trying to establish well-resourced female-only services? Certainly there was a problem, in that little existed in the way of female-only provision and to deny access to mixed facilities at times meant denying access to anything at all. But there were also indications that by negotiating step by step, facility by facility, by basing arguments in Islamic discourse and choosing words carefully, it was possible to make progress. One example was the nursing college in Jalalabad, where the local health authorities, faced with the prospect of a dwindling number of trained staff, found ways to resume admission of female trainees by ensuring segregation of courses. Despite the opportunity that this represented for Afghan women to receive better care, acknowledged by many Afghan professionals at the time, attempts by WHO to support the courses were greeted at the time with dismay by some expatriates.

Should we also, as Nancy Dupree suggests, have talked more to men?

> If men do not understand what you are doing with the women they are going to come up with some bizarre ideas. I remember a health project among the refugees where the women had six weeks of basic training. At the end of the training each graduate was given a plastic basin and a cake of soap. Immediately, the men were grumbling: 'What are they doing in there? They are training our women to be prostitutes! Why else would they need a basin and a bar of soap?!' ... If the women cannot go to the bazaar to buy soap, you must depend on the men of the household to do it. And if he does not understand the importance of it, he isn't going to buy the soap. The emphasis must be on the whole family, not on individuals. (Dupree 1998: 13–14)

The history of reform for women in Afghanistan is as old as the history of the state, and as contentious. Notions of female emancipation have long been associated with foreign interference, and have not only met with fierce resistance from tribal leaders but have not infrequently led to the downfall of the regime sponsoring change. More than a century ago, Amir Abdur Rahman Khan (1880–1901) introduced the first laws to attempt to align customary practice with Islam (Dupree 1984: 306). Using the dictates of the Qur'an, he forbade child marriages, forced marriages, the levirate (marriage of a widow to her deceased husband's brother), exorbitant bride-prices and marriage gifts. He upheld hereditary rights for widows and ruled that women could seek divorce. Despite this, customary practices prevailed. Amanullah, grandson of Amir Abdur Rahman Khan, took reform further, advocating monogamy, the removal of the veil, the end of seclusion and compulsory education for girls. He even supported higher education for females; and in October 1928, for the first time in Afghanistan's history, a number of women went abroad, to Turkey, to study nursing. Both Amanullah's wife and his sister spoke out publicly on the subject of equality for women. Speaking at the 1927 Independence celebrations, Queen Suraya said:

> Independence has been achieved. It belongs to all of us ... Do not think, however, that our nation needs only men to serve it. Women should also take part as women did in the early years of Islam. The valuable services rendered by women are recounted throughout history, from which we learn that women were not created solely for pleasure and comfort. From their examples we learn that we must all contribute toward the development of our nation and that this cannot be done without being equipped with knowledge. So we should all attempt to acquire as much knowledge as possible in order that we may render our services to society in the manner of the women of early Islam. (quoted in Dupree 1984: 308)

Afghan history is indeed full of accounts of heroic women whose actions and words rallied men at times of national crisis. From writer and political adviser Zaynab, daughter of Mirwais Hotak, standing at the bastion of Qandahar with her brothers when the city was besieged by the Persians, to Malalai holding her banner aloft at the battle of Maiwand in 1880 to prevent the tribal armies from retreating from the British, the poet heroine is an enduring symbol. Conservative leaders were not, however, much impressed with the lessons of history and they revolted against Amanullah. His successor, the Tajik Bacha i Saqao, insisted that women return behind the veil and it was to be thirty years before this imposition was once again removed.

The 1950s saw progress in schools and healthcare for women and the 1964 constitution gave them for the first time the right to vote. Increasing numbers of educated women began working in government and all manner of businesses (though, unlike southern Asia, not in manual labour, as this would dishonour both her and the male relative who let her do such a thing). Nevertheless, most urban women were still secluded even in the 1970s, and the changes had little impact on the countryside. While many women continued to exert influence, most did it indirectly through the men in their family. Many of the moves for reform continued to be spearheaded by progressive men, and there was little in the way of an indigenous women's movement (Dupree 1984).

Undercurrents of dissent continued to exist. In 1968 conservative members of parliament proposed a law prohibiting females from studying abroad, and in 1970 two conservative mullahs protested at public signs of the emancipation of women by shooting at the legs of women in western dress and splashing them with acid. It was not the last time such things were to happen, for at least one Afghan woman working on women's education in Peshawar in the 1990s had acid thrown in her face.

Despite the opposition, progress continued until the Saur Revolution of 1978, though much of it remained confined to Kabul. With the PDPA's takeover of power, women, especially young women, were mobilized to serve 'the cause', and in the internal struggles within the Communist Party women's issues were used by both sides in their claims to ascendancy. But reform ran ahead of society. Even in the urban areas people were shocked at the dress and behaviour of some women, while in the rural areas the campaign to eradicate illiteracy proved to be the spark that lit the fire of *jihad*: men were not having their women herded into literacy classes, and especially not mixed literacy classes. As the various *mujahideen* groups battled for power, between themselves and later against the Taliban, women's honour and their position in society again became mobilized as a rallying call.

Maybe a more careful reading of Afghan history would have taught us that change cannot be forced, from the outside or from within. The description by David Edwards (2002) of how the ultimate failure in Afghanistan of both the communist regime and its enemies was at least in part due to their failure to learn the lessons of the past, applied as much to the international community as to Afghans: 'There were many such lessons, including one about how Afghans treat outsiders who try to control their homeland and another about how they feel when people in authority interfere in their domestic affairs.'

This does not mean that Afghanistan is a society locked in its past, incapable of change. The same Afghans who fought a *jihad* against the communists in part because they forced through policies for educating girls, could, twenty years later, when faced with the rules of the Taliban, be heard defending the rights of their granddaughters to education. When asked why, most spoke of the experience of receiving education as refugees in Pakistan or Iran, of how it opened people's eyes from the narrow confines of their valleys. Change came because people saw for themselves, and made a choice.

The legacy of confrontation

The legacy of this confrontation remains with us to this day. The demonizing of the Taliban, as part of the campaign to justify the overthrow of the regime, has created a caricature of all who stand in the way of the new order. Not only have the battle-lines been drawn between the forces of conservatism and those of enlightenment, but dissenters are portrayed as the embodiment of all that is wrong with Afghanistan.

The confrontation led to an oversimplification of complex issues. Nowhere was this more clearly shown than with the controversy surrounding women's rights. Restrictions came to be seen simply as an imposition of the Taliban, a result of their obscurantist version of Islam. The underlying logic was that once the Taliban had gone, so too would the restrictions. This notion underpinned most outsiders' thinking on the issue, even though many aid workers would, if challenged, admit that it was not quite this straightforward. Not only were many of the restrictions rooted in practices that had long prevailed within the more conservative elements of Afghan society, but war had made Afghanistan more conservative. Even in urban areas many women could not go back to what they were doing ten years ago, and younger women in particular were likely to face restrictions. For many women, for example, a *mahram* was necessary if they were to travel; not because of the Taliban restriction but because their family demanded it. Now in post-Taliban Afghanistan, the edicts have gone but the restrictions remain, and some of the agencies that in the past shouted loudest about women's rights have failed to provide the conditions that would enable Afghan women to work. Consideration of where female staff would stay when they went to the field, or if they were asked to relocate to somewhere outside their home area, were simply not addressed by most agencies.

It is, perhaps, telling that the burqa, the compelling signifier of rights denied under the Taliban, remains an enduring symbol of what has not changed in the new Afghanistan. Images of shrouded women flooded the western press during that period, but the ubiquitous blue garments are still inconveniently visible. Even the Department for the Promotion of Virtue and Prevention of Vice remains, albeit that its methods of enforcement are now more subtle. Many women still wear the burqa out of custom, or say they have just come to feel more comfortable that way, but for many there is no choice, they say simply, 'We do not feel safe'. Even educated women do not always feel they can choose. Dr Annise Gul, a medical doctor and powerful defender of women's rights, now in charge of the Ministry of Women's Affairs in Badakhshan province, sheds her burqa only once within the safety of her clinic or office. When asked if she still has to wear it, she smiles ruefully, and says in a matter-of-fact way 'We do'.

The legacy of confrontation also lies in opportunities wasted. The sheer amount of time and effort spent on the cat-and-mouse game of principles with the Taliban was enormous. But time was not the only price. Expressing outrage may be cathartic, but it does not relieve anyone of responsibility to those who suffer. While there is no question that many of the Taliban's actions and policies constituted a denial of rights and were, both to many Afghans and by international standards, unacceptable, the strategy and tactics that were employed in the cause of change were all too often not those that were likely to benefit Afghans. As the UN's senior human rights adviser noted: 'Taliban gender politics had unleashed an aid agency gender war that was characterized by unending battles, skirmishes, and propaganda that further complicated the task of defining – and giving effect to – a workable policy framework' (Niland 2003: 19).

The value in UNICEF's denial for five years, in the name of principles, of support to education for Afghans inside the country came to be questioned by Afghan women and men who failed to see the logic of a policy that deprived boys of education in retribution for the Taliban denying this to girls. 'How', they asked, 'will a generation of uneducated Afghan men help in promoting women's rights?' 'Wasn't the lack of education in the refugee camps one reason so many boys went to the *madrasas*, the very institutions that helped to form the attitudes of the Taliban?'

Women's rights was not the only place where there was a price to pay. Western handling of the human rights issues connected with the war took a heavy toll on the West's claims to impartiality. In trying to link its humanitarian and political work, the UN increasingly jeopardized the humanitarian effort. By the time that the coalition declared war, the ground had been laid for animosity towards an assistance community that was seen as partial.[1] Just as the Taliban had become evil to the West, so too had western agencies become the enemy to them. The price for this is being paid today: UN and NGO staff are seen as legitimate targets for attack because they are deemed to be complicit with the US project.

Note

1 That the first international aid worker to be killed was an ICRC staff member sadly does not detract from this argument as, for all ICRC's cherished and well-maintained impartiality, neutrality and independence, at the end of the day we are all viewed in the same light.

4 | One size fits all – Afghanistan in the new world order

Reasons for war

A pick-up bearing formless, faceless women drives into the stadium. They get out and walk to their execution. The crowd looks on. Overlaying all is heavy music, heralding death.

Nothing epitomized the way in which the Taliban were portrayed in the West, and specifically in the USA, better than this clip from *Behind the Veil*. The film itself was one woman's story, the fragment of truth that belonged to that particular woman in one particular time and place, but it became representative of the oppression of all women in Afghanistan. There were other stories like it, but there were also many more that were different. This story, though, suited a purpose; it came at a particular historical moment when the West needed a narrative to justify war. For many, certainly, simple retaliation was enough, but not for all. Others had to be brought on board by an appeal at a different level; this was to be a humanitarian war, a war fought only for the best of motives and with the best of intentions. For this it was necessary that the Taliban were portrayed as the personification of evil, and Afghans, particularly women, as their victims. To underscore the point, the fragment of a fragment was endlessly repeated, over and over again at prime time on CNN and beamed around the world. In a way that was to be repeated before the US invasion of Iraq, the media coverage created a picture of a regime that was unremittingly brutal and from which its people had to be rescued. It served as a rallying cry for a war that had to be shown to have a moral purpose; it screamed 'We are justified'.

Such imagery did not, however, come out of a void, or in simple reaction to the events of 9/11, rather it was something that had been building momentum for several years. By the time the planes slammed into the World Trade Center, the Taliban were already imprinted on the world's media as unrepentant abusers of human rights, unscrupulous drug dealers and harbourers of terrorists; people beyond the pale. This enabled a whole range of people to feel righteous in their denunciations and ultimately justified in their war. Even though it was al-Qa'eda and not the Taliban that planned and executed the attacks, this caused little

6   *A woman who has been reduced to begging counts her takings during a lull
in the factional fighting in Darulaman, southern Kabul,1994. (Jolyon Leslie)*

concern; the terrorism of one was easily elided with oppression of the other, and the war on terror conveniently also became a war for the liberation of a people, its morality so hard to challenge that scarcely a voice was raised against it.

In the outpouring of solidarity with the USA that followed the attacks on the World Trade Center and the Pentagon, few stopped to question America's strategy of attacking Afghanistan. Yet if the United States' aim was simply to cripple al-Qa'eda and to kill or capture Osama bin Laden, this was an expensive and risky way to go about it. It was – or at least should have been – clear from the beginning that the chances of bin Laden escaping across the border into Pakistan, where he would be much more difficult to deal with, were high. The war was also of debatable legality and set a dangerous precedent: Israel was not slow to claim the war on terrorism as justification for its ever increasingly brutal attacks on Palestinians, and even for its raids into Syria. More effective, and far safer in terms of global security, would have been to do what any other country would have been expected to do: to pursue legal and diplomatic channels to bring the perpetrators to justice. The Taliban indicated that if the USA provided evidence that Osama bin Laden was involved in the attacks, they would be prepared to hand him over to a third country for trial, but at no time was this option tested.

A number of factors, each of which reinforced the other, seem to have lain behind the determined rush to war. There was the straightforward display of power, a deterrent to any other nation thinking of allowing its territory to be used as a base for actions against America. There was also the domestic agenda. Bush was a not very popular president who had gained office in an election widely thought to be fraudulent, and going to war has always been a good move for leaders with domestic difficulties. In the aftermath of 11 September his ratings soared dramatically. More than this, it has been cogently argued (Krugman 2003) that the war was shamelessly exploited not only to cover up misdeeds of the past but also to provide a smokescreen for a whole set of ruthless decisions which would hand great wealth to the people who put Bush in office. It was, in short, payback time hidden under the flag of patriotism. The war not only provided the perfect excuse for having turned a large budget surplus into a deficit, but it gave cover to Bush when he continued to push through huge tax cuts for the very rich despite this deficit. It justi-fied massive increases in defence spending, even though more defence spending would have made no difference to 11 September; that would have required better intelligence and better airport security. It enabled energy policies that dismantled pollution controls and allowed drilling in the Arctic to slide through with little debate, because to question the Bush administration at a time of war was to be 'unpatriotic'.

Yet somehow it seemed more than all these things. Although the attacks on the USA were the trigger for action, living in Afghanistan in the period up to autumn 2001 it seemed that America had for some time been gunning for a fight. Had the phrase 'the axis of evil' been coined then, Afghanistan would surely have been part of it. In a manner reminiscent of the run-up to the war against Saddam, or the bellicosity towards Iran, it mattered little what the Taliban did – they were damned. It is hard to pin down the host of ways in which it was made clear that they were beyond the pale, condemned utterly. The choice of language in itself is interesting; they were always a 'regime', a term intrinsically signifying illegitimacy, though in truth, to the people of Afghanistan, they were no more illegitimate than those they had succeeded. Nevertheless, two things stood out in particular. The first was the response to the Taliban's banning of opium production in accordance with international demands. As with Iraq and weapons of mass destruction, at first the USA refused to believe that their conditions had been complied with. Then, when the facts could no longer be denied, the goalposts were changed. Just as 'weapons of mass destruction' initially referred to nuclear weapons and then when none could be found it was redefined to include chemical weapons, so the demands on the Taliban were initially that they stopped growing opium poppy, and then when they did this the requirement shifted and became about their trading in it. The second, which followed on from the first and rubbed salt into wounds, was the one-sided arms embargo imposed as part of the second round of UN sanctions against the Taliban regime. To the Taliban it was, not unreasonably, seen as the international community joining in on one side of the conflict.

Early courtship

It had not always been like this. When the Taliban began their advance through Afghanistan, the Americans greeted them with a degree of welcome. Shortly after they took Kabul, acting State Department spokesman Glyn Davies said he could see 'nothing objectionable'[1] in the version of Islamic law the Taliban had imposed on areas they controlled. Assistant Secretary of State Robin Raphel urged all states not to isolate them, saying: "The Taliban control more than two-thirds of the country, they are Afghan, they are indigenous, they have demonstrated staying power.'[2] Twice in 1997 the Taliban met with State Department officials in Washington. They were then, it seems, seen as useful.

The reason for this courtship, which followed years of indifference to the country's fate, was its strategic position between the Central Asian states and international markets. While opening up trading opportunities with these new markets was in itself not insignificant, the really big profits were to be made from oil and gas pipelines. The Taliban's most important function was to 'provide security for roads and, potentially, oil and gas pipelines that would link the states of Central Asia to the international market through Pakistan rather than Iran' (Rubin 1997).

America has 4 per cent of the world's population and consumes more than 25 per cent of all energy, much of which it has to import (Kleveman 2003). Not only are very powerful interests involved in the oil industry, but without plentiful and secure supplies of cheap oil the American way of life simply cannot continue. The Caspian Sea and Central Asian states (collectively known as the Caspian region in the oil trade) have some of what are believed to be the last large unexploited oil and gas reserves in the world, and by the mid-1990s the scramble for a share of the profits they could yield was already under way. As Sheila Heslin, energy expert at the National Security Council, noted in a testimony to the Senate in 1997: 'US policy was to promote the rapid development of Caspian energy ... We did so specifically to promote the independence of these oil-rich countries, to in essence break Russia's monopoly control over transportation of oil from that region, and frankly, to promote Western energy security through diversification of supply' (quoted in Rashid 2000: 174).

Oil and gas are of no use if there is no way to get them out, and Afghanistan potentially offered advantages over all the alternative pipeline routes. Most crucially, it meant that a pipeline would not go through Iran, towards which the USA had long been antagonistic. By providing an alternative to existing routes flowing north through Russia, it would also serve to reduce the latter's influence in the region. The alternative route, from Baku across to Ceyhan in Turkey, was longer and meant traversing the unstable southern Caucasus.[3]

There was only one problem with the Afghan option: the warlords continued to fight. Insecurity was not good for business, especially the expensive business of building pipelines, and for a time the Taliban were seen as the answer, as a chance for stability. For as long as they were perceived as useful, their harsh interpretation of Islam and their denial of women's rights did not seem overly to bother the US administration. In the words of one US diplomat: 'The Taliban will probably develop like the Saudis did. There will be Aramco, pipelines, an emir, no parliament and lots of Sharia law. We can live with that' (Rashid 2000: 179).

Oil was a strategic as well as a commercial issue, and the Clinton administration weighed in heavily on behalf of UNOCAL in its tussle with the Argentinian firm Bridas over contracts to build pipelines through Afghanistan.[4] In February 1997, and again in November of that year, Taliban representatives were in Washington meeting both UNOCAL and State Department officials. UNOCAL estimated it had spent some $15–20 million on the pipeline project (ibid., p. 171), bringing in high-profile, ex-State Department officials to help devise its strategy with the Taliban. Among the experts it hired was Zalmay Khalilzad, an Afghan American who has been a key figure in the development of US policy towards Afghanistan and the Middle East. A member of the National Security Council, Khalilzad was appointed Bush's special envoy to Afghanistan at the end of 2001 and is now the US Ambassador in Kabul; so strong is his influence that Afghans joke that he, not Karzai, is the president of Afghanistan. Khalilzad served out the time of the Clinton administration working for the Rand Corporation and for UNOCAL, where he undertook an elaborate risk analysis for the Afghan pipeline project (Rashid 2000; Kleveman 2003). Since 2001, he also served as special presidential envoy to the Iraqi opposition, and from December 2002 as special envoy for the civil reconstruction of a post-war Iraq. Khalilzad initially urged engagement: 'I am confident that [the Taliban] would welcome an American reengagement. The Taliban does not practice the anti-US style of fundamentalism practiced by Iran – it is closer to the Saudi model.' It was only much later, after UNOCAL had put its Afghan plans on hold, that he shifted his stance to one of condemnation. Another figure from that time is President Hamid Karzai, who in 1997 represented UNOCAL in negotiations with the Taliban leadership.

Changing attitudes

By late 1997 US attitudes to the Taliban had changed. In a testimony to the Senate Foreign Relations subcommittee in October 1997, Assistant Secretary of State Karl Inderfurth spoke of America wanting to see an Afghan government that was 'multi-ethnic, broad-based, and that observes international norms of behaviour'. Visiting an Afghan refugee camp in Pakistan in the November, US Secretary of State Madeline Albright put it more bluntly: 'I think it is very clear why we are opposed to the Taliban. Because of their approach to human rights, their despicable treatment of women and children and their general lack of respect for human dignity.'[5]

While officially the reasons for this change of heart were women, drugs and terrorists, in reality it was much more complex and multilayered. Certainly the highly influential women's lobby had an effect. In a two-pronged campaign they targeted both UNOCAL and the president. The oil company was attacked in a high-profile lobbying campaign that helped persuade them that the public relations costs of continuing to court the Taliban were not worth it, especially as the drop in oil prices was beginning to undermine the pipeline's financial viability. Clinton, with his political career already rocked by the Lewinsky scandal, decided he could not afford to alienate female voters further, especially after Hollywood's liberal stars – key backers of the Democratic campaigns – made Afghan women's rights a *cause célèbre*. Yet given the United States' record elsewhere, it is hard not to question its real commitment to the rights of Afghan women. Saudi Arabia, for example, has an atrocious record on women's rights, and indeed human rights more generally. It has no qualms about stoning women to death for 'adultery', prisoners are routinely tortured, over 200 people were beheaded in 2000 and 2001. But Saudi Arabia is a friend, a guardian of the West's oil, and thus it has been decided that, 'a patient and discreet dialogue with the Saudi authorities is the best way to make progress' (Curtis 2003).

A further reason given for the tough stand taken in relation to the Taliban was their involvement in the production of opium. Yet as a reason for the change, it is less than convincing. The surge in opium poppy growing began in the 1980s under America's allies, the *mujahideen*, and little concern was then paid to it by the superpower. Drugs out and arms in proved too profitable a formula to interfere with, and as in Vietnam where the CIA ignored the drug trafficking of the anti-communist guerrillas they were financing, they ignored both the activities of the *mujahideen* and the involvement of the Pakistani ISI. The US Drugs Enforcement Agency uncovered forty major heroin syndicates in Pakistan at that time,[6] but not a single one was broken up (Rashid 2000).

The third reason, as put forward in the UN resolutions authorizing sanctions, was that the Taliban provided sanctuary for Osama bin Laden. The 1998 suicide bomb attacks on the US embassies in Dar-es-Salaam and Nairobi in many ways marked the beginning of the new phase in American relations with Afghanistan. The USA quickly retaliated with Cruise missile attacks on Osama bin Laden's training camps in Khost, an attack that inevitably brought outrage from some of the more militant Taliban supporters in the country. Yet here, too, the story does not quite add up. If the real concern was terrorism, far more attention ought to have been paid to Saudi Arabia. Osama was Saudi-born and known still to have links there, most of those involved in the 11 September hijackings were Saudi, and Saudi Arabia remains a key organizational base for al-Qa'eda. The Saudi connections were known, but they were also highly politically damaging for they led to the heart of American business interests.

Behind the issue of drugs, women's rights and terrorism, there seemed to be another more fundamental reason: the Taliban simply did not fit with how America thought the world should be run. For the USA there is only one acceptable model of statehood, as expressed in the recent National Security Strategy (2002): 'a single sustainable model for national success: freedom, democracy, and free enterprise'. But although this is being articulated ever more forcibly, the idea itself is not new. As has been shown consistently from America's involvement in the overthrow of the Arbenz government in Guatemala in 1954, and Allende's in Chile in 1973, to the long bitter struggle of Vietnam and its opposition to the democratically elected president of Venezuela, challenge to the dominant liberal capitalist system is simply not allowed. And if it is not to be allowed in countries that are relatively marginal in the global economic system, it is certainly not to be allowed in an oil-rich region. The Taliban's fault seemed to be less that they abused human rights (so do many others) or that they did not stop the growing of opium poppy (neither does Afghanistan's current government) but that their whole way of being was a challenge to western liberal democracy and free market capitalism. Their vision of returning Afghanistan to Allah and the rule of the shari'a was as radical a challenge as communism or the mullahs of Iran. Here was a country in an enormously strategic location for the global energy market, and its rulers simply weren't interested in playing the game. Nor could they be bought. For while the Taliban were certainly prepared to take money from the West, as was shown in their early dealings with UNOCAL, they did not want it enough to sacrifice their beliefs for it.

Antagonism to the Taliban began in the Clinton years, but it intensified after Bush became president. This is not surprising; those now in power had long been pushing for a much harder line towards the Islamic Middle East (from which, politically, events in Afghanistan cannot be separated). In 1992, Paul Wolfowitz, then Under-Secretary of Defense, wrote a document calling for intervention in Iraq and legitimizing pre-emptive attacks on other countries. Dick Cheney also endorsed this view, and although he later backed off in the face of public protest, he and others now in key positions continued to push throughout the 1990s for both a war on Iraq and the adoption of a policy of pre-emption (Krugman 2003).

As with the earlier courtship, so too were oil interests a driving force in the change of policy. The Bush government is dominated by oil-men. Dick Cheney used to be chief executive officer for the oil supply corporation Halliburton, Condoleeza Rice served on the board of directors for Chevron, acting as their principal expert on Kazakhstan; Robert Finn, the US Ambassador to Afghanistan in the immediate post-Taliban period, was a Caspian oil expert. Immediately after taking office, the administration made oil politics a new priority. In May 2001, Dick Cheney presented the National Energy Policy, which recommended that 'the President make energy security a priority of our trade and foreign policy'. It went on to say, 'our engagement will be global, spotlighting existing and emerging regions that will have a major impact on the global energy balance' (US Department of Energy 2001). Reliance on the Gulf, and in particular on Saudi Arabia, had long been a concern for the USA and this was becoming increasingly critical as alternative sources of production started to dry up. The corrupt and unpopular House of Saud is well known to be a key target of Osama bin Laden and the chance of it being overthrown and the rich oil reserves falling into the hands of an anti-US administration, as happened in Iran, must represent a nightmare scenario to the USA.

At the same time, developments in the Caspian region were increasing its importance to the USA. In July 2000 geologists discovered a massive oil bubble in the Kazakh part of the Caspian Sea. With a 25-mile-wide oil bubble, experts believe that this, the Kashagan oil field, represents some 30 billion barrels of crude oil. Only the Ghawar oil field in Saudi Arabia is larger. Not only does this represent huge profits, but it means that Kashagan has the potential to become what the industry calls a 'swing supplier', a supplier big enough to be able quickly to boost production to make up for any sudden cutbacks in supply. Currently only Saudi Arabia can do this, although Iraq (sitting on a total of 112 billion barrels) also has the potential. The US Department of Energy report reaffirmed Afghanistan's significance 'as a potential transit route for oil and natural gas exports from central Asia to the Arabian Sea'.

The war on terror therefore presented the USA with a double opportunity: to bring about regime change in Afghanistan, and to establish bases in a number of strategic locations in Central Asia. As Mahfouz Nedai, Afghanistan's deputy Minister of Industry, noted: 'Washington has sent their men into our government for good reason. The Americans have not come to Central Asia just for the terrorists' (Kleveman 2003).

Isolating the Taliban

Once it had been decided that the Taliban did not fit with US interests, the strategy shifted to one of isolating them in every way possible. This was pursued not only through normal diplomatic channels, such as sanctions, but also by a process of rendering them in the public eye as dangerous fanatics. Given a long history in the West of depicting the Orient as simultaneously exotic and barbarous (Said 1992), this was not an unduly difficult task. Nevertheless, no avenue was left untrod in pursuit of the objective: the meaning of security was turned on its head; the concern for human rights exploited; the use of assistance warped. Most of the media proved to be all-too-willing accomplices – again in keeping with a long history of misrepresenting Islam (Said 1997). None of this is to say that the Taliban did not have some very nasty characteristics; as Mark Duffield (2001b) notes: 'all discourse contains truths. It is in the nature of discourse, however, to select some truths and neglect others, and to rework those that have been adopted into a coherent and functional world view.' And the discourse built up about the Taliban was to prove very functional indeed.

After 1998, as Afghanistan became the focus of more political attention, the UN became the conduit for more direct censure. This culminated in October 1999 in the adoption of Security Council Resolution 1267, which imposed sanctions aimed at freezing Taliban assets while also withdrawing landing rights to the national airline. The measures were aimed at the Taliban rather than the population at large, although the demonstrations that took place suggested that this was not perceived to be the case by some Afghans. Key member-states were at pains to ensure that, at a time when the humanitarian situation was becoming the focus of international attention, such measures could not be portrayed as worsening the plight of Afghans. The second round of sanctions, imposed under Security Council Resolution 1333 in December 2000, put in place a one-sided arms embargo – which all members of the Security Council knew was unworkable because there was no way of enforcing the ban on cross-border supplies – on the Taliban. The military impact was thus minimal. By now the Taliban had come to the realization that, whatever they did, the western powers were against them, while ordinary Afghans felt increasingly isolated by the outside world.

The creation of a security problem One of the most striking things about the move towards isolating the Taliban was the way in which the security situation was manipulated. As NGOs and locally based UN staff repeatedly pointed out, the security situation under the Taliban was better for agency staff (and in many ways for ordinary Afghans) than it had been throughout the *mujahideen* time. For the first time in many years, it was possible to travel the roads at any time of the day or night without fear of being held up by gunmen. Yet one incident was to trigger a fundamental change in the way security was managed in Afghanistan. Once the news broke that the USA had launched a Cruise missile attack on the alleged sites of terrorist training camps in Khost, it was clear that there was the potential for trouble on the streets of Kabul. In consultation with their Taliban hosts, who were aware both of the risks of freelance retribution and their responsibility for the security of the small international contingent in Kabul, those in charge of UN security decided that all UN staff should be confined to their quarters until the situation was clarified. Despite this, an Italian assigned as a military adviser to UNSMA, Lieutenant Carmine Calo, and a French colleague took a marked UN vehicle out of the guarded UN compound, and on their way through the streets of Kabul were fired on after a staged accident. Both UNSMA staff were injured and Calo, though rushed to hospital, died some hours later.

Although the UN had experienced a number of other attacks over the previous decade and had still carried on working, and despite the fact that there was little to suggest that the general security situation had deteriorated, this tragic incident resulted in a complete evacuation of international UN staff from the country. It ushered in a new security era, as Afghanistan came to be portrayed as a dangerous country, where the security of foreigners could not be guaranteed. The UN took the unprecedented step of acceding to pressure to forbid US and UK nationals from serving in Afghanistan. After protracted negotiations with the Taliban, the return of UN staff to Kabul began in early 2000, followed by other areas, but with strict limits on numbers. While UN headquarters seemed unwilling to challenge the ban on UK and US nationals entering Afghanistan, some British staff in the field resorted to rediscovering their Irish ancestry, and one went so far as to buy herself a Somali passport. The policy appeared to be degenerating into a farce. Meanwhile, in the absence of any specific details about the alleged risks faced by USA and UK citizens, the ICRC politely resisted pressure to introduce similar restrictions on the deployment of its staff.

The UK went even further in its restrictions than the USA, with the Department for International Development withdrawing funding from NGOs that let international staff even visit the country. It is hard to know, even with the benefit of hindsight, how much this was due to political manipulation and how much it was due simply to ill-informed and prejudiced judgements. The Foreign Office insisted it had specific evidence that there were threats, but would never elaborate on what these were. From the beginning, NGOs strongly challenged the UK government line, pointing out that security was both better than it had been in the past and better than it was in many other countries where no such draconian restrictions were in place. The British refused to budge and most NGOs, believing the issue was more about politics than security, found their money elsewhere. The funding restriction was finally lifted by the UK in mid-2001, but only upon stringent security assessments of the agencies concerned.

While the result of all the regulations was to paint a picture of a country that was irredeemably dangerous, security on the ground actually remained quite good. Although there were some hold-ups of vehicles, mainly associated with the looting of Codan radios, the incidents were neither as frequent nor as violent as those that had happened in the past. Even after 11 September, when it was clear that Afghanistan would face retaliatory attacks, the Taliban stuck by the security guarantees they had given the international community and facilitated an orderly evacuation of international staff, leaving Afghans to face the American bombs alone.

Aid, rights and the US project

Aid has long been part of the strategy by which outside nations have gained influence in Afghanistan. But whereas in the 1960s and '70s this had been essentially a bilateral endeavour, and in the 1980s it had been linked to Cold War alliances, by the mid-'90s there was a move towards all organizations involved in assistance – donors, the UN and NGOs – pulling together in one system-wide effort in pursuit of peace in Afghanistan. Not all organizations bought into the Strategic Framework for Afghanistan (discussed in detail in Chapter 3),[7] and of those who did a number were somewhat reluctant partners. Nevertheless, officially at least, the assistance community aspired to 'speak with one voice'.

While the initial impetus for this effort came from the perceived need both to address the deep-seated conflict and to improve the effectiveness of assistance in what was seen as a 'failed state', once international policy became driven by efforts to isolate and demonize the Taliban, the modalities of the SFA could also be used to this end. The anchor for the common approach was seen as a set of shared principles by which decisions would be made as to when and how to give assistance. In the quest to define these, the notion of rights became central: people had a right to humanitarian assistance; a right to protection; women had equal rights with men. But the emergence of an assistance community bent on 'principled' and 'rights-based' programming at the very time that the Taliban were gaining control of the country and seeking to impose their own, rather different, notion of principles, meant that a clash was inevitable. This confrontation, though often stemming from a different set of priorities to the US agenda, played into the move to isolate the Taliban. For though the motives may have been different, the assistance community and the US body politic were both party to building up the discourse that the Taliban were evil and dangerous.

In part this was due to confusion on the ground as to how to achieve supposedly universal rights in someone else's country, one in which by custom as well as diktat these rights were not always recognized. But it was also due to overlapping agendas. The assistance community did not speak with one voice, not even within one organization. As the UN's senior human rights adviser at that time noted, any real progress on human rights issues was undermined by 'a high level of rhetoric at the international level that had more to do with external political agendas than development of interventions that would actually help erode discriminatory attitudes and practices' (Niland 2003).

One such example of how rights became an instrument of political agendas lies in a high-profile confrontation that seems to have gone down in international folklore as a truly heroic stance against evil. In 1997 Emma Bonino, then head of the European Community Office for Humanitarian Assistance (ECHO), visited Kabul, accompanied by celebrity CNN reporter Christiane Amanpour. They had asked to see the health facility, Rabbia Balkhi hospital, that the Taliban had declared would be dedicated to the provision of services to women. This followed a protracted controversy that had centred on allegations by the aid community that the Ministry of Public Health planned to centralize female healthcare, whereas in fact it had proposed the strengthening of one facility, which would be reserved for women. As would be the case in any other Muslim country, the visitors and accompanying press contingent were asked specifically not to film inside the hospital with a male crew. They chose to ignore this request, and proceeded to film at will in the female wards, whereupon the female head of the hospital called the police. Not surprisingly, the saga of the brief detention of Bonino became headline news. Inevitably, it was the Taliban, rather than the visitors, who were accused of unacceptable behaviour. Most aid workers in the city agreed with Afghan health professionals in seeing this as a crude self-serving stunt that served only to obscure the real story, which was about the need to improve health facilities for women. Apart from leaving the Afghans who were accompanying her on her visit (and who had tried to halt the filming) in detention, the legacy of Bonino was to make the work of Afghan medical professionals much more difficult. As the female head of the hospital said months later, 'the outside world has scored its points, but the ones who will pay the price are my patients'.[8]

Having decided that the Taliban were unacceptable, few opportunities were lost to point out their failings. The advocacy organization Physicians for Human Rights (PHR) (2001) launched a report claiming that 95 per cent of women in Kabul saw a decline in their mental health during the rule of the Taliban. Though they later admitted that the data collection was flawed, by then the damage was done.[9] The findings were highlighted in the press and soon became 'facts', to be used by a range of organizations and individuals as evidence of how bad the Taliban were. A later report issued by PHR, which drew a more nuanced picture and was based on much more thorough research, drew no press interest whatsoever. UN reports also regularly admonished the Taliban for not meeting some perfect moral standard. They were castigated for doing things that are the common behaviour of politicians worldwide, such as wanting to control assistance, or only spending their own money on public goods when it was 'roads and other infrastructure that benefits their supporters' (Leader 2000). While they were regularly denounced for what they did wrong, they never received credit for the things they managed well, most of which were quickly forgotten as inconvenient.

Hazarajat was a case in point. Some terrible things happened in this part of Afghanistan and they were rightly condemned. But some good things happened also. Women did not have to wear burqas, the Shi'a Hazaras were left in peace to pray as they chose, and when there were problems with the *kuchis* returning to claim their old grazing rights, the Taliban, at least in cases we knew of in Nawor and Panjao, helped to resolve them. And just as in the *jihad*, when NGOs were vocal about the crimes of the government side but anyone criticizing the *mujahideen* for their human rights violations was automatically seen as an apologist for the Soviets (Baitenmann 1990: 62), so now only the Taliban could be criticized. When the Taliban massacred 200 people in Yakawlang they were rightly condemned; but no one spoke out against Hizbe Wahdat for the initial attack on the town that precipitated this incident, even though Wahdat must have known they could not hold the town and that civilians would pay the price for their actions. The one-sided approach not only demonized the Taliban but it also allowed the other side to feel it had impunity, that whatever it did it would not be taken to task.

As in the fight against the Soviets, the USA was happy to ally itself with whoever suited its interests, whether it was the military or the propaganda war. This produced some interesting bed-fellows. The Revolutionary Association of the Women of Afghanistan (RAWA) is a hard-left group of urban, educated women of the type that establishment interests in the USA, conservative or liberal, would normally waste no time in condemning. Based in Quetta, it has always represented only a minority of Afghan women. In America, however, it became for many the voice of all. Its members were not slow to see the advantages offered to them by the interest of high-profile western women and a media hungry for the latest atrocity, and they used every opportunity they could to highlight the attacks on women's rights. On one memorable occasion, at a star-studded $1,000-a-ticket New York production of *The Vagina Monologues*, a shrouded RAWA delegate ascended to the stage, dramatically lifted her burqa and delivered a fiery speech to the cheers of the assembled audience (Thrupkaew 2002). The cynicism with which the women were, in turn, used can be seen in the way that, while in those days the USA thought their evidence against the Taliban credible enough to cite, today there is no mention of their documentation of the crimes of the Northern Alliance (Kolhatkar 2003). After 11 September, the crescendo of feeling against the Taliban accelerated. The American media, largely owned by the right, fell into line, with few dissenters. We were based in Islamabad in September and October 2001. Despite doing almost daily interviews with the international media, it was impossible not to observe how the US media almost never wanted interviews. It wasn't just that we were not American; even US colleagues received no callers. There simply was no room for views that might call into question, let alone be critical of, what the USA was doing. The British media tried harder. Locally based reporters searched out those who might tell a different story, who might know how it was for Afghans left behind, who knew something of the history of the country; but the BBC team reported that it fought a constant battle with London to present a more critical perspective – and, despite their efforts, those viewing the domestic news in the UK found little to challenge the party line.

Stitching up a country

The Americans won't ever give up their military bases in Afghanistan. From here they will control the entire region. (Farhang, Minister for Reconstruction, quoted in Kleveman 2003)

The events of 11 September presented the USA with the opportunity to start again, to build a pliable state in Afghanistan that would conform, at least outwardly, to liberal notions of 'democracy and free enterprise'. Given that the new administration was brought into being not by any political struggle but rather by the space opened up by American bombs, it was perhaps not surprising that it offered no coherent vision of what a future Afghanistan might look like. But if the Interim Administration lacked a clear ideology, the same could not be said for the country's 'liberators'. In the gap that ought to have been filled by political debate, they were already busy trying to establish a client state that would serve their interests.

At the same time as real political debate on the future of Afghanistan was failing to happen, the rhetoric of democracy was being used to hide the pursuit of western interests, not only in securing oil routes, but also in refashioning the whole economy in the market economy mode. Policies were being made on the ground by a few key ministers and their many foreign advisers. The Minister of Finance, Ashraf Ghani, was a long-time World Bank employee and devotee of the economic liberalization argument; the desire to parcel out the Afghan economy to the private sector ran through everything he touched. The draft National Development Framework produced in April 2002[10] was followed by the National Development Budget. Both were about turning Afghanistan into an economy where 'a competitive private sector becomes the engine of growth'. The government's role was seen as promotion of the private sector, government assets would be privatized and international firms were seen as partners in all major projects.

The documents sat well with the dogma of America and its favourite ally, the UK. In its National Security Strategy, America boldly declared it would bring 'free trade to every corner of the world', igniting 'a new era of global economic growth through free markets and free trade'. For the UK's Chancellor of the Exchequer, Gordon Brown, the poorest countries' 'obligations' were to 'pursue stability and create the opportunities for new investment'.[11] In a similar vein Margaret Beckett claimed Britain's businesses needed to be able to trade throughout the world 'without facing high tariffs, discriminatory regulations or unnecessarily burdensome procedures'.[12] How well such a strategy serves Afghanistan is another issue.

The USA and its allies, along with the international financial institutions, which they largely control, have long been telling developing countries that what they need is to open up their markets, to privatize their industries, and to end government's role as a service provider. Whether it is Argentina, Afghanistan or Angola, the message is the same. Yet while such a prescription is undoubtedly good for First World trade, there is little evidence to suggest that it will lead to growth in the countries concerned. On the contrary, all the evidence to date suggests that the private sector alone is unlikely to be a sufficient engine for growth. The countries where by far the highest levels of economic growth have been seen over recent decades have been those of East Asia, particularly China and South Korea, but also Vietnam, Thailand, Malaysia and Indonesia. Though all of these countries are very different and there is no one blueprint that can be drawn from them, they do show some interesting contrasts to the strategy being proposed for Afghanistan. None of these countries started its strategy for growth from the position of being a completely open economy; all had carefully structured barriers to protect their fledgling industries and only later, once industry was established, did they liberalize. Japan, somewhat earlier in the twentieth century, followed the same pattern, as of course did the USA itself. Even now, America quickly dumps its free trade policy as soon as its own industries are threatened. In January 2002 it introduced tariffs of as much as 30 per cent on imported steel in order to try and protect its steel industry; tariffs which were ruled by the WTO to be illegal and inconsistent with free trade.[13] In a similar vein it continues to grant massive subsidies to its agricultural sector, whose excess wheat then becomes food aid for the poor world, often depressing local prices and depriving farmers of their livelihoods.

In addition, East Asian countries not only invested heavily in health and education, but also in strategies that ensured that everyone had access to these essential services, thus producing an educated and healthy workforce.

Jobs for the boys While most Afghans have so far seen little benefit from reconstruction, US companies have been doing very well indeed. According to a report published by the Centre for Public Integrity, US firms received over US$8 billion in contracts for work in post-war Iraq and Afghanistan. The top recipient was Kellogg, Brown and Root, a subsidiary of Halliburton, of which Dick Cheney was chief executive officer prior to being chosen as George W. Bush's running mate. It was awarded contracts worth $2.3 billion. Almost all of the companies that won contracts in Iraq and Afghanistan were political players, giving some $12.7 million to the various Republican committees, and $7.1 million to the Democratic ones. George Bush alone reportedly received over $0.5 million. Although USAID has a public duty to ensure that taxpayers' dollars are used 'efficiently and effectively', an examination of contracts awarded would seem to suggest that other factors also come into play. In

January 2003 Creative Associates International Inc., an organization that had no experience of working in the country, bid for a major education contract as part of a consortium with two NGOs, neither of which was an expert in education. They won the bid over another consortium comprised of DAI and the three international NGOs that have the strongest track record of education development work in Afghanistan. Creative Associates is one of the many private consulting firms that developed in the 1970s and '80s in response to the US government's decision that it needed to subcontract much of its assistance work. Commonly known as 'Beltway Bandits', because they all have offices inside Washington's beltway, they are often staffed by former government employees and their main business is contracts from government organizations such as USAID. In addition to the Afghanistan contract, in March 2003 Creative Associates won an Iraq education contract worth up to $157 million. The organization, which has several former USAID officials on its staff, is the eleventh largest recipient of government contracts in Iraq and Afghanistan according to the Center for Public Integrity's analysis (CPI 2003). While it is the big fish that will clearly benefit most, even the smaller enterprises are confident of a killing. As the manager of a company bidding for the new US funds that were the talk of Kabul in early 2004 put it: 'We cannot lose – the guys in Washington have not only insured our assets in this place, but also our profits.'

Aid and the pursuit of liberal governance Aid, said USAID head Andrew Natsios in 2001, is 'a key foreign policy instrument'. And in case there was any doubt about what this meant, he elaborated: 'For eign assistance helps developing and transition nations move towards democratic systems and market economies; it helps nations prepare for participation in the global trading system and become better markets for US exports' (Kaplan 2003).

From a bilateral perspective this is perhaps neither surprising nor new. What is notable in Afghanistan is how far both the multilateral agencies, and even many of the supposedly independent NGOs, have been pulled into the free market project. This is in part only an intensification of a trend that has long been under way. For years now, liberal governance has made its way in the world via a whole network of agencies that manage what Mark Duffield (2001b) called 'the borderlands'. On the margins of the global system lie a whole raft of countries where poverty and long-running conflicts seem endemic. This, the excluded South, has for some time been seen as a danger to the international system because of the risk of conflict, criminality and terrorism spilling out over its borders. It also, to those concerned with justice, remains an unacceptable scar on the face of a rich world, an ever-present reminder that the policies work only for some. But in a unipolar world, where there is no longer any radical political challenge to the status quo, both those concerned with justice and those concerned with the advancement of the free market roll out the same solution: to try and manage the troublesome South through strategic networks that involve the UN and NGOs in a shift away from simply providing humanitarian assistance towards programmes to reduce conflict and increase stability.

Even so, 9/11 brought about a change of gear. The terms of engagement were set by Bush's famous 'you are either for us or against us'. The statement at a stroke removed the independent space in which the UN and NGOs might have been able to operate. While in the past it was often suspected that the UN was just part of the US project, undertaking its operational work in parts of the world where the US preferred to be 'hands off', now it was official. Agencies have been slow to realize the implications of this, and of how much more dangerous it has made the world for them. There is, it seems, at times a wilful donning of blinkers, a refusal to see the political project, far less the role they have come to play in it.

The UN in particular continued to pretend, even while the ever-increasing layers of razor wire on top of the walls of their buildings, the concrete bollards and 'no stopping' signs that surround them, showed that on one level it understood all too well. The price of this pretending was already being paid in Afghanistan, with an ICRC international staff member and a number of NGO national staff murdered, but it was not until the bombing of the UN's HQ in Baghdad that it seemed to sink in. Awful though the attack was, it was not, to anyone who has any understanding of the situation, surprising. The UN had not only overseen more than a decade of crippling sanctions, but had gone into Iraq in the wake of an illegal occupation of a country, and as such was bound to be a target. To pretend otherwise was, at best, dangerously naive. Yet at a memorial service in Mazar, held by the UN staff for their dead and injured colleagues and friends, the repeated question was: Why us?

A more courageous UN could, of course, have refused to accept this diktat, could have insisted on its independence and gone out of its way to prove this. But complicity is a hard habit to break, and co-option seductive. The post-Cold War dominance of a single world-view has made it if not easy, at least necessary, to persuade oneself that the only option is change from within. Once there it is all too easy to have one's critical faculties blunted. As Peter Griffiths notes in the foreword to his book about the World Bank, *The Economist's Tale* (2003):

> Some individuals chose to be incompetent, dishonest or downright evil. Some are pressed by the employers, their family or their society. Others tolerate incompetence, dishonesty or evil because they are afraid. They may be afraid they will lose their jobs and starve. They may be afraid that they will be beaten up or killed. Or they may be afraid that they will be seen to be making a fuss.

Human rights

Rights have long been a victim of the war in Afghanistan, but only sometimes have outside powers chosen to recognize this. The diligent concern for human rights abuses displayed by donors and senior UN officials when Afghanistan was under the Taliban evaporated with the signing of the Bonn agreements. In the months following, a number of frontline workers tried to raise human rights issues within the UN, only to be silenced. That rights are only ever invoked by mainstream politicians when it suits their purposes is not, perhaps, surprising; what is more shocking is the way in which the UN failed to challenge this. The overarching statements paid dutiful lip-service, stressing the importance of the full and equal participation of women in political, economic, cultural and social life. Action on the ground, however, suggested priorities were otherwise. The Special Representative of the UN Secretary General, Lakhdar Brahimi, stated that Afghanistan could not at this time have both justice and peace, and UN workers who tried to raise these issues found themselves blocked. An independent human rights commission was set up but was given little political support.

If one thing symbolized rights issues under the Taliban, it was the burqa. Images of shrouded women flooded the press, the embodiment of rights denied. Yet arriving back in Kabul in December 2001 one could not help but notice that every woman was still wearing it. As the months rolled by a few got rid of the burqa, but they were still in a minority. Outside Kabul, little has changed. By the summer of 2004 some women still wore it out of custom, or said they had just come to feel more comfortable that way, but for many there was no choice, they said simply: 'We do not feel safe.' Even those educated women who had been strong defenders of women's rights for many years did not always feel they could choose.

The burqa, of course, was always more symbolic than a substantive issue. For most Afghan women the rights to education and to paid work were far more important. But here, too, for all the publicity about girls going back to school, the actual improvements have been limited. In part that has been due to the lack of a coherent education policy, but conservative forces have also burned girls' schools and banned females from attending. Yet the international community has been largely silent.

A similar silence descended on the human rights abuses in the northern provinces. From Qunduz in the east to Faryab in the west, this area is a patchwork of different peoples with a long and complex history. At different times different groups gained access to land, displacing others and often themselves being displaced later, either by yet another group or by the return of earlier incumbents. In accordance with this long-established pattern, when the Taliban ruled in Kabul the Pashtuns were in the ascendancy in the north. Then, when the Taliban were defeated the Pashtuns bore the brunt of retributions, often for no other reason than that they came from the same ethnic group. Yet despite the fact that this situation was predictable, the international community failed to protect them and it was not until much later that the UN managed to intervene successfully to reduce the violence targeted at local Pashtun communities. Yet there were sizeable coalition forces in the north, and the Afghan forces accused of the violations were their military partners. Why did they not use their influence better to protect the civilian population? Why also did they not ensure protection for the hundreds of Taliban and other combatants who surrendered to the Northern Alliance after the fall of Qunduz and who are believed to have met their death either by suffocation in the containers in which they were transported or by summary execution? Bodies from this massacre, and from earlier ones, lie in mass graves in northern Afghanistan. Yet despite the fact that many believe that a proper investigation of the graves and a dignified burial of the remains are an essential part of any accountability and reconciliation process, so far UNAMA has been reluctant to act, stating that the decision whether or not to investigate lay with the Afghan authorities and the Human Rights Commission. Concern was also expressed that it would not be possible to protect witnesses and that responsibility to the living had to take precedence over justice to the dead. International human rights groups disagreed, as did the UN Special Rapporteur on Extra-judicial Executions, who visited Afghanistan in mid-October 2002 and called for an international inquiry into past human rights violations, including the graves in the north (UN 2002a). Finally, a decision was taken by the UN in September 2001 to authorize an official investigation into the sites but this was to be limited to 'finding and preserving evidence' and would have a 'low profile' since systematic and full investigations 'would seriously disrupt the fragile peace that the Government and international community are striving to foster and reinforce'. Since then a number of witnesses to the fate of Taliban captives at Dashte Leili are reported to have disappeared or have been tortured. As a human rights worker interviewed in December 2002 noted: 'Every time someone comes and looks, someone disappears.'

As with rights, so too have standards on security changed since the fall of the Taliban. The string of attacks on UN and NGO staff have included both expatriates – the gang rape of a female NGO worker in the north, the murder of an ICRC engineer in Uruzgan in early 2003 and a UNHCR worker in Ghazni in November 2003 – and Afghans, of whom many have been killed and many more wounded. Some of these attacks have been ugly in the extreme, with groups of workers hauled from their ambushed vehicles and summarily executed. Yet there has been no evacuation.

In Afghanistan, as in Iraq, the worsening security situation is conveniently blamed on 'remnants' of the old disorder. The truth is far more complex. The military intervention opened up a security vacuum, which the USA blocked an international force from filling as it feared it would interfere with its pursuit of al-Qa'eda. As a result, two distinct security problems now exist in Afghanistan. In the south and east, groups opposed to the current administration, many of which are finding shelter over the border in Pakistan, deliberately target anyone linked to the new administration. Their task is made easier by the political disenfranchisement of a large part of the population and the discontent caused by the heavy-handed tactics of the coalition forces. Meanwhile, in other parts of the country warlords who are nominally part of the government continue to fight each other. Those who recall the evacuation of UN staff in 1998, in response to a tragic but single casualty, can be forgiven for questioning the meaning of security when more than a third of rural districts are out of bounds to aid agencies and when, due to security concerns, all but one NGO has evacuated Qandahar.

NGOs – wanting it both ways

Beneath the cloak of having 'come to help', NGOs are also often part of the sell-off of the country's assets and the privatization of its services. The agencies themselves appear confused and uncomfortable with the position they find themselves in. Although unhappy at being associated with the government through involvement with projects such as the flagship National Solidarity Programme, they continue to take the money, slow to recognize the implications of the change in the political landscape. The years in which the *mujahideen* first fought for, and then fought over, Afghanistan left them the space to work as they chose, the Afghan government not being in a position to control their activities; the notion of independent NGOs working directly with communities took root. The Taliban days, if anything, entrenched this; NGOs were paid by donors to be 'independent' agencies working with communities in the face of a repressive government. They could retain their moral stance and be paid for it; for the agenda of donors and the agenda of NGOs was substantially one and the same. That is no longer the case.

Donors have clearly embarked on a political project to reconstruct Afghanistan in a certain mould, and while they are more than willing to fund NGOs to be implementers of projects within this framework, it is clear that there is no longer big money on the table for those who choose to remain outside. NGOs face a difficult choice, which few of them as yet seem to have recognized. The years of funding to do development work according to their own beliefs and priorities are over. Either they become part of the political project, with all its faults, or they retain their independence but lose large-scale funding and, perhaps even more importantly to some, a seat at the table of the power-brokers.

For USAID, the new role is clearly expressed in the shift from grants to contracting. Rather than being given resources to engage in development processes, agencies will now be given contracts to deliver to specified outcomes. Targets will be set – for example, the number of children to be vaccinated against measles – and if the agency does not meet them its funding will be cut accordingly. While this may be an attempt to get some accountability into the system, which in itself is no bad thing, it is accountability according to the donor's priorities, not the NGO's. To bemoan that more meaningful development indicators are not part of the picture is to miss the point – this is not a development process. For many donors, NGOs are now being funded not as development agencies but as subcontractors for specific programmes.

Failing the Afghans

The gap between the American values that are being pushed and the values of the majority of Afghans is enormous. For all America's attempts to promote its cultural values, the emphasis on individualism does not sit well with Afghan society. This is not just an issue of old versus new, rural versus urban, educated versus illiterate; even many well-educated, urban Afghans holding down well-paid jobs, those who are doing well out of the current dispensation and who could be called 'modern', do not subscribe to the US dream. They may not as yet have worked out a coherent alternative, but this does not mean they do not know that there is something wrong with what has been offered. Although for the moment America may still be more welcomed as liberator than hated as occupier, the line is a fine one. Already there are clear signs of unhappiness with what is happening. As one friend observed: 'The new generation of Afghans will not be really educated, but trained not to stand in the way of US interests.'

Meanwhile, for the majority of the country's citizens, the ordinary people who do not have access to well-paid jobs, there is simply a deep yearning for life to be better, to live in safety, to have healthcare and education, and the means of making a reasonable living. As yet, little has been offered in the way of meeting these aspirations. For all the fine words about economic growth relieving poverty, there is little indication that this might happen; nor are the models of services being put forward likely to produce much for the poor. The danger for America, with its all too visible presence in the country, is that it will be held responsible for these failures.

There is not only an immediate frustration but also a long-term problem of a lack of political leadership and of any vision as to how these aspirations could be met. This is more than just an Afghan problem; the absence of any models to challenge liberal capitalism is a global issue. At least until the 1970s alternative state-based models of modernity and of economic development existed, socialist and nationalist. Alongside them were models of political action by means of which people might hope to achieve change. Now all these have gone. In the 1980s economic liberalism increasingly became the dominant economic paradigm among southern elites as well as in the West, and coherent political action splintered into single-issue protest movements. While part of the reason for the decline of alternative modes of statehood was their own corruption and their failure to understand the systems they were trying to reform, their decline nevertheless leaves an enormous gap. To acknowledge that they had faults does not mean that their critique of the status quo was not valid. But, as Mark Duffield notes: 'From its position of dominance, liberal discourse has suppressed those aspects ... that argued the existence of inequalities within the global system, and most importantly, that the way in which wealth is created has a direct bearing on the extent and nature of poverty' (Duffield 2001b: 28). In its dominance, the West and the system it embodies has allowed itself to think it has the answers, even as it is failing so many people. Rather than ask how the system must be changed, the question has now become how to make southern societies fit the system. The notion that underdevelopment may be a function of the relationship between rich and poor countries has been more or less erased from the development discourse. The notion that any form of governance other than the market state might be valid has been excised from the global discourse (Gray 2003).

The danger of such a lacuna was ably illustrated by the outburst of a young Afghan friend. Karim is in his early twenties, a graduate of law from Balkh University and currently in a good job, giving him both a reasonable salary and interesting work. We were travelling together in the north of the country along the, admittedly dreadful, road between Pul i Khumri and Qunduz when he burst out: 'This country is completely corrupt, look at this road! What can we do – there is nothing for it but terrorism.' While it is unlikely that he would ever join up with al-Qa'eda, his burst of anger came from a deep well of despair at ever seeing any real improvement in his country. It was a powerful wake-up call to the price that will have to be paid if things do not get better. In the conversation about political change that followed, it became very clear that the models of political struggle and change that were part of the fabric of life for those of us who grew up in the West in the1960s and '70s, whether or not we were activists, no longer exist for today's young people. There is no longer a Mozambique with its brave vision of the future as it struggled to free itself from Portuguese colonialism, no longer a South Africa with its Nelson Mandela. The alternative visions of societies in which resources would be used to allow the poor to attain the basic requirements of a decent life, to be free of fear, to have enough to eat and safe water to drink, to have basic healthcare and education for their children, are no longer put forward. Yet the market state will never be able to meet the aspirations of most Afghans. Little wonder terrorism has a recruiting ground.

Notes

1 Voice of America, 27 September 1996.

2 Statement by Robin Raphel, head of US delegation, United Nations meeting on Afghanistan, 18 November 1996.

3 In 2002 BP Amoco finally took the decision to go ahead with this route. Construction will take about three years and is estimated to cost $3.2 billion.

4 The story is well documented in Rashid (2000).

5 Reuters, 18 November 1997.

6 In those days conversion into heroin was done in Pakistan rather than Afghanistan; the CIA's allies the ISI were heavily involved in the trade.

7 Notably, ICRC and MSF formally stayed outside, believing it compromised their neutrality.

8 Personal communication.

9 Personal communication with PHR senior staff member, 2001.

10 Ashraf Ghani was then head of the AACA, which produced the NDF. He became Minister of Finance after the ELJ issued in the ATA.

11 Speech to the Federal Reserve Bank, New York, 16 November 2001.

12 'Towards full market access', *Financial Times*, 10 July 1997.

13 'Fear of trade war after US steel tariffs ruled illegal', *Guardian*, 1 November 2003.

5 | The makings of a narco state?

Seeding recovery

Drive though Hazarajat in early summer and everywhere you look you can see people squatting in the fields, weeding. Two years ago there was no poppy in this area, now almost everyone grows it. Hazarajat has long been one of the poorest parts of Afghanistan, with its high mountains and patchworks of tiny fields. Traditionally its people dealt with poverty by migrating to the cities of Afghanistan and to Iran. The economic blockade imposed by the Taliban when they were trying to subjugate the area, followed by three years of drought, only intensified these trends. Now, however, people are returning.

The district of Dai Kundi, in the north of Uruzgan province, is probably the poorest district in the whole of Hazarajat. It lies two days' driving from Kabul over beautiful country and terrible roads; the steep hillsides are badly eroded and landholdings are tiny. Because of its remoteness it was almost completely ignored by international assistance agencies. In 1998, when Oxfam first opened its programme in the north of the district, the only other agency in Dai Kundi was Action Contre le Faim, which ran a health clinic in the south of the district. The UN never even visited. Most villages had never seen a foreigner. Three years ago whole villages were surviving only on remittances; now people are returning even to this most marginal of places because they have heard of the money to be made in poppy.

Afghanistan is the largest producer of opium in the world. Afghan opiates represent almost 100 per cent of those consumed in neighbouring countries and 80–90 per cent of the heroin found in European markets. The country's rise to this position is inextricably bound up with the course of the war. In 1979 it produced only a few hundred tons, by 2002 this had risen more than fifteen-fold to 3,400 tons, by 2003 it was 3,600 tons (UNODC 2003b). There are huge profits to be made but, large though they are, they represent only 7 per cent of the estimated final street value of US$35 billion (ATA 2004).

Although the country has long grown opium poppies, prior to the Soviet invasion and the uprising it provoked, the amounts cultivated were small and production confined to just a few areas of the country. During the years of the Soviet occupation, however, opium became an

7 *Lancing poppies outside a school in Darayem district, Badakhshan, 2003.*
(Chris Johnson)

important source of revenue for the opposition and cultivation expanded. Once the Soviets had withdrawn, production increased still further, in part because foreign sources of money for arms were less easy to come by and drugs profits were the obvious substitute. Commanders pushed farmers to cultivate poppy, while damage from the years of fighting reduced other income-generating opportunities. At the same time, Iran's ban of opium poppy cultivation in 1979 left a market gap just waiting to be filled. By 1989, the end of the Soviet occupation, production had increased to 800 tons, more than twice the combined annual production of Pakistan and Iran (Cooley 2000).

In the 1930s only three provinces grew poppy (even in 1994 it was grown in only eight), but by 2003 it had become an integral part of the rural economy, with twenty-eight of the county's thirty-two provinces growing it. All ethnic groups were by now involved, and the exponential rate of expansion was reflected in the fact that thirty-one districts cultivated it for the first time in that year. New areas accounted for about 10 per cent of total cultivation, while the percentage of cultivation concentrated in the top five provinces fell from 95 per cent in 2002 to 72 per cent in 2003 (UNODC 2003a). This broadening base and spread of networks and knowledge will make the job of eradication immeasurably harder, as it allows production simply to shift from one part of the country to another.

For many poor people, poppy growing is not only the most profitable activity available, but also the only way of meeting their needs. In many ways it is a miracle crop. It matures quickly, allowing double cropping in many areas, it is more weather-resistant than wheat, is easy to store, transport and sell. It is not only the profits that are important. Because opium can easily be stored it acts as a form of savings in a country that until recently was wracked by inflation; and because it is highly valuable, it can be used as collateral to gain access to credit in the absence of any formal banking system in rural areas. The rates are usurious, however, and can be repaid only in opium, leaving farmers trapped into growing more and more. Work done by UNODC showed that in 1998 over 60 per cent of the opium traders in the provinces of Qandahar, Helmand and Nangarhar provided credit to farmers against future opium production. Although the amounts loaned were limited, the repayment terms were harsh. Payments received in advance averaged just 42 per cent of the value of the opium at harvest time. This is the equivalent of an interest rate of 138 per cent for a loan obtained for just a few months. If the loan was not repaid at harvest time then rates doubled or tripled (UNODC 2003b).

The early years of Taliban control saw the production of opium rise again, with a crop of 4,600 tons, some 79 per cent of global production (ibid.). Then, in July 2000, the Taliban issued a decree banning the cultivation of opium poppy – though not, as was to be often pointed out later, its trade. The ban was too late to affect the 2000 harvest, but the following year cultivation fell to almost zero in the areas under Taliban control and total production for the country was only 185 tons, almost all of it in areas controlled by the Northern Alliance. Prices rose tenfold. However, while the Taliban had benefited from the opium trade, its structures remained essentially independent and they survived the ban without a problem; indeed, there are those who have argued that they actually benefited from it as the resultant rise in prices allowed even greater profits to be made from trafficking.

Once the Taliban had been removed from power, cultivation started afresh, and at unprecedented levels. While in some areas this was due to a spontaneous decision by farmers to resume growing, in the absence of any authority to stop them, the spread of poppy growing into the central highland areas of Ghor and Hazarajat was the result of a highly organized campaign to target new and remote areas. Traders came up from Herat and Helmand with seeds, credit and stories of the profits to be made. They promised to provide technical know-how and sent agents at harvest time to show local farmers when and how to score the poppy head to drain the resin. This is critical. Cut before full maturation of the head and the yield is much reduced; score too deeply and you cut the skin of the capsule, allowing the latex to oxidize in the capsule; score not deeply enough and flow of the latex is constrained.

This organized campaign was different to the way poppy growing had spread in earlier years. Then it was the itinerant labourers, who had worked on the crop and returned home with the knowledge to start cultivation in their native villages, who opened up new areas. In Hazarajat it was never going to happen like that. For the last two decades the area had been socially cut off from the rest of the country. The Soviets largely left it alone, finding it too marginal to be worth the effort to control. Then in the 1980s there was major internal bloodletting as rival groups struggled to gain ascendancy. The Hazaras who left the area largely ended up either in the urban centres or as refugees and had little contact with the poppy trade.

The first traders came in 2002, targeting the province of Ghor and the northern parts of Uruzgan. Take-up of the new crop was tentative. Most people tried it, but in a limited way. Farmers tried the poppy out on a small part of their land and planted only what the family itself could tend. The crop is labour intensive, but in an area of few employment opportunities family labour is in effect free, and the experiment cost little. The harvest was good and prices remained high, with farm gate prices across the country at the same level as in the years of the Taliban ban, some ten times pre-ban prices. News spread quickly to other districts, especially in neighbouring Bamiyan province. By 2003 all districts were growing poppy. In a district such as Lal, where farmers were growing for the second season, the irrigated land put to poppy was estimated to be double that of the previous year. Emboldened by their earlier success, families were paying labourers to help them with the crop, thus spreading the benefits even to those who did not have land. Wage rates in June were US$3/day, a previously unheard-of figure in this part of Afghanistan, where in the past people had laboured for as little as 25 cents; and that was only the beginning of the growing season – by harvest time they had risen to between US$5 and US$6. Many of those who did not have their own land but who had other assets, such as traders, were renting land in order to grow poppy. UNODC (2003a) estimated that over 2,000 hectares were put to poppy in Ghor in 2002, though this is almost certainly an underestimate as figures for the district of Lal, where many of the farmers grew poppy, were not included in the records.

Different districts managed production in different ways. In Lal, a district with strong elders who regularly intervened to solve disputes and stop open conflict breaking out, an agreement was made that none of the commanders would tax the crop. As a result the district saw more peace and prosperity than it had done for many years. 'They are too busy making money to fight,' said a friend. 'Even the Aimaq, they are our friends,' farmers said of the neighbours with whom they had always previously been in conflict.

Many people used the cash for very basic things: to pay off debts; to buy wheat, enabling them to become self-sufficient for the first time; to replace the animals they had lost in the drought; to improve their houses; and to marry. The wealthier bought minibuses, opened shops and even acquired TVs and satellite dishes. For the first time someone set up a large electricity generator in the bazaar and power lines could be seen stretching out to distant houses. The short-term effect was to jump-start economic recovery and render the employment creation programmes of the aid agencies largely redundant. Indeed, agencies reported difficulties in finding anyone to labour on them. Whereas in the past people had clamoured for such labouring opportunities, now the rewards were no longer attractive compared to what else was available.

Not everywhere was as peaceful and egalitarian as Lal. In the neighbouring Dai Kundi, district commanders fought for control of villages so they could take the 10 per cent *usher* on the harvest; in next door Sharistan, the two brothers who had controlled the district for the past two decades were reported to have collected 500 kg in tax alone in 2002, netting them something in the region of a quarter of a million dollars, in addition to substantial profits from their own fields.

The economic rewards of growing poppy are indisputable, at least if all goes well. Hazarajat produces the best-quality opium and, in 2002, a kilogram fetched US$400 at harvest time, $500 by the end of the season. A small farm of one *jerib* in size could produce 5–6 kg. Even if the farmer paid for labour, this made a profit thirty times that which he could hope to gain by planting wheat. By 2003, however, some of the downside was already becoming apparent. An insect-borne disease struck the poppy and proved resilient to the truckloads of chemicals brought in from Pakistan. Many Afghans believe that the disease was no accident, but a deliberate attempt to destroy their crops by outside powers opposed to poppy cultivation. Emboldened by the success of the previous year's harvest, a number of farmers had taken large amounts of credit on the basis the next year's harvest. Such loans are repayable only in opium and carry a high rate of interest. In addition land that would have normally grown wheat had been put to poppy, so people had to buy wheat – and at rising prices. There was also worry about what the government might do, as people had heard about poppy farms being destroyed.

Yet for all the worries, poppy still paid. As one NGO worker noted: 'They worry about addiction, but they like the money.' And even though farmers in Hazarajat harvested only an estimated 20 per cent of the predicted crop in 2003, they still made more money than they would have done by growing wheat, the regular staple. Meanwhile, the small town of Nili in the northern part of Uruzgan has become a centre for the opium trade, attracting traders from many parts of the country. 'It looked', said an Afghan friend who worked in the area and was a regular visitor to the town, 'just like the Taliban times, full of pick-ups and guns, and bearded men with black turbans.'

Or corrupting the state?

The scale of poppy growing in Hazarajat is, however, dwarfed by that of Badakhshan, and an analysis of the trade is particularly interesting because of its links to the heart of the current administration. Opium is believed to have been introduced into the province centuries ago by

Chinese traders, who used it for medicinal purposes. It is the one part of the country where opium addiction has a history, although this is almost entirely confined to Ismaili communities, mainly in Wakhan and Shegnan which, ironically, are not big growing areas. Cultivation has, however, never been at anything like its current level. In 2000 the total acreage under poppy was estimated to be only 2,358 hectares (UNDCP 2000), now this level is exceeded in single districts. In 2001, with the Taliban ban operative in the rest of the country, poppy growing increased by 152 per cent. It rose by a further third in 2002, and by 55 per cent in 2003 (UNODC 2003a). The profits involved are massive, especially as most of Badakhshan's opium is turned into heroin within the province, doubling its value.[1] Local farmers estimated that the district of Darayem would produce a staggering 210,000 kg in 2003, worth US$48 million as opium paste and around US$90 million by the time it has been turned into heroin. The district of Jurm, they calculated, would produce more than 140,000 kg, worth at least US$32 million, or US$60 million on conversion.[2]

Heroin manufacture in the province began to take place from the mid-1990s onwards. In 2003, eighteen factories were spread throughout the poppy growing districts. While the location of some of these factories is secret, others are astonishingly open. One commander built his right on the main road. The governor's response was that he knew he did not have the force to stop it, but please would the commander move it a little further away from the roadside. In another case, when Commander Donashee of Argu was security commander for the province, he destroyed all three heroin factories in Darayem and took the equipment down to Faizabad. The owners simply came to town and bought it back again. And, according to UNODC, the chief of police of Badakhshan had the largest heroin factory in the country in his garden.

UNODC analysis suggests that at least some of these laboratories have direct access to foreign heroin markets, rather than having to go through traders, thus greatly increasing potential profits. The persons operating such laboratories, frequently warlords and local commanders although there are also rumours of Russian mafia connections, have huge economic incentives for these activities to continue. They will do whatever they deem necessary to stop the authorities from destroying the laboratories. Such laboratories thus contain not only heroin-processing materials, but also sophisticated communications equipment and weapons of all kinds (UNODC 2003b).

Karzai's edicts against opium growing have made no difference here. 'Last year', said a local NGO worker, 'the governor of Badakhshan read out the official letter banning poppy, then told everyone they could carry on as normal.' He has reason to. In 2003 the chief of the traders was reported to be paying $10,000 a month each to the governor of Badakhshan and other important commanders in order to be able to run his business as he wanted. All the big commanders in this province are involved in the trade, via protection rackets if not in direct dealing.

That such high stakes in an illegal economy encourages a culture of violence perhaps goes without saying, yet the particular forms of such violence can be horrific. In a recent case in Khanaka village, not far from Faizabad city, a teacher from the district of Shegnan (a district with exceptionally high levels of education and one which has traditionally supplied teachers to much of Badakhshan) was asked by a local subcommander – now working for the Security Department – to take heroin down to Eshkeshem, the town near the border with Tajikistan. The teacher pleaded that he could not, having no experience of such work and being a poor man who could not afford to replace the goods if they were taken from him. The subcommander decided to kill him. He tied one end of a rope round his neck and the other to his vehicle and dragged him 10 km. At the end there was only his torso left. The subcommander then put about the story that he had done this because the teacher had tried to have sex with his nine-year-old son, at the school. The son, with amazing bravery, denied that this was so. The local mullah also testified that the teacher was a good man. The subcommander was put in gaol and President Karzai was believed to be intending to sign an instruction that he be handed over to the teacher's family for punishment, in accordance with shari'a law. On returning to Kabul some months later we inquired what had happened to him: he had been released.

The impunity that prevails in Badakhshan is indicative of how violence is embedded at all levels of government. Many of the former commanders are still in control, only their titles are different. Few people see any chance of this changing. Government appointments are made by a small group of people whose patterns of power and influence extend right into the upper echelons of central government. Although the Minister of Interior has tried to make some changes, he has little real power in Badakhshan, and people say of his appointees that they will be able to do little. Officials whom he has tried to move to positions out of the area because of the damaging consequences of their extra-state activities, have simply refused the posts they do not want. The ex-governor, a Rabbani man, was appointed special adviser to President Karzai; he refused to go to Kabul as he saw no advantage to himself. Those from within Badakhshan who have tried to speak out about what is happening say they have tried on many occasions to speak with President Karzai about the problems but have repeatedly been refused access.

Yet the money involved in the poppy industry has transformed the local economy. In the major poppy growing districts there are simply no longer any poor people. In Darayem, once one of the poorest districts in the province, a huge new bazaar has opened up. On a visit in 2003, one shop alone had twenty new motorcycles, still in wooden crates. In most other countries this would mean little; in Afghanistan, where such items are a luxury and most people in rural areas are lucky if they can afford a bicycle, it is an extraordinary sign of change. Two years ago this bazaar did not exist, and in the old one there was almost nothing. An Afghan friend who is a doctor and was restarting her clinic there after a number of years, had taken clothes with her to give to poor people; she could find no one to give them to. 'Three years ago,' she said, 'when I first came here, people did not even have bread to eat. There was no money for medicines, no money for a clinic fee. Now everyone has enough.' It certainly seemed to be true. In one small village, twenty-five families were planning on buying cars that year; previously nobody had owned one. In Jurm, daily wage rates at the beginning of July 2003, the height of the opium collecting season, had risen to US$12 a day plus three meals; this in an area where the daily wage in 2000 averaged less than a dollar, and even at that low rate there wasn't always work to be found. Not all districts were as high, but it was never reported at less than $5 plus meals. Many areas could not get enough local labour and brought in people from neighbouring districts and provinces. In Rustaq, in neighbouring Takhar province, the labour drain was such that it had created a crisis for the wheat harvest and the commander, in an attempt to entice people back, announced that sharecroppers could take the entire crop they had planted, rather than the normal practice of having to give the greater part of it to the landowner.

In the poppy growing areas almost everyone is cultivating; many of the mullahs preach against it – only to go out and work the fields. On the way to the airport in Faizabad, signs proclaim that the cultivation and trafficking of narcotics are against Islam – the signs are surrounded by fields of poppies. Unlike in Hazarajat, where people are still nervous about their new trade and will not talk to foreigners about it, here farmers discuss it openly. You can pull up and talk to any farmer and he will happily tell you what he made last year and what he hopes to make this. A few people are deeply against it, but the majority feels little concern about its immorality. Ordinary people rationalize it by their poverty: 'Islam says that pork is forbidden,' said one, 'but if you are starving the Qur'an says you can go out and eat pig.' Besides, the West is seen as responsible for sending the weapons that have caused Afghanistan so much misery. 'This is our export to the West', was a common refrain. Nor is the abuse of opiates and the misery it causes of great concern, for many ordinary farmers know and understand little of the problem. Abuse of opiates in Afghanistan, outside of specific communities in Badakhshan, is a recent problem and it is largely confined to cities and areas of refugee return. For those who do know and understand, particularly those who have travelled or lived in Europe or America, it is felt that the problem cannot be blamed on the producer but lies with the lack of a moral core to western society, with individualism and the breakdown of families that leave young people with little or no support. This is more than mere justification by those involved in the industry, it comes strongly even from those who themselves refuse to have anything to do with the poppy business.

The growing of opium poppy is seen by many small farmers as legitimate, even though they know it is illegal, because it meets pressing needs. 'It is the only source of solution to our many problems,' they say. In addition, the opiates business was not perceived to be an illegal activity in Afghanistan in the past; and now after so many years without government the whole concept of legality means little. After all, the new government is in far-away Kabul and has as yet made little difference to their lives, so its decrees mean little to them. And while its spoils are hardly shared equitably, they do produce for ordinary people, many of whom were very poor and deeply in debt as a result of the drought, a way not only to meet those debts but also a standard of living far better than they have ever seen in the past, or probably even dreamt of aspiring to. That others get immeasurably much richer is not – at least at present – a source of great concern, as long they themselves are benefiting also. The unwritten contract is that ordinary people are left in peace to earn a living, and are paid a good return on their labour. The uncomfortable truth is that many people will tell you they prefer to depend on poppies than on aid.

What is noticeable in Badakhshan is that small growers feel protected, because almost everyone in power in the province is involved in poppy, and the networks run right to the centre of government. Few people here believe it is possible to stop the growing, or think that the new governor will even try. By early 2004, only token efforts had been made by the government at eradication in this area. In Hazarajat, on the other hand, the contract is much more tenuous. Poppy growing is a new activity brought in by outsiders and, though local commanders certainly benefit, the really big players are from elsewhere. The lines of profit and control do not run to the centre of government but rather out to traders (and warlords) in Herat and Qandahar; the connection is to the periphery not the centre. People are therefore much less sure how much protection they have in their illegal activity, and are much more afraid of possible government action against them. Farmers in poppy growing areas of Hazarajat are wary of the interest that outsiders might show in their crops. They will insist they were growing wheat when their poppy fields can clearly be seen, and they will give information only to Afghans whose connections to the area they know well and in whom they have some trust. They were clearly worried about eradication campaigns: a common question was, 'We've heard on the radio that the government might come and pull up the poppy fields, do you know anything about this?' Workers in the north-west of the country, another area where poppy growing has extended into new districts, report the same wariness.

The poppy-pushing mafia have not had their way everywhere. They crossed from Wardak into Logar but the people would not grow it. 'It is *haram* [forbidden],' they said. 'Why should we grow it?' The same is true of the Shamali plain, where farmers see no sense in pulling up their prized vines for a crop that might be the focus of an eradication campaign at some time in the near future. Even in Badakhshan, in the heart of poppy growing, one commander from Upper Keshem resolutely refused to have it on his land, while in the Wakhan corridor, the efforts of the local leader to lessen the amount of addiction were reported to be bearing fruit. Similarly, in Nangarhar, one of the large landowners refused to see it grown in the area he controlled.

Understanding the opium market is far from easy, and estimates for the value of the opium economy as a whole vary widely. It is impossible to know how much opium was sold at harvest time, when the prices are lowest, and how much was held to be sold later at a higher price, or even kept as a form of savings. It is equally difficult to know how much potential income a farmer may have lost through taking credit on the basis of future sales. Not only can opium be 'dry' or 'wet', but the meaning of these terms can differ in different places. Different qualities of opium exist within and between areas and are traded at different prices, and, as with all agricultural production in Afghanistan, there are regional variations in the way things are categorized and measured.[3] Needless to say, few people are interested in telling the truth to nosy officials asking questions.

Nevertheless, some sense of the scale of the problem can be seen from the fact that UNODC estimated that for 2002 the gross income of Afghan farmers could have been in the region of US$1.2 billion, or an average $6,000 per farmer. While it declined somewhat in 2003, largely due to a decline in opium prices, it was still estimated to be in the region of $1.02 billion, or $3,900 per family (UNODC 2003a). This is in a country where per capita GDP is $170 (ATA 2004). Averages, of course, hide huge differences; nevertheless, even for small farmers the money to be made is well in excess of anything they could hope to get by a combination of cultivating other crops and taking casual labour as and when they can find it.

The really big money, however, is to be made in trafficking. Here, the trade seems to pass out of local hands, and there is little evidence of Afghan involvement beyond smuggling it out of the country. Ethnic links are crucial in setting up cross-border traffic, as is generally true of networks engaged in illegal trade (Duffield 2001b).

Badakshi heroin is believed to be trafficked along two main routes, one up into Tajikistan, the other down to Kabul. There are consistent reports, from numerous different sources, of military helicopters being used both to transport heroin to Kabul and, via Eshkeshem, into Tajikistan, from where the trade largely goes to Moscow. The Russians, who are still in charge of border security, change their border chief every month. Each outgoing chief allegedly briefs the incomer on his contacts. He then has one month in which he is paid very handsomely for keeping his eyes shut. It is said that a few honest policemen have tried to apprehend people; they have been shot. There are also consistent reports of government vehicles being used to transport the heroin by road. From Kabul the heroin is allegedly flown out of the country, some to Dubai and some directly into Europe. Many Afghans in Badakhshan believed that the coalition and ISAF were involved in this onward transport. Whether or not this is true, the very fact that it is so widely believed says something about the levels of international complicity that ordinary Afghans think exist. And not without reason; both history and current circumstances give cause for suspicion. The CIA was implicated in the drugs trade in the *mujahideen* days (Cooley 2000), while Kabul airport has since 2002 been under the control of ISAF.

Other regions in Afghanistan have links to their neighbours over the border. Abdul Rashid Dostum's involvement in drugs has been well documented, and there is little reason to believe it has changed for the better. As with the north-east, there are reports of it being flown across the border – and only influential commanders have planes. Regional warlords are known to be involved in the trade south to Quetta, while from the north-west there are links into Turkmenistan. A key group in the cross-border trade in the west and south is the Baluch tribes, who straddle Afghanistan, Pakistan and Iran, and to whom cross-border smuggling is entrusted. Working on flood relief in Zaranj during 1991, Jolyon was intrigued to see the number of stalls in the run-down bazaar stacked high with glass pickling jars. Asked what possible use the jars could have in this far-flung place, one of the local Red Crescent workers explained that they were filled with opium paste; and added a warning not to show – especially as the only foreigner in town – too direct an interest in either the merchandise in the bazaar or the long caravans of camels that crossed the desert. Many traders entrust the cross-border smuggling to the Baluch nomads, who are said to hand the goods over to Kurds, first in Iran and then through Turkey into Europe. Until recently, the effectively autonomous northern governorates of Iraq served as a useful corridor for transhipments.

While the big profits go to well-established networks, the poor also make a living from small-time smuggling. UN reports suggest that smuggling one kilogram of opium to Tehran in 2002 was the equivalent of two years of income, and smuggling one kilogram of heroin the equivalent of four years (UNODC 2003b). This, however, underestimates the real gain, for it assumes that the person could find labour every day, and this is highly unlikely. The benefits are clear. Many houses in the Gulran district in the north-west of Herat had satellite dishes on their roofs in 2002; all were bought with drug money. Yet with the death penalty for drug trafficking, smuggling to Iran is an extremely risky business. There are also costs to the family if a smuggler gets caught, for the traders will come and demand the price of the lost opium or heroin – a price that the family almost certainly cannot afford to pay. For many, the only way of redeeming this debt is for another family member to take up smuggling. Where there is no one to do this, families can lose everything they have, and sometimes even the young women of the family can be taken. Perhaps unsurprisingly, many prefer the lower but much less risky profits to be made smuggling to Central Asia.

In a major study of the narcotics trade published in early 2003, the UN estimated that the total narcotics revenue for 2003 could be as high as US$5 billion. The 2003 Opium Survey published later that year gives total farm gate income from opium as $1.02 billion and trafficking income as at least $1.3 billion. However, it says nothing about the profits being made from conversion to heroin, although it does note that most conversion is now done in country. Adding this in could easily take the sum to over $4 billion, compared to an official GDP of $4.4 billion.

While some of this money goes to support ordinary people, a very large amount ends up in the pockets of commanders, who benefit not only from their own production but also from a substantial tax rake-off and from the protection money paid to them. It is used for funding their militias and buying weapons; and the implications for Afghanistan's security are all too evident. It is also, if the anecdotal evidence is to be believed, funnelled into foreign bank accounts and investments, often in Dubai. In one transaction alone, a commander from Badakhshan was reported (by his ex-driver – and drivers usually know) to have taken US$64,000 to be deposited in his son's bank account in Dubai.

Few of the profits of the trade are invested in wider benefits to the community. In none of the poppy growing areas we have visited were there any signs of investment of even a small proportion of poppy income in things of public good, not even roads, which would benefit the traders themselves, let alone schools, clinics or drinking water.

Transitional attitudes

President (then Chairman) Karzai banned opium poppy cultivation and trade on 17 January 2002. By that time, however, most of the crops in the main growing areas had already been sown, and the high prices being offered by traders gave plenty of incentive to farmers to run the risk of continuing with the crop. Given how much was said about poppy cultivation at the time of the Taliban, it was politically important for the new administration to be seen to ban all aspects of the opium trade. However, it has as yet failed to get to grips with the impact that the problem has on every aspect of the country's development. A counter narcotics directorate has been set up as part of the National Security Council, but with a current staff of only fifty-two it is hard to see how it can make a real impact. Meanwhile, both donors and the government have failed to come up with an integrated strategy that would bring long-term jobs and development to rural areas. High poppy-related wages and profits undermine the government's attempts at short-term employment creation almost as much as they disable its efforts to bring security. Meanwhile, the free market economic policies being pursued are likely to bring little benefit to poor farmers in remote areas.

Writing in 1998, John Cooley noted how two conditions were necessary to suppress drugs. One was that there had to be internal and external peace and security. The second was that Afghanistan had to have one strong central power in control in Kabul with real authority everywhere. The second condition was to a large extent met by the Taliban; neither condition is met now. The current government's writ hardly extends beyond the environs of Kabul, and the drugs problem is inextricably bound up with the overall security problem.

Although the official line is that this government is against growing poppy, many of its members, from the Cabinet downwards, are involved in some way in the business. The *Washington Post* in 2003 interviewed a high-ranking narcotics official who had been asked by a US general for a list of Afghan officials who were involved in the drug trade: 'I told him it would be easier if I listed officials who weren't involved. That would be a shorter list,' the official was reported to have replied. It's the same at the local level. In one of the Hazarajat districts the head of the Department of Agriculture told visitors he did not grow poppy on his land, and even announced on the radio that it was against the shari'a, yet his sons were renting land elsewhere to grow the family crop. In Helmand, according to one well-placed informant, 'The governor cries, "Stop", and he says, "Grow".' Both the governor and the police commander grow on their own lands, so little concern do they have for the government ban.

For the government, the crucial issues are the impact of the narcotics business on security and its ability to corrupt politics at all levels. According to some sources, neighbouring Turkmenistan and Tajikistan already fit some definitions of narco-states, because both their governments sift profits directly from the drugs trade. 'Kirgyzstan also risks becoming a narco-state, as the low salaries paid to local government and security officials in the southern part of the country make them ripe for subornation' (Brill Olcott 2002). The same could well be said of Afghanistan, for while the formal government budget does not benefit from drugs income, government officials at all levels most certainly do. During the March 2004 meeting of the Afghan Development Forum in Kabul, Finance Minister Ashraf Ghani warned that if the Bonn agreement collapsed, Afghanistan would become a narco-mafia state. Yet in many ways it already is – the question is whether the mafia are inside the government or out.

People are also beginning to wake up to the looming public health crisis. So far, Afghanistan has been spared the major problems of drug addiction within its own borders but there are signs that this is changing. The relationship between growing and consuming is by no means straightforward; Sunni communities in Badakhshan have been growing opium poppy for years without using it. But these are socially cohesive rural communities; for urban youth, caught between cultures and with no prospect of a decent job, the risks are obvious. Already, increasing rates of addiction are being reported in urban areas, mainly linked to the return of refugees who developed the habit in Pakistan and Iran. It is difficult to get accurate figures, but one estimate is that Kabul alone has at least 20,000 heroin addicts. Smoking is still the most common method of consumption but, according to drugs experts, injecting is catching up fast, with all the attendant health fears. Already there are reports of increasing cases of Hepatitis A and B, and unless action is taken it can only be a matter of time before HIV rates start to rise and Afghanistan faces an AIDS-related public health crisis. Resources for dealing with the problem are totally inadequate, with Kabul's only facility for treating drug users in Kabul having just ten beds for its six-week in-patient programme. Staff also run education and advice programmes around the city, but they admit they are overwhelmed. 'It's nearly impossible to cope with the facilities we have now,' says Mohammed Raufi, one of the managers.[4]

Agency responses

Attempts in 2003 by some donors to tackle the problem by funding programmes that paid people to destroy their crops were an abject failure. People just took the money and carried on growing; sometimes they even grew more. Asked why there was so much poppy this year, people in Badakhshan would grin and say, 'Last year we were given 300 dollars a jerib to pull it up, maybe they will pay us again this year!' There were many ruses to win both ways. One was to cut the crop at the stem rather than pull it out by its roots. 'The UN showed us how,' farmers explained. 'Afterwards it grows even better than before, with bigger heads.' Enforcement officials would then declare the crop destroyed and, it was said, spilt the compensation with the farmer. Drugs officials were also reported to have cut deals with farmers, saying there had been 100 per cent eradication when in fact there had been only partial destruction of fields.

Assistance agencies meanwhile seem extraordinarily unconcerned about what is going on. Despite the fact that Jurm has a net income from opium alone (that is, before it is converted into heroin) of US$16 million, an NGO has signed with the Ministry of Rural Development to implement the National Solidarity Programme there, giving communities grants of up to $60,000. In another district an NGO asked the Ministry what they should do about poppy and were told: 'Just don't do irrigation works in those areas.'

Meanwhile, in 2003 the WFP was giving out wheat in a number of parts of the country, despite the fact that the UN had clearly stated in its reports that such programmes needed to be reduced in order to increase incentives for farmers to grow legal crops. A number of reputable NGOs in Badakhshan said they were put under pressure to sign contracts for programmes they believed were not only not necessary but also damaging. Oxfam staff, for example, claimed they were pushed to distribute wheat in Shar i Buzurg district at harvest time, regardless of the impact on local wheat prices. The WFP, it would appear, had too much wheat in Faizabad and needed to get it out. (Nor was it the only agency distributing wheat in the province.) The rationale was supposed to be that these projects would wean people away from poppy cultivation; in fact, they achieved the exact opposite – in Keshem people started growing poppy so they could get more projects. Afghan NGO workers in other parts of the country raised the same question: 'Why', they would say, especially after Afghanistan's bumper wheat harvest in 2003, 'if they want to distribute wheat do they not buy it from the local market? If farmers cannot get a good price for their wheat they will just turn to growing poppy.'

All this is in marked contrast to the Taliban years when much was made of establishing 'principled' positions and agreeing 'bottom lines'. Then, eradication of poppies was one of the key conditions laid down to the authorities.

A history of agency handouts has also created a culture where in some areas people feel no need to take responsibility for their community – everything, it seems, should be done for them. On the way up the Darayem valley lies a school. It is in a sorry state. Windows that have long since lost their glass swing on their hinges, battered benches are scattered in the dust. Few of the kids have books and in the classes visited no one could do even basic addition. Some classes appeared to have no teacher at all – they were out working on the poppy – though the kids, ever hopeful, sat there in anticipation. Inside the school compound, between the school building and the UNICEF tent and UNHCR plastic that were providing extra classrooms, grew poppies. If you looked out of the school windows, there was a sea of white and purple flowers as far as the eye could see. Yet the teachers asked the NGO that was working locally if it could provide them with a latrine for the school. The engineer suggested that maybe they could build a block of latrines with the profit from the poppy in their yard.

It is not like this everywhere. There are many communities where people, poor themselves, make huge sacrifices to support village schools or health workers. But neither the agencies nor the government appear to discriminate. The leaders of those communities that refuse to grow poppy are both irritated and puzzled as to why their attempts to support farmers growing legitimate crops have met with no support from the international community. In one area, for example, the WFP was asked to buy wheat for its programmes from the local market in order to help maintain good wheat prices and support keeping people away from poppy. They refused. While this may have been because the WFP had no money to buy food and only had donated (surplus) wheat from the rich world, such policies make little sense to Afghans. 'Why', asked a local landowner, an educated man who had spent many years studying in the West, 'does the international community not have proper coherent programmes; not just emergency measures, but support for mechanization and marketing that could make licit agriculture once again profitable?' His thoughts were echoed by others: 'I am afraid', said the head of one well-respected Afghan NGO, 'that if we ignore agriculture it will be a disaster. If agriculture is not made profitable, they will just grow poppy.'

Double standards – or caught in a bind?

Ninety-five per cent of the heroin sold on Britain's streets, and 70 per cent of that sold in Europe, is of Afghan origin. The end to growing poppy was one of the three key demands the international community, and in particular the USA, made upon the Taliban. Yet now, when it is being cultivated across more of the country than ever before, there is a new-found leniency.

In July 2002 the Taliban, as requested by the international community, banned the cultivation of opium poppy. It was verified by both UN and US officials that the poppy had indeed been eradicated from the territory they controlled. Yet far from getting any acknowledgement, let alone support for crop substitution schemes or other measures to alleviate the hardship for the poor who laboured on the crop, attention simply shifted away from the cultivation of poppy to the stockpiles of opium that allegedly enabled the Taliban to profit handsomely from the rise in market prices. The Taliban probably did benefit, but why did the USA and its allies not realize before they asked for the ban that this would be the likely consequence? Was it, perhaps, that they never expected it to be complied with? It may well be, as suggested by sceptical donors, that the Taliban never intended to maintain the ban, that it was just there for a year to get rid of stocks and raise prices. We will never know. What we do know is that a condition was laid down, that the Taliban met the condition, and that the rules were then changed. The country's leaders may well have been playing games, but the behaviour of the western powers gave them every reason to denounce them as having double standards. In a wonderful example of 'damned if you do and damned if you don't', the Taliban, having been blamed for the increase in poppy, were then blamed for the increase in prices when they banned it. They were also blamed for offering no alternatives. The total failure of the international community, who had pushed hard for exactly this ban, to provide any support for these alternatives, went unremarked.

In October 2001, just a few days before the start of the war against the Taliban, Tony Blair told the Labour Party Conference that 'the biggest drugs hoard in the world is in Afghanistan, controlled by the Taliban … The arms the Taliban are buying today are paid for with the lives of young British people, buying their drugs on British streets.' He repeated this claim a week later in the House of Commons, telling MPs that the Taliban 'is largely funded by the drugs trade' (McSmith and Reeves 2003). Then, even though production had been banned, it was a reason to go to war. Now all the excuses come out as to why Karzai's government is unable to make progress. Stated intent is now enough, at least that seemed to be the message of a Foreign Office spokeswoman who told the *Independent* that Britain was involved in a very ambitious anti-narcotics programme in Afghanistan, 'especially when you think of the lack of government infrastructure in large parts of the country outside Kabul' (ibid.). Never mind that the programme is a failure, it is ambitious, and the lack of infrastructure becomes somehow an excuse for the lack of success.

In line with its concerns, the British government assumed responsibility for coordinating the international effort to stop the drugs trade. As part of this it is spending US$70 million over three years on projects to eradicate poppy by providing Afghan farmers with another livelihood, and by training the police force. Yet when representatives from its Department for International Development visited Darayem, where it supports an NGO agricultural programme distributing wheat seed and fetilizer, the poppies were staring them in the face. It needed only a few questions to establish that the farmers kept the fertilizer, used it on the poppies and sold the wheat seed. Earlier in the growing season the British Ambassador had also visited the district and, while the poppies were not then in flower, it would have hardly been difficult to work out how much was growing. Privately, officials tell you they simply don't know what to do. Meanwhile their contribution to the Counter Narcotics Directorate for 2002–03 was just £97,000. The USA is no better than the UK. In 2003 its officials, including the US Ambassador, travelled through Jurm at harvest time; they could not have failed to see the poppy. Nor, if they had passed through the bazaar in neighbouring Argu, as they surely must have done, could they have missed the fact that it was full of clearly marked sacks of donated US and European wheat.

As one analyst notes, the USA has the intelligence and military capacity to destroy Afghanistan's drug stores and processing facilities if it wished to do so. Yet, it has specifically ruled out the Provincial Reconstruction Teams taking action on the drugs issue. The logic of this is somewhat puzzling, given that there is plenty of evidence to show that drugs money directly pays for terrorist activities and has enabled radical Islamist groups to become self-financing, not only in Afghanistan but throughout the central Asian region. Criminal groups in Pakistan also benefit, making between US$400 million and US$800 million year from trafficking.

To what extent the USA's ambivalence towards drug control is due to the powerful financial interests behind the drug trade and their influence on US foreign policy is unclear. Most of the large international banks and their offshore affiliates, it seems, have laundered narco-dollars (Chossudovsky 2002), and the CIA's complicity with the drug trade in the *mujahideen* years has been well documented (Rashid 2000). It does, however, leave US foreign policy faced with contradictory priorities: the need to keep America safe, and the need for the American institutions that keep the politicians in power to make maximum profits.

Of all the countries in the region, Iran is the one that has made the greatest efforts to eradicate the opiates trade. There has been a complete ban on growing in the country since 1979, drug dealers caught by the authorities face the death penalty, and the overall cost to the country of fighting the drug problem is estimated to be in the region of US$1 billion (UNODC 2003a). More than 3,000 Iranian law enforcement personnel have been killed in the last two decades while trying to stop the drug traffickers. Yet even this has not stopped the trafficking. Convoys of heavily armed trucks frequently leave south-east Iran bound for Turkey. They pass through every checkpoint without hindrance, their way reportedly cleared by people operating at the highest levels.

For the first two years of the transition, both donor governments and the media seemed to engage in a willing suspension of disbelief as to the levels of involvement not only of regional warlords but also key figures from the new administration. By the time they woke up to the problem it had grown massively. UNODC itself fell into the trap. Having accurately analysed the conditions that rendered the state and government ineffective in Afghanistan, noting the geo-strategic importance of its territory, the way neighbouring countries had vied for influence, and how the relationship between that and the fractures within the country had made the consolidation of the state impossible, their major report in 2003 on the opium industry goes on to say that these conditions 'do not prevail any longer' (UNODC 2003b). In a situation where there is ample evidence of all of Afghanistan's neighbours continuing to interfere, this is an extraordinary statement. The report's optimism about the possibility of Afghanistan controlling the drug trade sits oddly with its realism about the problem in central Asia and seems to be a case of politically correct thinking taking over from independent analysis. Similarly, a statement that '93 per cent of the area under poppy cultivation is restricted to six provinces that have not yet complied with the ban issued by the government in January 2002' (underlining in original), would seem to imply that the other provinces had complied. Yet until 2003 more than 90 per cent of Afghanistan's poppy cultivation had always taken place in just five or six provinces. Nor had any of the other provinces growing poppy complied with the ban. This massaging of facts in what is otherwise a detailed and thorough technical report, allied to a failure to analyse the political system and the links to government, leaves one wondering: were people just taken in by the 'spin' that Afghanistan was a success story, or was political censorship behind its production?

While it is easy to be cynical about the double standards that are being applied by western powers, there are no easy answers to the problem. There is much talk of eradication, but no one really knows how to go about it. Some half a million people are estimated to be involved one way or another in the opium business, many of them poor farmers. Removing their livelihoods would be catastrophic unless there was something to replace them, and the resentments engendered could easily inflame the security problem. Meanwhile, those making big money out of opium penetrate the political system in all parts of the country. The push in recent years to bring new areas into cultivation, along with the simplicity of conversion to heroin, means that the narcotics industry is now extremely footloose; both production of opium and its conversion can shift easily from one part of the country to another. Any attempts at eradication are likely to be met by increases in production elsewhere. In the areas of the south where there was some attempt at control in 2003, that is precisely what has happened. The reduction in Helmand was offset by an organized campaign to get farmers in the Khash Rud district of Nimroz to grow poppy. The district had never grown poppy before and is now full of it. Similarly, less poppy was seen along the main roads of Nangarhar and Laghman, but it had just moved up the side valleys instead.

Badakhshan, perhaps more than any other province, illustrates the difficulties of trying to control the narcotics business. The massive increases in growth, now sustained over the last three years, in themselves are some indication of the impunity people feel. In large measure this is due to the fact that the trade runs right to the centre of government. One of the Badakhshan commanders has 500 *jeribs* of land in Jurm and another 400 in the neighbouring district of Baharak, most of which has been put to poppy. His brother has a very high position in the security services in Kabul. Both heroin and opium are believed to be transported across the border to Tajikistan in military helicopters – something that can hardly happen without someone very high up in the Ministry of Defence being involved. Other supplies come down to Kabul in government vehicles. Even in the much smaller (legal) lapis industry, the local commanders always used to have to pay a third of the profits to Ahmad Shah Massoud; and the arrangement was passed on to his successor, Mohammad Fahim. How is it possible to imagine that in the narcotics business protection money would not have to be paid to those in power?

But it is not only Badakhshan – all of the regional leaders are involved. As one informant in Hazarajat said: 'If the government and big commanders were not involved no one could grow poppy. All of the commanders are linked in, you cannot operate in this country without their ensuring your safety.'

Indeed, it seems that there is a greater possibility of increase than of reduction. Neither the drop in opium prices in 2003 nor the high labour costs seem to have reduced incentives to plant. Indications are that an even larger area is being planted for 2004, despite attempts at eradication in 2003. Already new districts can be seen growing poppy for the first time, some in areas very close to urban centres – an indication of how confident people feel. Given that only 1 per cent of total arable land and slightly under 3 per cent of irrigated land is currently used for poppy growing, there is clearly plenty of scope for increase (UNODC 2003a). There is also a growing regional market, particularly in central Asia where the costs to the consumer are cheap – a shot of heroin in Tajikistan costs about the same as a bottle of beer.

On their own, none of the 'carrots' seems to offer much hope of weaning people away from the crop. Crop substitution schemes were potentially viable until 2000, but the massive hike in opium prices means there is now nothing else that can touch poppy for profitability. UNODC (2003b) suggest that as availability of labour is critical to the growing of poppy, one major aim of policy intervention could be to reduce the available level of labour at harvest time by timing labour-intensive works schemes to coincide with the harvest. Yet, with current wage levels in the poppy fields it is hard to see how this is any more viable than crop substitution. Rather, the reverse has happened; it is the government and the assistance agencies that have been unable to get people to labour on their schemes. When an NGO working on an employment creation programme in the district of Sharistan could not recruit enough workers because of the high wages being paid for working in the poppy fields, it sought to solve the problem by bringing in labour from other areas. The poppy farmers immediately offered higher wages to lure the new workers away. Raising rates to compete would completely distort the labour market – and in any case high rates would simply draw in more labour from further afield, rather than draw it away from poppy. Nor do ideas for increasing women's participation in the labour market seem realistic. In many areas women labour in the fields precisely because the fileds constitute the family farm, and culturally it would not be acceptable for them to enter the public labour market. Moreover, even when they do engage in the labour market it is not necessarily to the exclusion of working in the poppy fields – teachers in Badakhshan worked the poppy fields from 5 a.m. to 8 a.m., then went off to teach.

One of the few things that seems certain is that the growing of opium poppy will not be stopped until the rule of law is restored to the country. Concerned donor countries might well do better to focus their efforts on that rather than specific eradication schemes. Beyond that, economic growth that results in real development for the majority of Afghans will be needed. Proper long-term jobs, rather than short-term labouring, would draw some people away. More profitable agriculture would encourage some farmers to use their land for licit crops.

There are still some local leaders who are strongly against poppy cultivation, believing it to be both against Islam and deeply damaging to society. So far little has been done to support them in their efforts to limit the spread of the crop. The various incentive schemes may well be better used in this way rather than in government or agency-implemented attempts to wean farmers away from growing.

There is little real understanding of how decisions are made in relation to the narcotics industry in Afghanistan. Some of those study-ing the industry suggest that it does not appear to be controlled by a single cartel; but even if that is so it is little cause for comfort, for the implications of multiple players corrupting the political system is, if anything, worse than control by a cartel – being more fractured they will be even harder to control. It also leaves farmers making individual decisions as to whether or not they should grow poppy, which is likely to lead to the opium economy taking up more land and labour, and drawing resources away from more productive use. The large stocks of opium that were built up after the bumper harvests of 2002/3 seem, however, to be doing little to stem the spread in cultivation. The UN found that two out of three farmers intended to increase significantly their cultivation in 2004 (UNODC 2004). Despite widespread awareness of the ban on cultivation, and a more aggressive approach towards eradication, the UN concedes that the short-term benefits for farmers continue to outweigh their assessment of the potential risks. This is borne out by US predictions that a total of some 120,000 hectares might be cultivated in 2004.[5]

The poppy crop of 2004 has been the target of government eradication teams who set out to destroy up to 10,000 hectares of the crop prior to its harvest, but need the protection of the US-hired security guards. There is, however, a real risk of this selective campaign repeating the mistakes of the disarmament programme, as powerful interests seek to restructure the industry to their advantage. Even where this may not be the case, local perceptions about the focus and extent of eradication have already started to affect attitudes towards the forthcoming election among farmers in areas that have been singled out by the government in Kabul (Constable 2004b).

Given the extent to which the USA in particular needs a success in Afghanistan, donor governments are likely to present any reduction as a sign of the resolve of the administration of President Karzai. To anyone genuinely concerned with the eradication of opium poppy growing in the country, however, such a conclusion would be very premature indeed.

The West tends to see the fact that Afghanistan supplies most of Europe's heroin as a problem that belongs to Afghanistan. Yet when Turkey, Pakistan and Iran, which used to be the big suppliers on the world heroin market, successfully eradicated the crop, production simply shifted elsewhere. Even if by some miracle production were stopped in Afghanistan, there would always be another war-torn country to which it would relocate. In this the Afghans are right: the problem is located in the West. Shifting it on to Afghanistan may be politically convenient, but it will not solve the issue.

Notes

1 According to local sources, 7 kg of opium will fetch US$1,600; once it has been converted into a kilogram of heroin it is worth $3,000. UNDCP use a conversion ratio of 1:10 but admit 1:7 or even 1:6 is more likely.

2 It is difficult to cross-check locally obtained figures with UNDCP data as local people talk in terms of the new districts, while UNDCP uses the old district boundaries. The new district of Darayem was mainly carved out of Faizabad, although a smaller part of it used to be in Keshem. Old Faizabad included what is now Argu; Jurm used to include the new district of Khash. Inasmuch as it is possible to compare figures, the amounts given to us would seem not unreasonable given the very obvious increase in production in 2003. According to UNODC, Kishem and Jurm (old districts) were the two highest-ranking districts in the country for cultivation. Faizabad was ranked fourth.

3 For example, a *pau* (a unit of measurement commonly referred to when farmers are talking about opium prices) in Badakhshan is only half the weight of a *pau* in Kabul. In a similar way a Kabuli *ser*, the most common unit of measurement for wheat, is different to a Qandahari ser.

4 BBC World Service, February 2004.

5 Robert Charles, Assistant Secretary of State for International Narcotics and Law Enforcement, testimony before the House International Relations Committee, US State Department, 12 February 2004.

6 | State

The tribes consider the king rather differently to the Tajiks, the latter vesting the king with many powers, whereas for the tribes he has limited prerogatives; the tribes are largely self-governing. (Elphinstone 1815)

State and nation

A nation is, wrote Benedict Anderson (1991), 'an imagined political community'. Although the state exists as a political entity with recognized territory and institutions of governance, the nation exists in people's heads and provides a sense of belonging. Nationalism, the sense of attachment to a nation, has often been a driving force for state formation; a force that in recent times has had so many negative associations that it is hard to remember it was once viewed positively.

In some ways it is remarkable that after a quarter of a century of war many Afghans' imagining of their nation is still so strong. Despite the intense conflict people have been through and the fact that all ethnic groups except the Hazaras also spread across into neighbouring countries, people continue to see themselves as Afghans and do not generally wish to secede or to join neighbouring states. Yet the sense of nationhood is not equal across territory. What it means to an uneducated, older woman up a mountain valley is not what it means to a young man returned from the refugee camps of Pakistan, nor an educated person in Kabul. Nor are the geographical bounds of the nation always clear. The Pashtuns have ignored the frontier along the Durand Line in the south and east ever since the British drew it in the late nineteenth century. The physical porosity of the border – once off the main roads people travel across it as if it does not exist – is mirrored in the sense of belonging: the tribes here owe more loyalty to kinsmen across the border than they do to Kabul. This does not mean that they are not Afghan, nor that they want a separate state; rather, it is that being Pashtun is not a sub-set of being Afghan but a separate and overlapping identity – and, of the two, being Afghan is for many the less tangible, and therefore the less important.

Notions of belonging do not only change with distance, they change with education. Belonging for most Afghans is still created through the spoken word, through legend and story, parable and precept, and much

8 *Humpty Dumpty: originally reputed to have been built with a mortar of eggs, the historic Pul e Malan bridge, south of Herat, was restored in the mid-1990s. (Jolyon Leslie)*

of this goes from the local to the universal Islam, passing nation by. It is thus not surprising that those who have the strongest sense of themselves as Afghan – rather than, for example, as inhabitants of a valley or tribe – are those who have had access to education, and thus who can access more directly the world beyond. Where the non-educated, rural Afghan does connect to nation, it is often not in the sense of being part of a political community but rather through some form of engagement with its bureaucratic embodiment, the state, and this relationship is normally dealt with via a representative. Thus historically the state not only governed through the representatives of communities, but the whole concept of nation, and of the political legitimacy of its rulers, was mediated through these representatives. A friend in Qandahar, who is now the deputy head of the Electoral Commission, was asked in February 2004 whether people would register and, in the end, vote. 'If the tribal leaders encourage them,' he said. 'Otherwise it is impossible. If someone from outside tries, it cannot be done.'

This relationship sets the parameters of what the state today can be, and how it can operate. To envisage a state that has meaning only for a minority of educated citizens and then assume that it can somehow be rolled out to the whole of the country in the space of a couple of years is asking for problems. Yet that is largely what the Bonn agreement has set in train. It also has implications for how those who seek to rule the nation might gain legitimacy among its people. Legitimacy implies being regarded as an acceptable person for the job by those with influence, and at least having the passive acquiescence of the majority of citizens. Without this, conflict is likely to ensue. For, given the fractured nature of politics in Afghanistan and the endless scope for contenders to power – or even simply disenfranchised groups – to gain support from neighbouring countries, it is unlikely that any one group could rule by force.

Discussions about issues of legitimacy in present-day Afghanistan often prompt people to recall an idealized past. It remains unclear whether this is due to an innate conservatism – a fear of new political notions – or whether it can simply be put down to the evident failure of the politics of the last three decades. There is an overwhelming sense that the political actors that have dominated in the recent past lacked legitimacy in the eyes of most of the population, who also find it hard to have much confidence that the present is any better. The gun is seen to rule, the term 'faction' is used rather than 'party' – and factions are associated with guns, not with politics. It was the failure to provide even basic security that more than anything undermined the legitimacy of the *mujahideen*, and conversely it was their ability to provide this most essential condition that gave the Taliban some legitimacy in the eyes of many, despite dislike of their other policies.

In Afghan history the state has tended to be regarded as having legitimacy if it fulfils three requirements: it embodies the concept of Afghanistan as an independent Islamic territory; it acts as a broker between clans, tribes and ethnic groups – although not necessarily on equal terms; and it provides a certain level of benefits to citizens, including security and access to public services and infrastructure.

A presumptive leader needs to straddle two worlds: to understand, be part of, and value tradition, and balance this with the requirements of a modern state. The notion of a hereditary ruling class is part of Afghan political culture. With the exception of the very brief reign of Bacha i Saqao, members of the Durrani tribe led the nation from 1747 to 1978. David Edwards (2002), writing about the PDPA takeover of power, notes that the fact that Nur Muhammad Taraki was the son of a poor semi-peasant, semi-shepherd family, about whom little was known before he became president in 1979, was a marked departure from previous practice and highly radical in terms of a society where background was extremely important. The most profound innovation introduced by the PDPA, he writes, was not land reform or women's rights, but 'the notion that kinship didn't matter, that literally anyone could lead the nation'. The perception that where a person comes from is important still persists. Commenting on the current political situation, a highly educated and well-travelled clan leader from the Jalalabad area spoke of how: 'Rootless people are now in power. In the West the root is education. We do not have that, so the root was those who were known, the *khans*, the *malik*, business people. People who come from poverty to be king, they only work for their own and those around them.'

A short history

The history of the Afghan state extends back little more than a hundred years, to the reign of Abdur Rahman Khan (1881–1901) who, with the help of British cash, created a well-equipped army and used it ruthlessly to crush internal dissent and turn Afghanistan from a tribal confederacy into a centralized state. However, the tribal areas were never brought totally under central control and continued to retain a measure of independence. The country's borders conformed more to imperial needs than internal logic; its northern frontier was the outcome of negotiations between the British and the Russians, while the Durand Line reflected the strategic fringe of imperial India.

Succeeding rulers opened up the country to trade, undertook land reform, regularized taxes, improved roads and increased educational provision. Yet tribal society remained strong and, as none of the leaders was prepared to use might to govern to the same extent as Abdur Rahman Khan, the state remained weak. In a pattern that was to be repeated throughout the history of the modern Afghan state, Abdur Rahman Khan was able to build a strong state only by dint of foreign financial backing. The price of this, in the wake of the second Anglo-Afghan war, was the ceding of control of external affairs to the British. After the First World War, resistance to this outside interference in the country's affairs grew and led to the assassination of Abdur Rahman Khan's son and successor, Habibullah, in 1919. His son, Amanullah, seized the throne, declared the country's independence which, after a brief war, the British conceded. Amanullah tried hard to transform Afghanistan into a modern nation-state, reversing the isolationist economic policies and opening up the country to trade. He undertook land reform, regularized taxes, improved roads, increased educational provision and, in 1921, gave the country its first constitution. But his ambitious plans were ahead of both the state's capacity to implement and of society's acceptance of direct state intrusion in family or community affairs. Amanullah's attempts to shift power away from village elders and the religious establishment and his liberal stance on women's issues led in 1928 to a series of regional insurrections which finally toppled him. It was a movement led by the Tajik Bacha i Saqao that was the first to move on Kabul and seize power. The rule of this Tajik usurper, however, lasted less than a year, before Nadir Khan, eldest of the Pashtun Musahiban brothers, deposed him. Thus began a dynasty that lasted until 1978.

The strategic position of Afghanistan, first as a buffer state between the Russian and British empires, then as a site of Cold War politics, allowed Afghanistan to develop as a classic rentier state. From 1956 to 1973 foreign grants and loans accounted for 80 per cent of the country's investment and development expenditure (Rubin 1995). This relieved the state of the need to confront resistance to taxes from rural landowners and merchants in order to build up a domestic taxation base and so made it less important to set up governmental structures to control the country. In Amanullah's time, taxes on land and animals were believed to represent some two-thirds of government expenditure (Fry 1974); by the 1950s they did not even cover the operational costs of local government. Instead, external funds were used to build a modern state sector in Kabul that bypassed the rural power holders, leaving them with a large measure of local autonomy. The political elite neither organized the rural majority, nor represented their interests. Far from attempting to govern the country effectively, they simply acted as one link in a chain of patronage for a few areas that were deemed to be of strategic importance. Just as it had been at the turn of the century, Afghanistan's rulers continued to fragment tribal power and manoeuvre round it, rather than confront it. Part of that manoeuvring was to bring the tribes into government. From Abdur Rahman Khan onwards, the business of politics was conducted through informal, vertical channels of client–patron relations and kinship networks were important in obtaining state posts. It has resulted in what one writer has called the 'tribalisation' of the state (Shahrani 1998), a process which aimed to de-tribalize society by co-opting key players into the state structure.

Meanwhile, at village level, people continued to rely on local power networks; the state had little authority and largely used local leadership to govern. A contract existed: a minimal level of loyalty for a minimal level of services. As an NGO worker put it: 'The government made roads, built *karezes*, planted gardens and made a school in the district centres. What it did not do was interfere in the domestic sphere.'

The provision of these services, along with the continued maintenance of Afghanistan's independence and a reasonable level of security (even if in many cases this had more to do with traditional structures than the state itself) gave the state a certain measure of acceptance. This, however, was always liable to be contested, and a sense that there was a need to increase legitimacy among key constituencies, for example urban intellectuals and rural traditional leaders, led to provisions for elected upper and lower houses of a consultative parliament in the 1964 constitution. However, the legislation permitting the existence of political parties was never signed, and the king retained control over the executive, which was neither selected from, nor responsible to, parliament. Parliament was seen not as an institution for nationwide democracy but as a means of gaining legitimacy and political support. At this it failed. Although those interested in politics had more freedom than at any time in the past, in the absence of formalized parties to regulate political conduct, politics was both disorderly and inefficient. At the same time, the bureaucracy of government was highly dysfunctional (Maley 2002). In addition to endemic financial corruption, there were serious problems of nepotism (Kakar 1978). Finally, the state's failure to respond adequately to the famine of 1972 underscored just how little concern its leaders had for the Afghan people. This paved the way for the overthrow of Zahir Shah by his cousin and former prime minister, Mohammad Daoud.

For all his energy, Daoud failed to stem the disillusionment with the old order. In some ways his regime was seen as even less legitimate than the one that preceded it. Traditional authority at least still carried some weight, but in dissolving the monarchy Daoud forfeited this association with the authority of the ruling class while failing to develop alternative sources of legitimacy. There was increasing suppression of opposition; it was at this time that the infamous Pul i Charkhi prison was built, in which many opponents of this and succeeding regimes were incarcerated or lost their lives. Daoud co-opted the language of revolution (*inqilab*) without backing it up with much-needed reforms, despite allying himself with radical groups such as the extreme leftist Parcham group, whose members would later betray him (Maley 2002). Like those before him, he needed foreign cash for his strong state and therefore became increasingly dependent on Soviet aid. The state, however, continued to fail to bring visible benefits to the majority of the population. Ironically, greater access to education served only to increase frustration. Universities were full of students experiencing for the first time the dislocation between their rural, traditional backgrounds and life in a big city; and once graduated, jobs in keeping with their skills and aspirations remained scarce. The oil boom of the early 1970s also led to unprecedented opportunities for labour migration, even for those without formal education, and this altered patterns of social control and exposed people to new ideas. The time for change had come.

The principal communist organization in Afghanistan, the People's Democratic Party of Afghanistan (PDPA), overthrew Daoud in the Saur Revolution of 27 April 1978 but was immediately beset by internal struggles. In addition to the personal differences of its leaders, the Parchamis wanted a more gradual approach to change, while the Khalqis wanted it now (Maley 2002). Although the Khalqis initially won the struggle, there was little popular support for their ill-conceived programme of radical reform, and no state machinery capable of properly implementing their ambitious plans. Unsurprisingly, botched efforts at land redistribution and attempts to radically reorder gender relations soon led to revolt in the countryside. The reforms not only threatened the status quo but were perceived by conservatives to challenge Islamic values. Meanwhile in the cities, in one of the worst periods of internal oppression that Afghanistan had experienced, those deemed to be opponents of the regime were imprisoned, tortured and sometimes executed. Alarmed by the growing disorder and fearful of an attempt by the USA to regain in Afghanistan the influence it had recently lost in Iran, Soviet President Brezhnev sent troops across the border in December 1979.

For many Afghans, this was to destroy any last shred of legitimacy that the PDPA government might have retained, for despite the fact that the troops had technically been 'invited' by the Afghan government they were widely perceived as foreign invaders. Afghanistan had lost its independence, and resistance to the occupation soon spread. From 1979 until the mid-1980s the Soviets virtually controlled the Afghan state structure. All major offices were staffed with Soviet advisers and, in economic terms, government-controlled Afghanistan became a Soviet republic. The USSR paid the government's deficits and gave financial and technical assistance to state investment. Afghanistan's natural gas supplies, developed with Soviet money and expertise, were sold directly to the USSR at sub-economic prices. As with the Soviet Union itself (Lieven 1999), the nature of the Soviet-controlled Afghan state was as a social network providing access to goods, services and patronage; a base of political power in its own right. As the conflict deepened, the contrast between the plight of rural and urban communities was stark. Because the war had led to shortages of food and fuel in Kabul, the Soviets provided 100,000 tons of wheat annually as a gift, and the same again in exchange for goods. Despite continued political repression, the major cities became enclaves where the state continued to function relatively well, markets thrived, people had health services, jobs, food rations and education. Thousands departed to undertake advanced studies in Soviet countries. Even though they lived under constant fear of rocketing, for many urban Afghans it was, comparatively speaking, a good time.

The political war, however, was lost. In sacrificing Afghanistan's independence, the regime also lost its legitimacy. Despite removing the more radical elements of PDPA and moderating their policies, nothing the Soviets could do – short of leaving the country – could redeem it.

One last attempt was made. The old Soviet protégé, Babrak Karmal, was in 1986 replaced by Najibullah, who had been head of state intelligence, KhAD. Under the banner of 'national reconciliation', Najibullah publicly embraced Islam as the religion of Afghanistan, abandoned plans for the transformation of the countryside and proclaimed the importance of the private sector (Rubin 2002). The old Soviet ideology of class struggle was replaced with the concept of nationhood through cooperation. But it was too late. Kabul and other government-controlled cities were increasingly vulnerable, as Soviet support began to dry up; while across the frontlines the *mujadiheen* increasingly used revenue from opium to supplement the foreign assistance that was funding their wars. In order to maintain military control of key enclaves and access to the highways, Najibullah increasingly had to cut deals with local militias, rather than rely on the conventional chain of command. In the end they sealed his fate.

Finally, faced with the huge cost of the conflict, and the internal political changes that were taking place in the USSR, the Soviets gave up. The signing of the Geneva Accords paved the way for Gorbachev to order his forces out, and by February 1989 the last Soviet troops left northwards over the Amu Darya river. Their departure allowed factionalism to come to the surface within government ranks, but Najibullah used the military assets left behind by his sponsors to retain control for another three years. To this day, many Afghans refer to Najibullah as the last strong leader they can remember, whose regime they believe had the potential to establish a stable state had it received wider international political support: 'Najib was very smart, if he had had support from the western powers he could have brought peace to Afghanistan, he was flexible. The UN should have forced the neighbouring countries to reach consensus and to stop supplying weapons to Afghanistan.'

Even his past, it seems, could be forgotten by some: 'One big weakness was that Najib was head of KhAD. People remembered this and at first they did not trust him. But then gradually people started to trust him – everything has a time and when it has gone it has gone. For the US and the UN it would have been a good opportunity to support Najib: systems were established, even corruption was low.'

But support was not forthcoming, and it soon became clear that Najibullah's government was being undermined from too many directions to survive. As things began to unravel, the discipline of those involved in state structures was affected. And there was a corresponding loss of faith in government:

> People expected the government to bring stability and security. From the state they expected health and education. But the people were weakening every year, they became so war-hit that in the end they were not much interested in education: 'we are hungry, we have no future', they would say. After 12th grade they would join the army; it was a bleak future. Teachers were very poor. In the government no one was working, they were just sitting, chatting, talking of the government.

And yet as the *mujahideen* drew closer to Kabul, many of those involved in the state also became afraid of the future. The account of a friend captures something of the fears and feelings around at the time:

> I was thinking, 'this [Soviet] regime is terrible'. At that time we had to go to the army, we couldn't go to our villages. There was lots of propa-

ganda from the West, through the radio, against the Soviet Union. We were thinking of freedom. There were leaflets, saying that the *mujahideen* were heroes, and we expected freedom and a flow of money. We were dreaming of the time the *mujahideen* would come. But there was also concern that if the *mujahideen* came there would be many assassinations, that was the big worry. In the village there was no protection, the *mujahideen* came, took the father in the night and killed him. The things that happened at that time, it was terrible, it is hard to tell those stories, they were brutal, men killed in front of people. Human rights? Where were they? Not only the *mujahideen* but the Communists also, torturing anyone connected with the *mujahideen*.

Despite the international recognition of the new Islamic State of Afghanistan, made up from the *mujahideen* groups, the departure of Najibullah signalled the effective end of a functioning state. In its place, the struggle for territory and political power seemed to become an end in itself for the various factions. It was as if the *jihad* justified each faction's exclusive, and therefore fruitless, claim to power.

Graffiti that appeared on walls in central Kabul months after the fall of Najibullah perhaps summed up the feeling of many. Referring to Najib's student nickname of 'the cow', and the track record of the incoming administration, it said simply, 'Give us back our cow, and take away your donkeys ... '

Although the *mujahideen* parties had had varied success at organizing at a local level while in opposition, like those before them they subscribed to the concept of a centralized state and once in power immediately began to battle for its control. Kabul had both symbolic and actual value, for which the factions competed and in the process tore the city apart in a frenzy of fighting and looting. Across the country, ethnic and tribal alliances were used in the pursuit of power (Roy 1986; Rubin 1995) and, with no single force strong enough to take control, they led to the disintegration of the state.

With the division of Afghanistan along largely military lines, the state fragmented into autonomous units with their own networks of power; fiefdoms that were largely based on regional groupings of commanders or factions. Some of these worked better than others. The Shura e Nazar, or Supervisory Council of the North, which had been set up precisely to be a counter-balance to Najib's government, proved unable to cope with the shift to real political power (and responsibility) in Kabul. In the north, on the other hand, Dostum ran a virtual mini-state, centred on Mazar i Sharif. His rule was often authoritarian and brutal, but this ensured a relative security which enabled the bureaucracy of the state to continue to function. Trade with the CIS states was buoyant and Mazar i Sharif came to be regarded by many foreign aid agencies as an island of peace and prosperity in an otherwise turbulent country. Having established a separate currency for the region and even his own airline, few people in those days called Dostum a warlord. In the east, the Nangarhar shura in Jalalabad, under the leadership of Haji Abdul Qadeer, also looked across the frontier for the means to maintain its autonomy from Kabul, raising significant revenue from the transit trade with Pakistan and establishing a virtual air bridge with the Gulf, which was reportedly also used for the illicit export of narcotics.

The war saw civilian authority become subordinate to military authority, which was often highly abusive. It was this abuse of power, which went on at all levels, coupled with a serial failure to provide any benefits to the wider population, that destroyed the legitimacy of all those who pretended to govern. There was no reason to trust the country's leadership any longer. Some rural areas continued to run their affairs without a state, with justice being dispensed by elders or a *shura* of commanders. With a few exceptions, services, where they existed, were provided by aid agencies, primarily NGOs. Other parts of the country, however, were under the control of rival commanders who looted, pillaged and raped. This was certainly the case in Qandahar, where the factions preyed upon the population to the extent that, in the words of a friend, they 'were happy for *any* change'.

The Taliban state

Thus was created the space into which came the Taliban. In response to the chaos and anarchy of the *mujahideen*, their avowed goal was to reassert central control by some form of state structure, initially in Qandahar. Although the picture often painted of their rule is one of unrelieved oppression, it was in fact more varied than that. While in many places they governed harshly, even brutally, in others – whether because these palces were marginal to their project or because they recognized their inherent ungovernability – they negotiated compromises with the local leadership. As did many regimes before them, they often left the remote areas to govern themselves. 'Tribal people just carried on their own affairs,' as one elder from Zabul put it. On the other hand, elders in a village close to Qandahar spoke of how, 'during the Taliban time no tribal system could function, they didn't want it'. Others, too, saw that they had failed their people: 'The Taliban became cruel, threatening people, not respecting order, not wanting educated people, making forced conscription. People were fond of music, but they stopped all celebrations. They forced the people to grow beards and brought them to the mosque for prayers. They took money from people. Village leaders were afraid of the Taliban, but they could do nothing. The Taliban wanted to finish such people.'

Reactions to their rule were similarly varied, and at times surprising. Some Pashtuns felt betrayed, as hopes of a better government proved ill-founded, local customs and ways of working were not respected, and increasing numbers of foreigners joined their ranks. Moreover, many recalled how the Taliban had said they would bring back Zahir Shah, which is why they had given their support.

Yet in some places in Hazarajat, where the Taliban's arrival had been anticipated with real fear, they governed better than people had anticipated. Not in the towns of Yakawlang and Bamiyan, where the persistent struggle with Hizbe Wahdat for control led to a string of atrocities, but in the rest of the region where they effectively passed control to local leadership. In contrast to Kabul and urban centres, aid agencies often found they could circumvent rules and regulations. 'The Taliban, they didn't ask us what we were doing,' said a worker from Oxfam, 'they just said, "Are you an agency?" We said, "Yes, we are an agency." They never bothered us. Only with one district governor did we have problems. He said, "You cannot have a girls' school." We said, "It is not a girls' school, it is a mosque." He said, "OK".'

For those of us who lived in Kabul at the time, the image of the Islamic Emirate of Afghanistan that the Taliban established after taking over Kabul in 1996 seemed at times to owe more to conjecture on the part of the outside world than to the reality of policy enacted on the ground. Despite impressions of an intolerant regime that swept away everything connected with previous administrations, change was far from wholesale and there was a good deal of flexibility in practice. Aspects of the old state apparatus that were deemed not to compromise Islamic precepts were simply left alone. As well as being expedient, this allowed the Emirate to reclaim the formal authority of the state, whose specific policies were then defined or clarified by edict. The fact that these edicts often emanated from Qandahar rather than from Kabul, and that they usually bore the imprimatur of a group of *ulema* or similar religious au-thority – rather than that of the presumptive head of state and protector of the faithful – served to make the whole process of governance seem all the more mysterious to Taliban-watchers at that time.

In addition to the young foot-soldiers who gave the movement its name, the Taliban drew upon disaffected – and in some cases opportunistic – *mujahideen*. As a result, the administration inevitably faced pressure to reconcile the interests of disparate groups, based on religious, factional or geographical affiliations. Where this situation differed from the earlier *mujahideen* administration, however, was in the general acceptance, at least initially, of a primary loyalty to the Emirate, which should come before personal or factional interests.

Having failed to understand the phenomenon of the Taliban movement, the regime that they strove to put in place was quickly characterized by the western world as 'failed'. As the deputy leader, Mullah Rabbani, pointed out in response to a question from a UN envoy about human rights during 1999: 'You do not seem to understand that we are Afghans. We try to take responsibility for our people, while those who you choose to recognise as representatives of Afghanistan sign international agreements on behalf of their people, while having limited control. You treat us like an armed faction, while expecting us to behave like a government.' Yet although often publicly dismissive of the opinion of the international community, the issue of UN recognition seemed to remain curiously important to the Taliban leadership.

While abhorring the excesses of the regime – and ridiculing both its presumptions and its apparently simple operating practices – there was an enduring fascination on the part of outsiders as to how the Taliban maintained control with such ruthless effect. The primitive outward face of the Emirate in fact hid a somewhat more worldly structure that was integrated into regional trading networks that provided them and others with an important source of revenue. There seems little doubt that these networks grew in strength during the mid-1990s, and that this involved a web of commercial players with far better international contacts and market access than the Taliban themselves.

Aid and the state

Aid has long been part of the strategy by which outside nations have gained influence in Afghanistan. This is not unusual. From the 1950s onwards, the global pattern was for official development aid to be given as part of a post-colonial framework that was not only concerned with reducing poverty in the South through economic growth but also fitted with the interest of western countries in maintaining their influence in the world. Thus, in Afghanistan in the 1960s and 1970s, countries from both the West and East jostled for influence, adopting the different departments of Kabul University and funding a raft of development projects. Many of these were part of the state's modernization project, and many were failures – or at the best only partial successes.

The Soviet invasion changed the nature of things. Thereafter, the battle lines of the conflict were mirrored in aid flows, as Soviet aid to the Kabul government was pitched against western aid to the *mujahideen*. Though presented as solidarity aid to freedom fighters engaged in a just cause, the truth was that the aid to the *mujahideen* was often an instrument of government policy, and NGOs were established as fronts for this. AfghanAid, for example, was set up largely to implement the agenda of the UK government, while the Swedish Committee for Afghanistan emerged from anti-Soviet feelings among the public, tinged with a hard-line Calvinist edge. Few questions were asked about the nature of the cross-border operations, and neither the fundamentalism of the *mujahideen* nor the conservatism of rural society appeared to be an issue to those who two decades later were to decry the Taliban and seek to use aid as a means to moderate their behaviour. On the contrary, it provided an unassailable – and romantic – *cause célèbre*. Guests at dinner parties in Peshawar were entranced by stories about the 'inside' from heroic aid workers who, dressed in local garb, had trekked over the mountains with bearded *mujahideen*, battling against the might of the Soviets. In many ways, NGOs followed the factions, competing both for territory and the protection of their commanders, apparently with little idea of how much this compromised them in the eyes of the population. The fact that much of the humanitarian assistance was given in ways that were deeply damaging to the future of the country passed the majority of NGO staff by.

At this stage of Afghanistan's history, aid not only supported war but contributed to the future fragmentation of the state. Individual commanders boosted their standing by the aid that they could bring to the areas under their control. While efforts were latterly made by donors to create a unified structure among the *mujahideen* that might form the basis for a future government, this was secondary to the overwhelming need to destroy the Soviets.

The UN and the failed state model

By the mid-1990s, the rationale that had been driving global aid since the 1950s was looking distinctly flawed. Bilateral development aid depended on having a government to give it to; yet in a number of the poorest countries of the world the nation-state had all but disintegrated, or at least was the site of serious conflict. Afghanistan was a case in point. Meanwhile the humanitarian crises associated with such long-drawn-out conflicts – variously known as complex emergencies, complex political emergencies, or situations of chronic conflict and political instability – called into question many of the assumptions of classic emergency aid. As crises stretched out across the years, the notion of what was development aid and what emergency aid became blurred. Rather than being an operational distinction based on types of need, it now frequently became a political issue of recognition. Debates became polarized between the notion of giving aid for 'humanitarian' purposes, argued by its proponents to be free of politics and based only on need (at least in intent, though most would recognize the practice as being more complicated), and the attempt to take account of outcomes – the extent to which giving or withholding aid might improve the situation of the beneficiary group. A critique of humanitarian assistance was developed that highlighted how aid could do harm as well as good (Anderson 1996).

At the same time, the need to address the issue of conflict became a central concern of development policy (Duffield 2001b). Part of the role of international organizations came to be seen as rebuilding war-torn societies in a way that would help to avert future conflict, such engagement being seen as necessary if peace and stability were to prevail. In line with this, the UN started to reconsider the role it should be playing in long-term conflict countries. The problem was that, in the absence of any form of local representative political organization, the desired outcomes were decided by outsiders, as was the means to reach them. Unlike in South Africa, where the ANC clearly articulated the way in which it wanted assistance to support the struggle for liberation, in most crisis countries there was no movement to speak on behalf of the people. The benchmarks to which these outcomes were therefore tethered, and which were their claim to legitimacy, were the various international instruments that indicated some bottom line of welfare and security. It was in this context that the notion of rights came increasingly to be heard in the debate about aid.

The evident collapse of much of the state bureaucracy, the descent of parts of the country into chaos, and the continued internecine fighting in Kabul prompted the UN to characterize Afghanistan as a 'failed state'. The long-standing humanitarian emergency had now become an 'emergency of governance'. While special envoys continued to shuttle between factions in an effort to find a political solution, the UN agencies moved into the vacuum to assume responsibilities as an almost surrogate government. They not only provided assistance but also attempted to take on system-wide policy and planning functions and acted as the country's spokesperson in dealings with journalists and foreign diplomats. In keeping with the global move towards addressing issues of conflict, the UN developed a new approach, the Strategic Framework for Afghanistan (SFA), designed to bring together the political and assistance wings of the UN in common pursuit of a peaceful solution to the Afghanistan crisis.

Adopted in 1998, the SFA aimed to provide 'a more coherent, effective and integrated political strategy and assistance programme' through a 'common conceptual tool that identifies key activities ... on the basis of shared principles and objectives'. The overarching goal of the UN was articulated as one of facilitating 'the transition from a state of internal conflict to a just and sustainable peace through mutually reinforcing political and assistance initiatives' and ensuring 'no "disconnects" between political, human rights, humanitarian and developmental aspects of the [international] response'.

The UN's work in Afghanistan was seen as having two components: an assistance pillar and a political pillar (in later versions there was a third pillar, human rights, whereas in the earlier version human rights was seen as integral). Within the assistance pillar the key operational element was known as Principled Common Programming. Although an intent of this was to agree common principles to which the aid community could sign up, thus establishing 'bottom lines' for negotiations, both donors and agencies found this difficult in practice. Not only were there many different sets of principles – Common Programming principles, agency principles, donor principles – but there was no agreement as to what took precedence when principles contradicted each other. Was the imperative, for example, to provide humanitarian assistance or to support women's rights?

In order to realize the goals of the SFA, a comprehensive restructuring of aid coordination mechanisms was undertaken after 1998. This, it was felt by donors and agencies alike, would result in greater coherence and effectiveness through processes of collective analysis and common operational programming. In keeping with the aims of the SFA, this restructuring envisaged more systematic links between the wider humanitarian community and political actors within the UN. The extent to which opportunities for consultation between the political and aid wings of the UN were taken up, or resulted in greater coherence, was limited, due in part to the failure of the UN to undertake comprehensive reform of the management within and between the agencies concerned. By not undertaking reform, the UN also limited its ability to determine a common position on a range of key assistance issues.

An examination of aid behaviour between 1998 and late 2001 suggests that, regardless of the SFA, donor policy and practice in Afghanistan were driven by priorities set in capital cities, rather than by collective positions agreed on the ground. Furthermore, most donors maintained a degree of ambivalence towards collective positions, especially where these might compromise their independence of action. Funding priorities were found to bear only an incidental relationship to the priorities articulated in the SFA and PCP. Instead, funding patterns appeared in many cases to relate to specific issues of concern to the donor country and its broad political attitudes towards Afghanistan. The lack of commitment to a collective position was perhaps the most evident at the Afghanistan Support Group meeting in Stockholm in 1999 when, in response to efforts to define an appropriate process of engagement on rights issues, the USA assertively stated its intention to act unilaterally if necessary.

Even as the Taliban asserted the authority of their central administration, and took on an increasing range of functions of government, the UN continued to pursue the failed state model in its dealings with the country. While this might partly be explained by the fact that only three countries had accorded formal recognition to the Emirate, there was evident confusion on the part of key UN member-states as to how to respond to the presumptions of the Taliban, and an increasing dislike of what they saw of their policies. Donors and aid agencies alike tied themselves in knots over how to deal this. On the one hand they refused to recognize the government's existence, yet on the other they insisted it should be responsible for the provisions of international treaties signed by previous Afghan governments. This led to what one commentator described as a

> strange absence of authorities as authorities. The Taliban appear as the object of advocacy and of conditionality, but not as authorities that are in fact already engaged in the running of a country. It is as if UN assistance activities can continue in a vacuum without engaging the authorities except to advocate to them. The fact that they are not recognised means almost that they are not seen, a situation bound to lead to unrealistic goals. (Leader 2000)

Even though most member-states of the UN did not recognize the Taliban government, the operational agencies ended up working with them. For if the UN wanted to work in Afghanistan, which it clearly did, there was no alternative: by the end of the 1990s the Taliban controlled 90 per cent of the country's territory.

Nowhere was the confusion about how to engage with Afghanistan more apparent than in the issue of what was called 'capacity building'.

Despite the fact that investments had in the past been made in strength-ening a range of institutions, inside and outside the formal state, donors and the UN now came to perceive that 'capacity building' of government departments risked lending legitimacy to the Taliban state. As a result, UN official policy as stated in the SFA indicated that:

> Institution and capacity-building activities must advance human rights and will not seek to provide support to any presumptive state authority which does not fully subscribe to the principles contained in the found-ing instruments of the United Nations, the Universal Declaration of Human Rights, the Convention on the Rights of the Child, the Conven-tion on the Elimination of Discrimination against Women and Inter-national Humanitarian Law. (UNOCHA 1998)

This implied working where possible with communities rather than authorities, in effect to try and bypass the Taliban. Yet aid agencies wanted to deliver humanitarian assistance to a country in long-term need. For this to happen, departments had to function, at least to some extent, and the UN and other agencies had to engage with them. Con-structing a mode of service delivery that ignored state structures simply wasn't feasible. So, for example, UNICEF implemented its expanded programme of immunization with and through the Ministry of Public Health, UN-Habitat conducted its water and sanitation work through municipalities, UNHCR had joint projects with the Ministry of Martyrs and Repatriation, FAO had a contract with the Ministry of Agriculture for seed multiplication and WFP programmed its food through the Ministry of Rehabilitation and Rural Development and the Ministry of Public Health.

Assistance that was provided to sustain, even if not build, the capacity of relevant departments to undertake this work included both techni-cal and salary support; for civil servants continued to be paid next to nothing and, without some remuneration, could hardly be expected to work. This led to a remarkable set of double standards. In order to sustain health structures at a time when support from the central or regional administration was negligible or non-existent, direct payments of 'incentives' to public health professionals and support staff became routine throughout the 1990s. Following the controversy about female healthcare in Kabul in 1997, and more general concern about the dis-criminatory policies of the Taliban, some donors expressed dismay at payments to civil servants through presumptive governmental structures, while others went as far as specifically to preclude any such payments from their contributions. In order to maintain support for public health staff providing vital services, therefore, both UN agencies and NGOs began to pay such incentives to individuals, rather than through the local health structures. However, despite their attempt to register disapproval of the Taliban administration, at least one major donor who had restricted payments via UN and NGOs continued to fund the ICRC to pay incentives for hospital staff. The payment of these incentives was generally acknowledged to have been instrumental in ensuring continued access for female patients in the two largest hospitals in the city. As was noted at the time, the

> combination of a formal policy which does not accommodate the political realities of the situation, and a multitude of UN agencies with their own mandates, has led to a situation where policy ... is confused and indecisive. This confusion is most apparent in terms of engagement with the administrative structures. In effect, each agency has pursued its own line in determining if and how it will work with the authorities. (Leader 2000)

The legacy of centralization

By 2001, when the international spotlight again focused on the nature of the Afghan state, Afghanistan had been through a number of different versions of statehood, ranging from the modernizing 1960s and 1970s, through the Soviet model, to the accommodations of Najibullah and finally, via the collapsed state of the early 1990s, to the Taliban's strict version of an Islamic state.

Throughout all, however, the model of statehood remained that of a unitary central authority; the devolution of power from the centre has never been part of the Afghan political imagining, much less practice. Even at the time when the factions were dismembering the country, a central state remained the ideal, and the prize to be fought for. One of the key reasons given by Afghans for this has been that a strong state is needed to save the country from interfering neighbours. Yet history has shown that whenever the Afghan state was said to be 'strong', it was a strength that was bought with foreign money – and at the price of foreign interference. Moreover, these resources were used not against Afghanistan's neighbours but against its people. From Abdur Rahman Khan, through Daoud, the communists, and finally the Taliban, administrations that have aspired to be strong have also been politically repressive.

The bureaucracy of the state is extraordinary in the degree of centralization of its formal structure and fiscal arrangements. Provincial authorities have neither tax-raising powers nor can they raise loans. Outside central government, the only tax autonomy is at the municipal level, and that is minimal. Provinces do, of course, collect taxes – most notably customs taxes – but that is theoretically on behalf of central government, and should be remitted to Kabul. The provincial government structure is a mirror of the central structure (although not all ministries are represented) and heads of departments report to their parent ministry in Kabul rather than to the provincial governor. The districts again replicate the same system, although even fewer ministries are represented – indeed, some districts have only an *uluswal*. Staffing establishments are set centrally, as are rates of pay. In the past, particularly in the communist times, budget requests were prepared at the provincial level, and the governor and heads of departments would review proposals before sending them up to the centre. This no longer happens and the entire process is now top-down, with the provincial budget being simply the sum of various ministry decisions. That in other countries systems exist where significant budgetary and tax-raising powers are devolved to the local level is a matter of surprise to many Afghans.

Another legacy of the succession of centralized administrations is that local politics has often been used less to deal with local issues than to increase the influence of dominant groups at the centre. The central mountain region of Hazarajat was effectively split up and apportioned between different provinces in order to prevent Hazaras developing a strong regional voice that could make itself heard at the centre. All groups have gerrymandered provincial and district boundaries whenever they have had the chance. The Pashtuns did it to ensure they dominated the liberal parliament in the early 1970s; in the 1980s and 1990s the Tajiks split Badakhshan into ever more districts and the Hazaras created new districts in southern Hazarajat. The trend continues today, with the creation of a new province of Panjshir and another of Dai Kundi. The actual interests of regions, far less communities, has been of little concern to those seeking to pursue their interests in this way.

The challenge facing those involved in reconstructing the 'new' Afghanistan will be how to rebuild a recognizable state from the threadbare institutions and systems that survive. This implies not only a functional state that actually works for ordinary people but also a symbolic state that represents the interests of the many, and can therefore be a source of confidence and pride.

7 | Bonn and beyond, part I: the political transition

'The task of state building as an emergency response seems self-defeating. It is impractical –within a short space of time – to re-establish an executive, legislature and judiciary that did not work, or to construct them without historical foundation and where no conditions prevail for their animation,' wrote Jarat Chopra (2002) in relation to East Timor. The same could be said of Afghanistan. While there is undoubtedly a need to establish a functioning state, and for it to develop a minimal degree of legitimacy among its people, the fully-fledged liberal democracy envisaged as an outcome of the Bonn agreement was always a pipe dream. As the previous chapter has shown, the state that existed prior to the Saur Revolution of 1978 was weak in many ways, and barely touched the lives of many in the countryside. Since then, a continuous contest for power has fragmented it and further eroded its authority.

Yet rather than engage in some hard-headed thinking about what was both necessary and possible at this stage of the country's history, the international community went on a fantasy tour, imagining a state that could not possibly exist and on this basis constructing plans that were doomed to failure. As a result the country has been left in a tangled heap of broken promises and recriminations. The plans were doomed, first, because it is not possible to rebuild in two and a half years what it took more than two decades to destroy. Yet the international community is deluding itself into thinking that it can do more than this, and that it can fast-forward history. It is not just the Afghanistan of the late 1970s it wants to piece back together, but a fully representative, gender-sensitive state – something Afghanistan never was. Where the state failed to function, people had long relied on traditional systems of governance to try and bring some order to their daily lives. As explored in Chapter 2, these worked on different sets of principles to those of western liberal governance, yet the international community made little effort to understand these or how they might form the basis of a state-building strategy. The result, as in East Timor (Hohe 2002), was a formal process that continues to become increasingly dislocated from the lives of ordinary Afghans.

The plans were also doomed because the international institutions

9   *A heavily armed, unmarked, ISAF group attracts the curiosity of young Afghans in suburban Kabul, 2004. (Jolyon Leslie)*

that were charged with assisting Afghans have neither the capacity nor the political backing to deliver to such ambitious targets. The result has been to fail Afghanistan far more than if they had gone for less ambitious targets and achieved them.

Inauspicious beginnings

The problem started with the Bonn agreement itself. It certainly represented a new era of international engagement in Afghanistan, but it was an engagement that took place in the shadow of a massive military campaign in retaliation for the events of 11 September 2001. Although the agreement that emerged is often referred to as a 'peace agreement', the circumstances that gave rise to it were not those from which peace agreements are usually forged. The meeting at Bonn hardly represented the resolution of a diversity of interests, for these had still to be negotiated. Nor, given the way in which Bonn was brought about by outside actors, did it signal recognition by the major protagonists that negotiation now served their interests more than continued fighting. The major party to the conflict, the Taliban, was not even at the table. Rather, the Bonn agreement was a victors' sharing of the spoils of war in the wake of the forcible removal from power of the Taliban. The victors, however, had fought each other as much as they had fought the Taliban; and just as the military campaign to remove the Taliban created opportunities for the old rivalries to re-emerge and scores to be settled, so too Bonn allowed certain factions to establish themselves on the new political stage.

In the euphoria of victory, sponsors of the new Afghan order seemed to forget the interests that the Taliban represented. Their inevitable military defeat was widely assumed to be the end of a dark era in Afghan history, with any talk of a possible resurgence regarded at the time as far-fetched. That this was not the case should have been obvious from the beginning; but it was only in mid-2003, when forces opposed to the Bonn process had inflicted substantial casualties on both civilian and military personnel and put more than a third of the country out of bounds to UN and other aid agencies, that the gravity of the situation was finally acknowledged. Even then, no coherent response about how to deal with the opposition was forthcoming – the only strategy was intensified search and destroy operations that further alienated the population.

Had Bonn been more openly acknowledged for what it was – the best deal that could be obtained at the time – and had the UN and member-states examined what steps were needed to advance the cause of peace on the ground, the transition might have had a chance. The challenge was less to oversee an agreement than to negotiate a strategy for securing peace and ensuring the minimum conditions in which people could begin to rebuild their lives. This required a cold, sober analysis of the situation in the country, of the political will of member-states, and of the capacities of international organizations to deliver. Aid needed to be used strategically to support the peace-building process, rather than rushing headlong into an attempt at reconstruction, based on false premises.

Any strategy for building and sustaining peace requires a number of interlocking elements. First and most crucial is a transition to good security. This point was made over and over again by Afghans in all parts of the country, and was reiterated in endless studies. Yet it was to be the international community's greatest failure. The US decision to engage certain factions to pursue its ground war not only returned to power the very people who had been responsible for Afghanistan's plunder, but also ensured that they obtained significant supplies of new arms and useful quantities of hard currency. Kabul reverted to the control of Shura e Nazar, while in the provinces regional warlords battled for control. Second is the need to build legitimacy. Although this might in part have emerged from improvements in security, it also required other things: some minimal level of representation of all of the country's main ethnic groups; an end to the excessive levels of corruption; the beginnings of service delivery, most notably in education; and a few key, visible development projects, to signal that things were improving. These were, and remain, formidable challenges. But the imagining of peace allowed those concerned with the transition to skate over a whole number of unresolved issues that were obstacles to actually securing the peace, and to plan for reconstruction as if nothing lay in the way.

Imagining a state

If the international community imagined a peace agreement, so too it imagined a state; both what it was (a *terra nullis* on which they could set to work from scratch) and what it should become (a liberal democracy). The text of the Bonn agreement sets out the eventual goals of the transition as 'the establishment of a broad-based, gender-sensitive, multi-ethnic and fully representative government',[1] with all of the implications of human rights protected, services for its citizens and a modern justice system. Would that it could be so. The reality is that Afghanistan is far from all these things and they cannot be wished into being over a period of two and a half years. Nor is the country a blank canvas on which the outside world can paint the colours of its choice, but a territory staked out by powerful players who have their feet in the past and their eyes to the future. Key figures tasked with supporting the transition were clearly aware of the realpolitik on the ground, but seemed not to, or chose not to, understand fully the implications of maintaining warlords in government, or how this might affect popular perceptions of the international project. A study in mid-2003 by the Stimson Centre, which examined Afghanistan against fifteen key variables that had been found to be crucial in sustaining peace in other post-civil war situations, indicated that this was far from an 'effective transition' (Durch 2003). Yet filled with a certainty and a belief that the Americans had won the war and that that was the end of the story, they rushed headlong into trying to construct a country that could not be.

'We want a strong state' Almost wherever you go in Afghanistan this is what people say. It lies at the forefront of people's longings; a strong state that will deter foreign powers from interfering, for whom they blame much of the trouble of the last quarter of a century, and put an end to the warlords, whom they hold equally guilty. This desire is bolstered by the filtered memories of a golden past, which is remembered as a period with a strong central state, although in reality it was often far from this. The 'strong state' sentiment is echoed by President Karzai and his American backers. The reasons are understandable, but the wish for a strong state begs many questions. What should such a state look like? Who should control it? How and when can it be realized?

The strong state idea has been seized upon as a possible model for the new Afghanistan by western analysts, partly as a counter to the liberal democracy model, which they rightly claim is a fantasy. Yet the notion of a strong, central Afghan state is an equal fantasy. How might such a state be established? Amir Abdur Rahman was clear: he was ruthless, and anyone who got in his way was suppressed. But in the days of international scrutiny and human rights concerns, such ruthless suppression of dissent would not be possible, even if it were desirable, which it clearly is not. Should the USA then bomb a strong state into being, fighting every conflict on behalf of the central government? History suggests that this would leave it in the same position as the former USSR, a beleaguered occupier, confined to the cities, flying from enclave to enclave because the roads are not safe. Already we are too close to this scenario for comfort in parts of the south, where the US presence on Afghan soil serves as a rallying point for those opposed to the government. In the north, meanwhile, the state and its foreign backers cannot control even Dostum and Atta. Can they realistically think of taking on Ismail Khan?

For all the apparent consensus on the need for a strong state, there is little agreement once one gets down to details. Everyone identifies warlord-ism as the source of the country's problems, but some of those most vehemently advocating the end of it are themselves seen by others as warlords. Some of these are now ministers. It is also true that everyone wants a state that is representative and a leader that is 'fair and not ethnically biased' (Johnson et al. 2003; Malikyar and Rubin 2002). Yet in present-day Afghanistan it is inconceivable that anyone could satisfy all players on that account. This suggests a need for alternative centres of power where local leaders feel they can exert a measure of control and influence.

In the post-Bonn period, the central state model offered the option only of an American puppet state or a Shura e Nazar state. Both would provoke resistance. The Afghan state was from its creation a Pashtun state. With the exception of one very short period, Pashtuns ruled Afghanistan until, with the departure of Najibullah, the state fell apart. By all reckonings, Pashtuns remain the single largest ethnic group in the country. A non-Pashtun strong state would, therefore, be impossible without a completely unacceptable level of coercion, which would have to be aided by outside powers; and the more heavy-handed outsiders are in pursuit of a 'strong' state, the more of a problem external intervention will become. In any case, Western powers have from the beginning shown themselves unwilling to commit troops on a significant scale in Afghanistan.

Yet while a strong state without the Pashtuns is impossible to envisage, so too is a state in which the interests of other ethnic groups are not fully taken on board. The changes in the political landscape that have resulted from two decades of war mean it is unlikely that the rest of the country would any longer accept Pashtun dominance of government. The Pashtuns are also compromised in the eyes of other groups by their association with the Taliban, and any attempt by them to take over the state will be met with resistance from those who claim to have defeated the former regime. Moreover, those Pashtuns who are in government are largely there as individuals, rather than as representatives of tribal networks. With no army and no tribal backing, they have only the might of the USA and international political support to keep them in place. This might suit the likes of the erstwhile UK ambassador, who once said, 'They are ethnic westerners – we know how to deal with them', but many of them have been outside Afghanistan for a long time and are out of touch with the realities of their country. The historical precedents are obvious: through the 1960s and 1970s Afghanistan had a state that was dependent on foreign aid and foreign advisers, and this contributed to a situation in which the government was not only largely unaccountable to its people but also increasingly distant from them. The evident detachment of the technocrats in the Transitional Administration is resonant of the circumstances that led to the coup of 1978. Now as then, however, the sponsors of reform are unwilling to challenge the particular 'Afghan voice' to which they choose to listen, and go along uncritically with the ambitions that the strong state notion represents, regardless of the fact that neither they nor their clients have the means to realize it.

While it is true that decentralized models of government will have problems establishing control and that a decentralized and criminalized economy is no basis for genuine social and political legitimacy (Cramer and Goodhand 2003), neither is a centralized and criminalized economy – nor one that has ceded control of its policy to outsiders. And as Rubin and Malikyar note, 'It is far from certain that the popularity of centralization would survive its implementation'. When you talk to people about what they really mean by a strong state and why they want it, what they really want is a non-corrupt state and the end to warlord power. They want a state that will bring some security so that they can get on with their lives, and which provides a basic level of services, so that their children can go to school and they can get healthcare. The call for centralization is instrumental not fundamental, and if it does not deliver it could easily be rejected in turn.

For the state to bring stability it has to be effective in acting as a broker to maintain a balance of power at the local level and solve disputes that cannot be managed by local structures. This implies a degree of trust that will not be achieved by an extension of central authority that seems to rely more on enforcement than any political accommodation. Flawed as local structures might sometimes be, and open to abuse by commanders and other power holders, there is at present little alternative but to build on these. The state has no capacity to manage directly, nor is it conceivable that it will have for many years to come. A centralized state that reduces the status of tribal and other local leaders will quickly find that it has no means of governing.

Part of the problem is that the nature of 'strength' has been misconceived. It has been read to mean one person, in the role of president, rather than any form of coalition; or rather than a strong bureaucracy that is not corrupt. It fits with the agenda of a certain group and it fits with the USA's limited vision of government; but the only way this model of strength can survive in Afghanistan is through the backing of US force – which is hardly a sustainable project.

The principal alternative that has been put forward to the strong central state is federalism. This either–or approach reflects a failure both to explore the range of alternatives available and to deal adequately with the fundamental questions that the centre–periphery relationship raises. This failure derives both from a lack of political vision on the part of the sponsors of the transition and from Afghanistan's own political history. The reality of Afghanistan is a large measure of de facto decentralization – and this will not be altered simply by a constitution that formalizes a centralized state. The challenge is to transform the transition into something that Bonn was not: an agreement on a process of power-sharing.

The years of war have seen the emergence of multiple authorities and these cannot just be ignored. The most notable is Ismail Khan's statelet in Herat, complete with social welfare for its citizens, significant control over the affairs of neighbouring provinces and direct international diplomatic contacts. Other regional power holders also enjoy substantial autonomy, combining both administrative and military power. Assistance has often legitimized this, whether intentionally or not, by the way it has worked. It is easy to denigrate these people by calling them warlords, yet Ismail Khan remains legitimate in the eyes of many of his people. As a colleague in Herat noted, 'The educated people do not like him, but the ordinary people, to them he is a *jihadi* hero.' In terms of basic security, his firm grip on power instils confidence in many people in the region. As a Herati driver carrying 10,000 gallons of gasoline on a road leading out of the city put it, 'On Ismail Khan's roads, you can drive at any time without a problem' (Bearak 2002).

The fragmentation of central authority is manifest on the ground. Unlike in the past, when provincial governors were always appointed from other parts of the country, most governors are now from the factional groups dominant in their areas. Attempts since 2002 to impose appointees from Kabul have often been the focus for conflict. Even in places where governors have been formally sanctioned by President Karzai, they owe their positions to their existing military control: they have their appointments because they have power, not power because of their appointments. Governors in turn appoint *uluswals*, although in places where the governor's military authority has not extended sufficiently this has caused local conflict. In Shindand district of Herat, for example, Ismail Khan's attempts to impose his appointee as *uluswal* provoked resistance from local Pashtuns, who felt excluded from power in Herat. They in turn drew support from Pashtun power holders in Qandahar, thus enabling them to sustain the stand-off. This has in some cases been exploited by neighbouring regional power holders seeking to extend their influence. Where Kabul has attempted to replace governors, as in Qandahar, the new appointees have struggled to assert their power as established interests continue to work behind the scenes.

For all the attention that has been given to the regional power holders, the real problem for the state lies not so much with the periphery as with the centre. Ismail Khan might be withholding from Kabul customs revenue raised in Herat, but he is not contesting the central state. Dostum and Atta both need it, as does Khalili. None of the regional warlords is contesting state power, but rather attempting to ensure that they dominate their regions and retain the ability to extract wealth from them. Warlords such as Sayyaf, on the other hand, are trying to shape the nature of the central state; in his case through the enormous influence he wields over the Supreme Court and parts of the judiciary. The role of Fahim is particularly problematic because of his control of the Ministry of Defence, where his evident self-interest undermines any efforts by the Karzai administration to build domestic credibility, particularly through disarmament and the creation of a national army. The central state cannot work if it is not seen as a (reasonably) honest broker. Yet, Fahim continues to treat the Ministry as the fiefdom of his clan within Shura e Nazar, and to claim that this is their entitlement after the long *jihad*. Ninety out of the 100 generals appointed by Fahim in early 2002 were from his group (Manuel and Singer 2003).

President Karzai used his closing address to the delegates of the Constitutional Loya Jirga on 4 January 2004 to justify proposals for the instruments of a strong state, and issued an explicit challenge to factional leaders to compete with him for the presidency. In making an argument for a presidential system of government, he sought to portray the alternative parliamentary system as one that risked the country being 'divided among political parties which are formed along ethnic lines, or split into small parties, which are disposed to forming alliances and coalitions along ethnic, sectarian or regional lines in order to be able to govern'. It is a description that seems quite accurately to sum up the status quo of the military groupings that now dominate the political landscape in the country. Curiously, he went on to claim that the parliamentary system, with all of the participation and debate that this implies, would 'limit the possibility of the emergence of national, inclusive political parties'. Quite how the centralizing of powers that this *loya jirga* finally endorsed will be used to erase ethnic or sectarian divisions is far from clear.

The political transition

Nature of the current state Both the Interim and Transitional Administrations have been sites of contest between those striving for power. Those struggles have not for the most part been about the political direction the country should go in – the shape of its economy, its foreign policy, the development of services – but have been about individual and group advancement. For many ordinary Afghans there is a profound sense of disappointment at the failure of the leadership, despite intense international involvement and scrutiny, to rise above the self-serving behaviour of previous regimes. What they see behind the mask of government is the reassertion of informal, robust networks of individual power-relations, aimed at protecting personal or group interests. Although the rhetoric is one of rebuilding the state, many of those in power seem set on extracting from it as much as possible, as if there was no tomorrow.

One of the starkest examples of this is urban real estate, which since early 2002 has become the transitional stockmarket for the rich and powerful in Kabul. Exiled home-owners who have not seen the city for years have returned to Kabul to evict tenants and oversee hasty repairs in order to profiteer from the sky-high rents paid by embassies and international agencies that compete for space for their expanding offices and homes. From the clerks in the municipality who deal with building permissions, to the ministers who quietly offer visiting donor missions their house to rent (payable offshore, of course), everyone is on the make. The willingness of international organizations to pay New York prices simply fuels the greed of the landlords, who price the middle classes out of the centre of the city. Market forces have swung into action.

It was only a matter of time before the unscrupulous also set their sights on government land. Like others before them, commanders wasted no time in occupying land on the outskirts of Kabul, distributing some of it to their hangers-on, who paid off municipal staff to obtain legal title, and then quickly sold it on. The most brazen recent land-grab was initiated by the Minister of Defence, who unilaterally redesignated official land in Sher Pur for private residential development and then got the chief of police to clear dozens of families living in the area to make way for his plans. Plots were offered to his military cronies and members of the cabinet at knock-down prices. The Afghan Independent Human

Rights Commission reported that $1,500 was paid for 'documentation' of plots, some of which are worth up to $170,000. All but four cabinet ministers accepted the offer, in the full knowledge that the process was illegal. While President Karzai pledged at the time to take firm action, and appointed a commission of inquiry to investigate, lavish villas were already rising above the new walls that surrounded the plots. The fact that these villas will soon be let to embassies or international organizations will be of small comfort to the estimated half a million Kabulis who are waiting for distribution of government land on which to build themselves homes.[2]

Processes of transition The Bonn agreement laid out three major steps in the transition process: an Emergency Loya Jirga (ELJ) to be held in June 2002, which would decide on a transitional authority, including a broad-based Transitional Administration; a Constitutional Loya Jirga to be convened within eighteen months of the establishment of the transitional authority, in order to adopt a new constitution; and finally the election of a fully representative government by June 2004.

The emergency loya jirga As the first milestone in the transition process, this *loya jirga* represented an important step towards the creation of a legitimate state. Held in June 2002, it was mandated to choose the head of state, decide the structure of the successor Transitional Administration and agree on the composition of the cabinet. A huge effort went into preparing for it, with meetings held in all parts of the country to select local representatives, who then went on to vote for delegates to the *jirga* itself. UNAMA, which organized the process, was widely acknowledged as having done a good job, and there is little doubt that the many Afghans and internationals who facilitated the process at the local level were committed to making it a truly democratic process. Nevertheless, given the power relations that prevailed and the lack of law and order in the country, it was inevitable that the process came under significant pressure from local power holders. This included intimidation, the exclusion of women and, in some cases, direct violence. Many Afghans were extraordinarily brave in standing up to this, and helped to ensure that the elected delegates did in the end represent a range of political, religious and ethnic interests within Afghan society. In addition to the elected delegates there were additional appointed delegates; while some of these were also selected through equitable processes, such as the representatives from refugee communities, many appointees were representatives of military factions, and were responsible for much of the intimidation that went on during the meeting. Despite all the problems, however, 'It was', said a woman interviewed in the north in the summer of 2002, 'the most democratic thing Afghanistan has ever seen'.

Sadly, democracy stopped at the door to the tent where the *loya jirga* was convened in Kabul. This was largely due to behind-the-scenes orchestration, but was exacerbated by procedural confusion and poor chairing. The exact substance of decisions to be made had been vague since Bonn, and this lack of clarity was exploited by those wanting to adjust the agenda to suit their own ends. The problem was compounded by the fact that the Loya Jirga Commission failed to produce clear procedural rules. The result was several agenda-less days, chaotic speakers' lists and delegates frustrated at not knowing what, when or how they were to decide issues. Delegates were given little opportunity seriously to address the issues before them. The *loya jirga* was seen by many to have been manipulated, particularly in the way in which the king was prevented from standing for office. This not only cast a shadow over the legitimacy of the event but also raised questions about the whole political process. 'If they stopped the king from being elected,' said a group of village elders, 'how can we believe in free and fair elections?' Finally, the move towards greater representation that so many had hoped for did not happen, and power remained largely in the hands of Shura e Nazar.

Despite the evident problems with the process, the international community seemed unwilling to present it as anything but an unconditional success. Even though many UN staff in the field were themselves critical of the manner in which the delegates had been intimidated, or how the meeting had been chaired, these views were suppressed by a system that seemed unwilling to rock the boat. The UN Under-Secretary-General for Political Affairs acknowledged irregularities in the *loya jirga* process but went on to call on the Afghan authorities to 'address instances where democratic rights have been abused by those who still equated power with violence and force' (UN 2002b). Given that a number of those now in power were responsible for the abuse, his words were little comfort to those who looked to the United Nations to censure those responsible.

The constitutional process The pattern of manipulation that was started with the Emergency Loya Jirga continued with the constitutional process. The Bonn agreement provided for the setting up of a Constitutional Commission within two months of the establishment of the Transitional Administration. The ATA, however, chose not to establish this at once but to start by appointing a nine-person technical drafting committee. The committee, it was proposed, would work for up to six months producing a draft of the new constitution, which would then be put before a larger commission of up to thirty-five members prior to being submitted to the Constitutional Loya Jirga. Following on from the experience of the ELJ, this departure from the terms of the Bonn agreement immediately gave rise to suspicions that the constitutional drafting process would be manipulated.

The manner in which the process was handled thereafter served only to increase those suspicions. For a long time there was uncertainty as to how the delegates to the CLJ would be selected. In the end they were chosen from the larger pool of delegates to the ELJ. Given the intimidation that stifled participation at the ELJ itself, a number of delegates stated that they did not feel it was worth the risk of standing again.

Public consultations on the constitution took place in June and July 2003, but through a questionnaire rather than on the basis of a draft of the proposed constitution. Although such a draft was widely known to exist, and critiques of it were circulating, the official reluctance to release it inevitably gave rise to speculation that there was something to hide. Had an open-ended consultation on broad ideas and principles been held in 2002, before the drafting process started, people could have understood it as informing the work of the drafting committee. To hold such a process when it was known that a draft had been prepared fuelled fears of another stitch-up.

Despite the fact that the consultative process was an integral element of the transition, the entire operation was rushed, which affected both the extent of outreach (UN 2003c) and the way in which discussions were handled in the focus groups that were convened. Many community leaders were, it seems, never consulted at all. With limited public education on the issues, certainly outside of Kabul, many of those who were consulted found the questionnaire perplexing in the extreme. As a respected headteacher in a village near Bagram explained, 'These are very complex issues that they are asking us to comment on in weeks. It would take me much longer to respond, maybe months, after reflection and discussion with my people.'

People talk of meetings that were little more than lectures from local power-brokers, who warned the participants (and in some cases the facilitators) not to challenge their views. A friend who heads an NGO which had been commissioned to undertake consultations in Helmand was hauled in by UNAMA political officers in Kabul to explain why two Taliban had been allowed to participate in consultations that his staff had held, in the belief that they should be as inclusive as possible. The UN were, it seems, unimpressed by his assurances that the two had contributed to a lively debate on the role of Islamic law.

In the end, however, the consultative process probably made little difference to the final document. Between the end of September 2003, when the Constitutional Review Commission submitted its final draft to President Karzai, and 3 November, when the draft was first released to the public, substantial changes were made. The most important of these were to concentrate more power in the presidency, and it was clear even before the CLJ started that this was the model that was going to be pushed through; the only question was what price would have to be paid for its acceptance. The final product was, as it was always going to be, the result of deals made between Karzai and his US backers and the *jihadi* groups.

As before, the evident problems were glossed over. Minister of Finance Ashraf Ghani, writing in the *Financial Times* (1 April 2004), described the adoption of the constitution as 'the third big step in empowering the people'. In an editorial, the *Washington Post* (24 December 2003) described how the delegates 'have spent the past 10 days peacefully debating the draft of a new constitution that would make Afghanistan an electoral democracy for the first time in its history'.

The constitution certainly has positive aspects. It explicitly recognizes women as well as men as citizens of Afghanistan and with equal rights and duties under the law. It provides for the election of at least two women from every province to the Wolesi Jirga (House of the People), giving a minimum of 25 per cent of women in the house – far more than in most western democracies. It recognizes the country's various minority groups and for the first time in an Afghan constitution allows for the use of Shi'a jurisprudence in matters of personal law. Hanafi jurisprudence retains the residual role it was given in the 1964 constitution (that is, used when there are no other laws or articles of the constitution governing the matter in question) and Shi'a law for the first time is recognized in relation to disputes involving only Shi'as. This provision had been under attack by conservatives who had wanted Hanafi jurisprudence as the sole source of law. However, much in the constitution is very general and will be referred to the courts for interpretation. It is here that the price for the acceptance of the strong presidency will be paid. The Supreme Court is run by conservative Islamists, who appeared to have gained power over the judiciary in the bargaining that went on over their support for the more liberal provisions of the final constitution.

Elections 'Free and fair' elections are the intended culmination of the process set in motion at Bonn. They are also the holy grail of western transition formulas, providing moral cover for exit: 'hold an election and withdraw from and abandon the territory', as one analyst put it (Chopra 2002). Yet as a route to peace they have proved deeply problematic. From Sierra Leone to Angola, elections that have been held too early have served only to return the country to war.

Elections that are free and fair entail the right and the opportunity to choose one thing over another. This implies certain conditions. It means that both voters and candidates should have freedom of movement, assembly, association and speech, as well as freedom from intimidation. Rules must be set and then applied in an unbiased fashion, the distribution of resources among competitors should be reasonably equal, there needs to be an independent electoral authority, impartial voter education, fair media access, secure polling stations and ballot boxes and appropriate, transparent scrutiny procedures that might be subject to review (Elklit and Svensson 1997). None of these is achievable in the current situation in Afghanistan.

The electoral system itself will need to allow for representation of Afghanistan's diversity, and give all contenders for power enough of a stake in the system that they remain bound to democratic politics. First-past-the-post systems, which exaggerate the rewards to the winner, clearly cannot achieve this. Given the factionalized nature of Afghan politics, the primary goal should be to produce reasonable proportionality, by which each group secures a proportion of seats broadly in accordance with the number of votes received. In addition, the widespread distrust of political parties requires that voters should be given the chance to vote for individuals, rather than only parties. Voting procedure will also need to be simple and transparent; illiteracy and innumeracy limit the complexity of possible voting systems, and inexperience with voting also means that results must be easily explicable.

Successful electoral processes build on a culture in which elections are seen as a legitimate means of constituting a leadership, and outcomes are therefore accepted even by those who find them disappointing (Kumar and Ottaway 1998). Such cultures cannot be conjured up overnight.

Competitive elections are not part of Afghan culture (see Chapter 2) and the notion of political opposition as an end in itself is meaningless, for the opposition needs to be able to deliver something to its constituency if it is to have legitimacy (Edwards 2002). The idea of voluntarily ceding power, or that political control might only be temporary, is unfamiliar. Most of those who currently hold power in Afghanistan came to it by the gun, and persuading them to give it up to the ballot box will not be easy.

While democratic mechanisms can be an effective means of managing conflict, holding elections too early could undermine the entire transition, destabilizing the fragile equilibrium between factions and plunging the country back into war. Election campaigns typically produce intense political contention, and in fragile polities can increase distrust between parties, tempting them to step outside the framework of constitutional politics if they emerge from the voting as losers. Nor can the entire burden of change be placed on an election. Experience from recent post-conflict elections shows that big shifts in power can easily result in a return to war. The move towards a more broad-based government needs to have started before the election, and politically there are strong arguments for moving into an electoral phase only after other key tasks of state-building have been successfully accomplished (Ottaway and Lieven 2002; Snyder 2000).

Building state failure

'State building requires both a legal framework and the political relations that support it' (Malikyar and Rubin 2002). By the beginning of 2004, more than two years after the signing of the Bonn agreement, there had been the beginnings of the legal framework through the new constitution, but little serious effort to sort out the underlying political relations. Instead, the provisions of the Bonn agreement – the ELJ, CLJ and finally elections – seem to have been treated as a series of events that have to be organized, to be ticked off as markers passed. Passing the milestones has in itself been hailed as a sign of the legitimization of the centre, and this has been allowed to conceal the fitful nature of the political process. The energy that has been put into the moulding of the Kabul administration has been at the expense of consideration of how legitimacy might be achieved at the local level, and how this might result in a more robust state structure. The need to create a political space in which people can express their views free of intimidation has been largely ignored.

The experience of the second major milestone of the transition, the Constitutional Loya Jirga, leaves one wondering whether it made any sense to invest such resources in deciding a new constitution at a time when there was still no security in the country and no rule of law. A constitution alone cannot solve Afghanistan's problems. There remains a fundamental struggle for power in the country, and until that is resolved any form of constitution may well be meaningless. Just how meaningless was demonstrated within ten days of the endorsement of the constitution, when a broadcast performance by the Afghan singer Salma saw the deputy Chief Justice Fazl Ahmad Manawi declare, 'We are opposed to women singing and dancing as a whole and it has to be stopped'. That this view was expressed while there was no case before the courts, and was based on no existing law, suggests that a strict interpretation of the clause in the new constitution that states that no law should be contrary to the 'beliefs and provisions' of Islam could easily wipe out the gains apparently made for women in the process (*New York Times*, 26 January 2004).

This came after the experience during the CLJ of Malalai Joya. Malalai, a twenty-five-year-old female delegate from the south-western province of Farah, stood up early in the proceedings to denounce the *mujahideen* leaders as criminals, suggesting that they should be tried in an international court for their deeds against 'bare-footed Afghans'. She spoke for the feelings of many, and in the days that followed many ordinary men and women in Kabul spoke of her as the 'new Malalai', in reference to the famous heroine who rallied the Pashtun forces against the British troops at the Battle of Maiwand in 1880. Some in the tent, however, were outraged and called for her to withdraw her claims, while the chairman, Sibghatullah Mojaddedi, tried to have her expelled from the convention. In the end, she had to be placed under UN protection. Malalai's fate was a disturbing reminder of the threats issued by the same people against a member of the ELJ Commission who also had to be bundled out of the ELJ and provided with UN protection after having been too outspoken in his criticisms.

Both incidents seem to point to the international community's unwillingness to confront the impunity of factional leaders. The political manoeuvring that has gone on to reach agreement has in many ways further entrenched the warlords as part of Afghanistan's political landscape. All of the real decisions were made behind closed doors, through negotiations with the men with the guns. It does not bode well for democracy and it does little to render the transitional administration legitimate in the eyes of its people.

In opting for a purely presidential system, the constitution does little to provide for meaningful democratic governance, for any form of power sharing or for a system of checks and balances. It is true that in the current situation it is easy to see problems with *any* form of constitution. A parliamentary system could result in an unstable government, and a semi-presidential system with a strong prime minister could increase the likelihood of conflict between two rival power centres. Yet the presidential system carries enormous risks. The concentration of power in the hands of one person is potentially dangerous in an unstable political situation as it increases the rewards of illegitimate capture of the presidency, and thus heightens the risk of this happening.

For a presidential system to work well there needs to be trust in the electoral process, for this is the principal brake on the unbridled power of the head of state. Given the lack of security, the intimidation that has accompanied both the ELJ and CLJ processes, and the fact that electoral politics has never really been part of Afghan political life, this trust is unlikely to exist in the early years of the new government. By driving this particular model through, the USA either has a peculiar blindness about systems other than its own, and the risks that such a system faces in Afghanistan, or it is determined to ensure that it takes control of Afghan politics; it must also be convinced that it has the means to manipulate the electoral outcome, and that its man will stay alive.

While the constitutional process seems to have consolidated the position of the technocratic, modernizing Pashtun element within the administration, there is little guarantee that this will either result in more effective government or bring better security. This element is a Kabul-based elite, out of touch with many of its own people, in conflict with other groups, and wholly reliant on US power. America may have supported the technocrats for their professional competence and (for the most part) freedom from corruption. It may also have been a result of belated US efforts to take action on some of the perceived problems of warlord power within the government, and in particular to try to marginalize Fahim. However, if the USA pursues what becomes seen as Pashtun dominance, it risks deepening ethnic divisions within the country. This increases the chances of the formation of an anti-Pashtun (and by implication anti-US) bloc on the old basis of 'the enemy of my enemy is my friend'. Rather than promoting reconciliation and building a truly strong state, the outcome of the CLJ risks sowing the seed of deeper alienation.

'Why should I vote?' By the beginning of 2004 it was abundantly clear that none of the prerequisites for a successful election could be in place in time for elections in June, as was envisaged in the Bonn agreement. Not only had the basic elements of state building not been accomplished, but there was little progress on the procedures that needed to be put in place if an election were to be viable. Reliable census data were not available, electoral districts were disputed and the country still had to adopt an electoral law. Yet it was a shortfall in the $122 million required for the registration exercise (UN 2003c), rather than more fundamental issues, that for a long time was portrayed as the major constraint to the electoral process.

The UN had began to draft in international volunteers to supervise voter registration in November 2003, but by late January 2004 only some 500,000 out of the 10 million Afghans eligible to vote had actually registered,[3] and only twenty out of the planned seventy supervisors had in fact been fielded.[4] Yet somehow the process continued to be portrayed as being on track. The very fact that by the beginning of 2004 the registration process was confined to eight urban centres, in a country where three-quarters of the population lives in rural areas, should have called into question the reality of the timetable.

The most important issue in deciding whether to go ahead with elections in 2004 should clearly be an assessment of whether they would push Afghanistan's peace process forward by reinforcing participation and the legitimacy of the central government, or back by upsetting the fragile equilibrium that currently exists between the factions. Although there are concerns that prolonging the life of the ATA by postponing elections could bring back memories of Rabbani's attempts to hang on to power during the mid-1990s, the greater danger is that an election held in poor security and without adequate preparation risks triggering more conflict.

As early as July 2003, the UN acknowledged that 'blocked access to even a few key districts, as is currently the case, would compromise the outcome of the process as a whole' (UN 2003c). Yet no one in Qandahar we spoke to in February 2004 felt elections could take place in more than about half of the districts in the south. Even the UN's Special Representative, Lakhdar Brahimi, whose mission was mandated to oversee the process, had by the time of his departure in early 2004 concluded that 'elections should not be organized as long as armed factions are in control of the country'.[5] This followed his unusually frank admission of the risks in an interview with the *Financial Times* a month earlier, when he said that 'if you know an election is going to blow the whole place up, you don't do it just for the sake of respecting a deadline'.

Yet throughout 2003 and the early part of 2004, the Americans pushed hard for elections to be held according to the timetable agreed at Bonn. As it was already far too late to overcome the basic procedural obstacles to having a full election for some form of national assembly, direct presidential elections were presented as some form of compromise. Yet an election for a single position, with no means of balancing the power this gives, is the process most likely to increase tension in the country.

For many Afghans we spoke to, as for many international commentators, it seemed that the driving force had less to do with Afghanistan than how elections would serve George Bush's need for a success story in time for the US presidential elections. Then suddenly, in mid-February 2004, the USA changed tack and having pushed elections for so long seemed to be having second thoughts. On 16 February the *New York Times* ran an article entitled, 'US Aides Hint Afghan Voting May Be Put Off', which claimed that the Bush administration had begun 'suggesting' that Afghanistan's elections 'may have to be postponed because of security problems and failure to register enough voters'. On the same day, the *Washington Post* also ran an article about elections, reporting on the slowness of preparations and the dangers of increased ethnic tensions if presidential elections went ahead without a parliament to balance the president's power. It quoted a registration worker in Kabul saying, 'We are all 100 percent sure it will have to be delayed, but that's not a problem. If after 23 years of war, if a delay is in the interests of the nation, nobody will mind' (Constable 2004a).

Many Afghans, not surprisingly, feel deeply cynical about what is going on. Asked what she thought about many women not being able to vote for cultural reasons, a thoughtful and highly educated Pashtun friend replied:

> Why should I vote? By what means will these people be selected to be candidates? Who will they represent? This election is for you not for us. You will have it and then you will go, leaving us with a system that has no roots in our country. You can grow new systems, yes, but it takes time; they need to put down roots. And the Pashtun women in the countryside, they will be herded like cattle to the voting stations. They will be just voting fodder. What meaning does this have?

Enduring security?

> Without genuine and lasting security in Afghanistan, nothing will be possible, let alone the establishment of a new government. (SRSG Brahimi, briefing to the UN Security Council, New York, 13 November 2001)

> Security sector reform, in short, is the basic pre-requisite to re-creating the nation that today's parents hope to leave for future generations. (Hamid Karzai, Kabul, 30 July 2003)

We now know that our future security, wherever we are, depends on Afghanistan's security. (Jaap de Hoop Scheffer, NATO Secretary General, Kabul, 8 February 2004)

Over and over again Afghans say the security transition is *the* priority, the single most important thing that needs to happen in their country. It has, to date, been a failure. As a result, the country is slipping back into a familiar pattern, with the state in effective control of only the capital and a few other towns, and with tenuous negotiated control over the roads that link them. Many reasons have been put forward as to why this is so: it has been because of the intransigence of the Ministry of Defence, the interference of regional states, the slow pace of reconstruction and delivery, and growing Pashtun disaffection (Sedra 2003). All of which is true enough – but so is the fact that all of these factors were entirely predictable. Despite this, donors and the UN embarked on a process of planning for the reform of the security sector that seemed not to take into account the realities, and clearly had no strategies for dealing with them.

The problem would seem to lie in a mixture of politics and incompetence. The imagining of a peace agreement led easily into the imagining that the process of disarmament and the formation of a national army would follow. The need to present the defeat of the Taliban as a definitive victory obscured the fact that there was still a war going on in the country. Indeed, as explored in Chapter 1, attempts by the USA simultaneously to pursue that war and build a peace continue to be incompatible, and represent one of the greatest obstacles to effecting a successful security transition.

Security sector reform in Afghanistan centres on five 'pillars', agreed in Geneva in April 2002, each with its own donor lead: military reform (USA), police reform (Germany), disarmament and demobilization (Japan) counter-narcotics (UK) and judicial reform (Italy). While few would have imagined that the progress in each of these sectors might be easy in such circumstances, the patchy performance of certain lead countries, coupled with an acute lack of coordination, has held the overall process hostage as much as any resistance from key power-brokers.

Just as has been the case in the support they provided for reconstruction, donors have chosen to select an aspect of security sector reform that they choose to fund, often with little consideration as to its relevance to the wider goals of the process (Rubin et al. 2003). While Germany seems to have provided an effective lead in supporting training of officers for an eventual national police force, confidence in the process of reform has been affected by the disparities in levels of pay offered by different donors, some of whom have declined to pay 'their' police at all (Goodhand and Bergne 2003). With a government wage of US$30, this almost ensures that corruption, which deeply undermines the credibility of the force, continues. As a senior police official in Mazar in 2003 put it: 'I have four children, they are all at school. Each child needs at least 1,000 Afghanis a month; tell me, how can I not be corrupt? We cannot live on 1,500 Afghanis [US$30] a month – it is not possible.'

The Law and Order Trust Fund that was set up to pool contributions for security sector reform, including police salaries, had by July 2003 received pledges of only $40 million out of the $120 million requested, with actual contributions significantly lower still. As in other sectors, the initial focus of reforms has been on Kabul, so trainees from outside the capital have been expected to return to unreformed police forces in the provinces, where their effectiveness is limited (UN 2003b).

The lack of coherence in the way that support is being offered by the international community is, however, not the only obstacle to police reform. In an attempt to reduce Shura e Nazar dominance of the administration, Yunis Qanooni, Minister of Interior in the Interim Administration, was persuaded to step down at the Emergency Loya Jirga. He was replaced by the elderly Wardak, but was then given a new position as Special Adviser on Security, from which he called the shots through his network within the factionalized police force. With Wardak clearly ineffective, Ali Ahmad Jalali, a US-trained military professional, was persuaded to return from the USA to take up the post of minister in February 2003. Since then he has repeatedly challenged factional interests but with only limited success, and their continuing resistance still slows down the pace of reform. Just as with the dispute about control of regional customs revenue, the battle-lines seem to be drawn within the Transitional Administration between powerful factional interests and the westernized, technocratic elements who are the strongest advocates of security sector reform (Rubin 2003a).

Given the layers of self-interest that prevail, there is clearly a need for a convincing deterrent – the robust force posture[6] that was advocated in the landmark Brahimi report on UN peacekeeping – if real change is to take place. This is a view shared by the Afghans who, with a wry reference to the much-feared department that enforced the strict regulations of the Taliban, continue to refer to the B-52 bombers that were used in the early stages of the US military campaign as 'vice and virtue'. The next element of deterrence that was put in place, as foreseen under the Bonn agreement and mandated by UNSC resolution

1386, was the deployment of the International Security Assistance Force (ISAF) to Kabul.

Keeping the peace Squatting beside the main road between Kabul and the north on an icy day in December 2001 with a group of elders from a village near Qarabagh, the discussion centred on how they had dug possessions out of the ruins of their homes that had been flattened by the US bombing of the nearby frontlines. This was the road along which the departing Soviet troops had finally left, and that we had used to reach areas outside government control during the early 1990s. It was also a route along which many returning refugees from Pakistan had subsequently travelled, only to be forced out of their homes by the Taliban, who in 1999 embarked on a scorched-earth policy in areas close to the frontlines. It was therefore with some curiosity that we watched a line of camouflaged Land-Rovers – with apologetically small Union Jack stickers in the front windscreens – approach. There were tense expressions on the faces of the squaddies who peered at us through the tinted windscreens, and we waved at them from the roadside so that they might feel more at home. At this, the front vehicle stopped, and a side-window opened a crack. Given that there was only one road to Kabul, we assumed that they did not need directions. As we walked towards the convoy to see if they needed assistance, a voice from inside the vehicle barked out: 'I say, are you all right?' 'Yes, fine – are you? Perhaps you'd like to come and meet our Afghan friends, and explain why you're here.' There was no response, and the window was quickly rolled up, before the vehicle accelerated away, to be followed by the rest of the convoy. Returning to the perplexed group of village elders, it only remained to try to explain that this was in fact the vanguard of international peacekeeping in Afghanistan. ISAF had arrived.

Contrary to undertakings that had been made to the USA, once the Taliban retreat began the forces of Shura e Nazar moved quickly from the north to occupy all major installations in the city. By the time the ISAF peacekeepers rolled into Kabul, they were faced with the option of fulfilling their mandate to de-militarize the city, which would mean dislodging Shura e Nazar troops by force, or accepting the status quo. They chose the latter, in a move that clearly signalled a lack of international resolve that continues to dog the security transition. Apprehensive at the return of armed factional fighters to the streets, Kabulis looked to ISAF to ensure that the city did not lapse back into the lawlessness they had witnessed between 1992 and 1996. For this to happen, they knew that ISAF must confront Shura e Nazar forces. The

British commander of ISAF acknowledged in January 2002 that factional fighters were more of a risk to Kabul's security than the remnants of al-Qa'eda and the Taliban, yet the failure of his force to de-militarize the city effectively at this early stage allowed factional interests again to become entrenched. As an elder in the western district of Dashte Barchi – where the looting, some say, is as bad as when it lay between factional frontlines in the mid-1990s – put it: 'The commanders run circles around the peacekeepers. They loot and rape at night, and discuss security with ISAF by day.'

While many would agree that ISAF has made an important contribution to building public confidence, Kabulis can be forgiven for wondering whether this is in fact enough. It clearly was not enough for those students of Kabul University, involved in November 2002 in a peaceful protest about poor living conditions, who were assaulted and arrested by the secret police as ISAF looked on. The failure of both ISAF and the UN to act, despite requests from the Afghan Independent Human Rights Commission, on alleged threats issued by intelligence agents against wounded students who were hospitalized hardly suggests a robust approach towards abuses of rights by factional elements within the administration. The Military Technical Agreement which sets out the terms of engagement for ISAF envisages the establishment of 'a stable and secure environment in Kabul and the vicinity'. While their hi-tech displays of force on the city's streets are welcome, the credibility of ISAF will hinge on their willingness to live up to their responsibilities and deal with lawlessness and intimidation, especially from factional elements within the Transitional Administration.

The original aim of the deployment of peacekeepers to Kabul was to secure the space in which the transitional process could unfold. The transfer of the command of ISAF to NATO during the summer of 2003 coincided with a growing number of calls – most notably by the UNSRSG in July 2003 – for the 'ISAF effect' to be extended to fill the security gap in other parts of the country (UN 2003b). If the international community saw fit to provide a peacekeeper for every fifty Kosovans, it was argued, how could one peacekeeper per five thousand Afghans be effective? (CARE 2003). The experience of ISAF in Kabul, however, raises questions as to whether more peacekeepers will in fact be able to ensure an effective security transition in other parts of the country.

Notes

1 'Agreement on Provisional Arrangements in Afghanistan Pending the Re-establishment of Permanent Government Institutions', 5 December 2001.

2 Interview with UN Special Rapporteur on Housing, IRIN, September 2003.

3 UN News Centre, 22 January 2004.

4 IRIN News, 5 February 2004.

5 UN Wire, 28 January 2004.

6 Acknowledging the need for peacekeepers to do more than bear witness, but also act as a credible deterrent to the warring parties (UN A/55/305-S/2000/809, August 2000).

The state: who is in control?

One of the most important questions facing any state is what kind of economy the country will have. It is a question that ought to be the subject of heated policy debate, yet in Afghanistan there has never been a whisper that there might be alternatives to the thinking of the international financial institutions, which moved to ensure that they were in a position to influence the country's economic development before the Bonn agreement was even signed.

Since the Soviet invasion, the World Bank had kept only a watching brief on the country and the Asian Development Bank had not even had that, but this did not deter them from asserting their role from the start. At the end of November 2002, together with the United Nations Development Programme (UNDP), they organized a conference in Islamabad to consider the future of Afghanistan, which paved the way for the formulation of a joint preliminary needs assessment. Both authors participated in the UN team for the assessment – an experience that was to prove instructive. The exercise, which aimed to produce a report outlining national rehabilitation needs for presentation at a donors' meeting in Tokyo by January 2002, faced enormous constraints, not least of which were restrictions on access to the country. Nevertheless, there existed in many people a real commitment to seizing an opportunity to help draw attention to the situation facing Afghans. Whatever we felt about the way in which the situation had come about, few of us doubted that this was the best chance for peace that Afghanistan had had for many years.

After a series of preparatory meetings, a draft report was produced that looked at Afghanistan's needs holistically, rather than along the conventional sectoral approach. This, we believed, was how Afghans lived their lives and how services could best be delivered by a low-income state, particularly to scattered rural communities. Moreover, we (naively, as it turned out) felt that such a framework would provide a basis for a much deeper process of consultation with Afghans at provincial and district level as a means of harnessing the immense energy that existed for peace and reconstruction. This approach was endorsed by the World Bank and

UNDP. They had not, however, reckoned with the Asian Development Bank, whose staff in Manila were determined to keep to the old ways of working, and who restructured it into sectors while the other two team-leaders were in Kabul consulting the authorities. It was not just an issue of presentation, however, for one of the consequences of this change was that ordinary Afghans were never consulted – at least not in a way that enabled them to decide whether scarce resources should go first into education, or roads, or agricultural extension. In follow-up missions choices were only ever presented within sectors, resulting in a stream of specialists visiting communities, largely near Kabul, often to ask the same basic questions.

Meanwhile, the international financial institutions were soon lending and making grants in all sectors in Afghanistan, from health and education to transport and communications. The International Monetary Fund looked into fast-track reforms in the Central Bank, while a band of international consultants set up offices in the Ministry of Finance. Western interests were soon shaping all aspects of policy development.

Given the limited capacity that existed in the Afghan administration, it was inevitable that external advisers would play an important role, yet the extent to which policy was set by people who knew nothing about Afghanistan was frightening. It could have been anywhere. That political, social and economic history is important in determining what is possible in a country was not part of the thinking; it was simply cut and paste. Many of those responsible for the writing hardly left their offices in Kabul, and never ventured outside the city. Some of them hardly stayed long enough for the entry stamp to dry in their passports. Breaking off an interview to attend a press briefing for the launch of the new Afghan currency in autumn 2002, the governor of the Central Bank was approached by a young consultant from the Adam Smith Institute and asked for a briefing on the economy. Clearly irritated, his words were sharp: 'Why do you keep sending new people? You are the third person in a month. You come, I spend time with you, you stay a couple of weeks, and then you go again and someone else comes. We do not have the time to act like this, to keep telling new people how it is. Stay and learn something, only then can you help.'

The reliance on external consultants was also driven by the agendas of donors. Hoops had to be jumped through to get funds and layers of oversight consultants were designed into projects to ensure money did not go astray. While concern with transparency and accountability is understandable, it seemed that the processes were designed to meet the needs not of Afghanistan but of the donors, whose systems were

10 *Curious villagers in the war-torn Shamali plain surround a UN convoy, 1993. (Jolyon Leslie)*

simply too complicated and expectations of quick-delivery too fast for the existing structures. Given the chronic lack of capacity at all levels, it inevitably resulted in ownership being taken away from the people of the country, despite all the fine words in the mission statements of donors or agencies.

The US move, announced in the wake of the invasion of Iraq, dramatically to scale up its reconstruction assistance to Afghanistan has brought yet another wave of consultant advisers to the ministries, whose budgets have been quickly revised upwards in the hope of attracting US largesse. Meanwhile, the clan of contractors who dominate the bidding processes have begun head-hunting Afghan staff. An acquaintance who had recently returned home to Kabul from Europe to head up a technical department, where she is finding it difficult to find resources to retain her staff, was taken out to dinner by one of the largest contractors and offered a monthly consultancy fee that was more than the quarterly operational budget for her entire department.

Along with the money and the projects came an unseemly haste to write everything anew. It was as if everything from the past either no longer existed or was simply bad. While there may be much that is wrong with the inherited policies in Afghanistan, the rush to rewrite them all in the space of a couple of years, before there is any political stability in the country, let alone a legitimate government, shows little concern for the democratic process.

Meanwhile, the real interests of the international financial institutions became clear in their attitude to debt relief. By 2002, Afghanistan had accumulated arrears of $45 million for loans made in the pre 1979 period. Rather than forgive these and start anew, the institutions insisted that all loans be paid off before there could be any new lending. This was done using money donors provided by the Afghan Reconstruction Trust Fund, a total of $56.9 million being settled by February 2003 (Carlin 2003). Interestingly, the World Bank at the same time claimed that: 'Another risk, which could impact on World Bank assistance to Afghanistan, would materialize if *forgiveness of bilateral debts is less generous than hoped, reducing the debt-sustainability of planned/pledge concessional lending to Afghanistan by IFIs*' (World Bank 2003 – emphasis in original). So, it seems, bilateral donors are meant to forgive the monies owed to them and also pay up for the money owed to international financial institutions.

The privatized economy The key document articulating the thinking on the economy is the National Development Framework (NDF), and its successor the National Development Budget (NDB). Here the goal is clearly spelt out as one of economic growth, and the private sector is seen as the route to that growth. According to the budget document, 'a competitive private sector becomes the engine of growth' and also, 'the instrument of social inclusion'. The government's role is seen as promotion of the private sector, including 'the use of external assistance to build the physical infrastructure that lays the basis for a private-sector led strategy of growth'.

While few would dispute that growth is important, unless it leads to a reduction in poverty it will not bring stability; and unless it occurs in a regulated manner it is more likely to result in a criminalized state than a democratic and socially inclusive one. Ever since the preliminary needs assessment, the rollback of the government has been promoted as a vital condition for market reform. Yet in many ways what Afghanistan needs at the moment is not *less* state but *more*. The country is currently one big free-trade zone, with a nation of traders well able to take advantage of any opportunities going. The state, far from having too much control, has too little. The absence of regulatory frameworks is already leading to political power being pursued through control of markets and accumulation, as has been seen in other parts of the world (Stiglitz 2002). Furthermore, if Afghanistan is fortunate enough to attract foreign investment – and this is by no means certain – it needs to happen in a regulated manner. Unregulated investment carries a heavy risk of bringing instability to the economy, as money flows in and out in pursuit of quick profits. The NDF does make reference to the government being a regulator, but at present there is little sign of this being put into action; it has the air of necessary rhetoric rather than realistic policy.

Privatization Both the NDF and NDB lay a heavy emphasis on privatization, making it clear that as the Afghan private sector lacks capacity, international firms are seen by the administration as its partners in all the major projects. Any policy of screening international firms is quite clearly ruled out of order. It is, it seems, open season. As part of this drive, the government will 'assist in the reconstruction of key industries', if necessary 'dispos[ing] of other assets' in order that privatization may go ahead. For example, Afghanistan's priorities in energy and mining include: to facilitate private sector management and investment in the sector, in part by privatizing most state-owned enterprises in that sector (ii); to assist in the reconstruction of key industries ... where such industries can be run by the private sector on a viable basis (iv); and supporting the construction of gas and other energy pipelines (v). The government will also be responsible for 'ensuring private sector involvement in telephone, IT and media areas' and will 'privatize the public transport fleet, and in time the national airline' (Transitional Government of Afghanistan 2002).

Privatization has long been one of the three pillars of economic orthodoxy in relation to the developing world; a policy pushed on poor nations by the World Bank, the International Monetary Fund and the US Treasury, whether they like it or not. While in some cases it can make sense, applied as a blanket formula it rarely has much to offer. In place after place it has been shown that privatization undertaken too early can be a disaster. Without regulatory frameworks and competition it all too often leads not to growth but to asset-stripping, not to benefits to consumers but simply to high prices. The advocates for privatization argue that these other things can come later, but once a vested interest has set in, it has the incentive and the resources to maintain its position, and will distort the political process in order to do so (Stiglitz 2002). While the World Bank and others suggest that privatization can be the answer to both government inefficiency and corruption, the evidence is that if a government is corrupt privatization will not solve the problem. Indeed, privatization processes have often simply served to make government ministers very rich indeed (Reno 1999). And despite the trust placed in the private sector by the authors of the National Development Framework, the evidence is that privatization without regulation has no effect on growth (Stiglitz 2002).

The International Monetary Fund reports that Afghanistan currently has eighty state-owned enterprises, none of which is profitable, or even self-sustaining. Nevertheless, they are still public assets and should not be just sold off cheaply to make a few people wealthy, as happened in Russia and many of the ex-Soviet countries. The new investment laws being proposed contain no guarantees that the assets will not be stripped, nor that 'corporatized' foreign-owned privatized industries will not simply take advantage of tax breaks to repatriate profits. The problem is likely to be particularly acute in the natural resources sector where, rather than using the wealth these represent to support investment and development, the new owners might simply take the opportunity to appropriate the quick profits to be made. Current forms of extraction of timber, gems and natural gas – along, of course, with the narcotics industry – allow people to become rich without investing anything. Consequently they do nothing to foster long-term economic growth. While the new constitution affirms that these resources belong to the state, it says nothing of how they might be developed.

Attracting them in ... In its wish to attract private capital the government seems set to remove all forms of control. The National Development Framework promises to 'not consider any philosophy which is based on screening and approval of foreign investment applications', to apply a 'low company tax rate to all investors', and to 'establish a free trade regime with low and predictable tariffs'. In pursuit of more private sector economic activity in Afghanistan, the government passed a new law on Domestic and Foreign Private Investment, which grants tax waivers on investments, exempts all exports from taxes for the first four years of production, and allows for tax-free repatriation of funds (Carlin 2003). The previous requirement that investors deposit $50,000 to obtain a commercial licence, and that domestic investors deposit half the value of the proposed investment, has been abolished. As a result, unscrupulous business people would be free to run if their business got into trouble, leaving both workers and creditors unpaid.

While lifting trade barriers certainly suits the rich world, how well it will serve Afghanistan is another issue. As with privatization, dismantling all barriers in the early stages of a country's development is not the way to encourage growth. Those countries that have been successful in lifting themselves out of poverty have done so behind barriers of protection, which have only been lifted as development progressed. Successful developing countries like those of East Asia opened themselves to the outside world slowly, and in a sequenced way. They phased barriers out only after jobs had been created, and they took a role in promoting enterprises. China is only just dismantling barriers now, twenty years after it started its march to the market. Russia, by contrast, rushed to dismantle all controls; but globalization did not produce the promised results, it brought only unprecedented poverty. For Afghanistan, sitting close to the advanced economies of China and India, there will be little chance for indigenous firms to become established if there is no protection for the early stages of their development.

Moreover, foreign inward investment has often undermined democratic processes in countries because it flourishes on privileges granted by government or, more accurately, bribed government officials (Stiglitz 2002). Already the rot is setting in. 'You cannot get a contract in Afghanistan unless you pay a bribe,' said an old friend with his own engineering practice. 'And I will not do it,' he continued, 'so I don't get much work.'

As a strategy for growth, the pursuit of private capital is doubly flawed. Not only does it bring a host of problems, but there is not even much evidence to suggest that foreign capital will invest in peripheral economies, except where they have raw materials that are needed by the global economy. Russia has seen very little outside investment except in energy. Sub-Saharan Africa, with the exception of South Africa, has seen almost none at all except in key raw materials and exotic tourism (Duffield 2001b). Afghanistan currently seems to be going the same way.

If there is a problem with the too early liberalization of trade, there is an even greater problem with premature liberalization of capital and financial markets. Foreign banks have a primary commitment to their shareholders, and once a country encounters problems will start to pull in their loans, thus exacerbating the difficulties and frequently pushing the country into crisis. It was too rapid liberalization of capital and financial markets that led to the global crises of the 1990s. Worst of all is what is known as 'hot money', which has nothing at all to do with development but which simply speculates on exchange rates. With its financial markets liberalized long before it has a stable economy, Afghanistan lays itself wide open to such abuse. The only interest that will be served is that of the financial market (Stiglitz 2002).

Nor do such banks always provide money where it is needed. The fact that Standard Chartered was the first western bank to establish a branch in Kabul was hailed in 2003 as a significant economic step. But it is difficult to imagine that Standard Chartered will provide the loans that Afghanistan's farmers and small and medium-sized businesses will need if growth is to become a reality. The case of Argentina showed all too clearly how foreign banks can actually contribute to lack of growth. Before the collapse of its economy in 2001, the banking sector was dominated by foreign banks, which lent readily to multinationals, and even to large domestic firms. Small and medium-sized enterprises, meanwhile, faced problems in getting credit and this was a major brake on growth, the lack of which was pivotal in the economic collapse. Bolivia similarly suffered when a major foreign bank pulled back on lending, plunging the country into a deep economic downturn (ibid.).

Privatizing services In the rush to the market economy even the health service is being largely stripped away from the state. Beneath a glowing account of the success of Afghanistan's health policy (*The Lancet*, 13 September 2003) is hidden the fact that the health service has essentially been primed for privatization. Services have been parcelled out to NGOs in performance-based partnerships, with the Ministry of Health as contract manager – and with a residual service delivery role only in those districts where no one else wanted to work. The current 'window' of donor interest, which everyone agrees is unlikely to last for long, is being used not to build up the capacity of the ministry as a deliverer of services or regulator, but as a contract manager. The question of what will happen once donor funding to NGO implementers ends has been glossed over, although a senior UNICEF official privately admitted that the answer is likely to be cost recovery. Yet, as he acknowledged, cost recovery has proved to be notoriously inefficient in poor countries where, in order not to exclude the poor from services, costs have to be set so low that schemes often cost more to administer than they raise in revenue. Neither NGOs nor the private sector are likely to find the provision of healthcare to remote rural areas commercially viable unless the state steps in with funding. And if it does that, then it raises the question as to whether it would be cheaper and more effective to do the job itself, in addition to the legitimacy gained by being seen to provide services for its people.

As significant as the process of privatization itself is the fact that these changes are being made largely without any debate, through which Afghans might have the chance to make a choice on the shape of service provision in their country. The debate that did occur – and it was a long, and at times acrimonious, one – seems to have been essentially between donors about the technicalities of how the performance-based partnership scheme should be set up, not the fundamental question of whether this was the right way to provide the service. In keeping with the 'one size fits all' approach to policy development, this system of health service delivery was decided upon before a World Bank study into provincial-level administration had even set foot in the provinces, far less prepared their report. When the team did finally travel they concluded that local departments were functioning to a much greater extent than had been expected, and that what Afghanistan needed at that time was not to change the way everything was done but to improve the functioning of the existing system.

Once again, past imagery had fuelled both the assumption that 'we know best', and that the state had entirely disintegrated. Years of presenting Afghanistan as a 'failed state' with 'collapsed public services' made it very easy to assume that nothing remained. Yet, of all the ministries, health was the one that remained the most functional. Even through the time of the Taliban, when external support was withheld from most ministries and the UN and NGOs worked largely independently of what would normally be their government counterparts, humanitarian considerations maintained the inflow of funds for health, which helped to ensure that the ministry retained a group of experienced and dedicated medical professionals. The requirement that female health services be provided only by women also ensured that female health staff could continue to work, unlike other ministries. Moreover, a long-standing agreement that government doctors could have a private practice ensured them an income, while retaining them within the public health system. Not only did government hospitals and clinics function, but the ministry itself managed to plan services in cooperation with its implementing partners.

The government's major programme to provide employment opportunities to vulnerable people, while simultaneously improving rural infra structure, has also got caught up in the privatization frenzy. Rather than, as in the past, seeking proposals for works to be undertaken under the programme, all work will now be awarded through a competitive bidding process. It sounds fine, until you realize that in most of rural Afghanistan the key requirements for the market to operate efficiently are simply not there. There is no regulatory framework, and even if such a thing is signed into law in Kabul it will be years before it can become a reality in many areas. There is a complete dearth of information according to which people could make informed decisions; and recommendations on bids are being made by unpaid and poorly qualified officials, for whom the temptation of corruption will be enormous. Yet when we asked whether it might be more sensible to introduce the process in a phased way, we were told that this government would not countenance such a thing, everything had to be done everywhere at once; no matter that the government does not have the means and the plans are ill conceived. It seemed oddly reminiscent of the Khalqis.

Rolling back the state The push to roll back the functions of state extends well beyond the provision of conventional public services, to new programmes that aim to strengthen local governance. The flagship of these programmes is the National Solidarity Programme (NSP), which provides grants of up to $60,000 to local communities, conditional upon the election of a committee to oversee the identification and implementation of projects. For one of NSP's chief architects, Samantha Reynolds, the programme is fundamentally about local governance. Based on previous work with urban community organizations, known as community fora, Reynolds sees the role of NSP as being 'not there to solve problems but to set in place a governance framework, a structure through which communities can be involved in decisions'. The idea that communities might be linked to the state, and might be so via a mechanism more democratic than the old *maliks* and *arbabs*, is important. However, it is unclear how communities will in fact relate to an administration that currently provides only very limited services outside Kabul, and whose provincial and district health and education departments continue to be starved of resources. In these circumstances, what decisions can communities be involved in beyond how to spend their one-off grant from the programme? Far more likely is that NSP will actually function as part of the rollback of the state, taking scarce resources away from the development of services, while buying off any potential public pressure for their provision. Communities, many of which are unused to getting anything from the state, will undoubtedly be delighted to receive a grant, but that is hardly a measure of success of the programme. Many of the issues identified as priorities by communities require far more than just a grant. A school building is of little use unless there is money to train, manage and pay teachers, develop a curriculum and supply of teaching materials, and therefore all requests from communities for such facilities have to be referred to the appropriate ministry. While community participation is vital, one wonders therefore whether school buildings might not be better undertaken as part of Ministry of Education programmes, and linked to their planning processes.

The question is not whether local governance is a good thing but whether the National Solidarity Programme, as it is currently configured, is an effective way to achieve it. The scheme risks becoming a donor-funded version of the old system of patronage, rather than a genuine mechanism for participation. Those NGOs who have gone along with it suggest that there is at present no other way of getting development funds for rural communities. Yet many have doubts: 'We shall do it in Zabul, in districts we have long worked in,' said the head of an established NGO in 2003. 'We have to try – but it is too ambitious.' By 2004, he and other workers in the southern provinces were suggesting that in the deteriorating security conditions, it was not possible to implement NSP in most districts.

In a country where many community structures have been taken over by commanders, there is a serious risk of misappropriation of resources. It is a problem that is compounded by pushing through programming too fast, as a result of having significant sums of money to spend within a short time-frame. This has required expensive layers of facilitating partners and oversight consultants, while hours of NGO and departmental time have been spent discussing details of a scheme which some believe to be unworkable. While strict criteria have been developed for the election of committees, a study of the similar World

Bank-funded community empowerment scheme in East Timor showed, elections can easily be subverted and real decisions can be made outside formal structures (Ospina and Hohe 2001). As an Afghan colleague noted: 'There should be open elections, but overnight we cannot get it. It will take two years. If we do it now they will elect warlords, because they are scared.'

Gaining fiscal control All of the government's plans will ultimately be of little avail if they cannot achieve fiscal control. Due to both the poverty of the country and the weakness of government institutions, collection of income or land-based taxes is unlikely to generate significant revenue. Afghanistan's main source of internally generated income will therefore, at least for the foreseeable future, remain the customs taxes on goods crossing its borders. While there is potential to raise taxes on natural resources such as timber, gems and natural gas, the government currently has control of none of these.

In effect, Afghanistan currently has two tax regimes, a weak and ineffective formal one, and a highly effective informal one – controlled by the real power-brokers in the country. Both regional commanders and some ministers in the current administration control financial resources considerably in excess of current state revenues. These include customs revenues, taxes collected from the population under their control, the proceeds of a variety of industries, legal and illegal, including gems, drugs, timber and natural gas extraction. At the district or sub-district level, a variety of commanders also extract taxes from populations under their control. This not only enables the warlords to remain independent of central government but also enables the lesser commanders to exercise considerable autonomy from those above them, while undermining attempts at security sector reform or the establishment of law and order.

Without its own sources of revenue, the government will be for ever dependent on foreign aid, with all that this implies for control over policy and accountability to its people. Foreign aid pays only for the things of its choosing, and it exacts a charge even for this: the price of our money is to do things our way. Moreover, it rarely pays for basic things such as the salaries of policemen and teachers; and even when it does, different donors pay different amounts. It makes it impossible to build a coherent national system. But without proper payment for the country's civil service there is no hope of rooting out corruption; and without an end to corruption, no chance of legitimacy.

The size of the problem is substantial. In 2002/3 government expenditure was estimated to be $349 million, while recorded domestic revenue was in the order of $132 million (IMF 2003). The gap was covered by donor funds. The 2004/5 government recurrent budget was set at $609 million, while domestic revenues are unlikely to exceed $300 million. The Finance Minister, Ashraf Ghani, is more than aware of the problem, but it was not until early 2003 that President Karzai moved against the regions, summoning the various commanders and governors to demand that they remit customs revenues to Kabul or he would resign. His ultimatum had the effect of increasing the proportion of recorded customs revenue passed on to Kabul, but few would claim that this represents the total collected. The Ministry of Finance envisages that with stricter enforcement, by international peacekeepers if necessary, the administration will be in a position to finance the wage portion of its recurrent expenditures in five years and the entire recurrent budget in nine years.

The battle over revenues will, however, not be an easy one. Through the course of the war, regional power-brokers have established strong trading links with neighbouring countries. They have been careful to take their money out of the country, not only depositing it in foreign bank accounts, but also using it to build up substantial offshore investments. Afghan financial interests in Dubai and other Gulf states, and beyond, are immense.

The response of wartime entrepreneurs to a peace settlement is usually to take capital abroad, while at the same time taking advantage of the minimum levels of state regulation to continue to exploit illicit activities or to invest in speculative construction projects or the poorly regulated finance sectors (Cramer and Goodhand 2003). The implications of this response on the exercise of political power in Afghanistan seem not to have been examined. In one of the few pieces of work to look at the problem, Frederick Starr, writing in the BICC briefing on Afghanistan's security dilemma, underlines how the Karzai administration is undermined by powerful political foes, who far from being sidelined are 'daily gaining in power' (Starr 2003). Key to this power are the mafia-like networks that have control over the drug industry and other key economic resources. Given the known levels of mafia-style corruption in Russia (Lieven 1999; Stiglitz 2002), it is easy to imagine how pernicious this could turn out to be.

Re-establishing the rentier state Despite early rhetoric about a Marshall Plan for Afghanistan, the levels of assistance to Afghanistan are below those provided to other recent post-conflict countries. The USA even forgot to put a sum in its budget submission to Congress in January

2003, causing some red faces and a face-saving supplementary request later in the year. Of the US$87 billion set aside for Iraq and Afghanistan in November 2003, only $1.6 billion was earmarked for reconstruction in Afghanistan. Yet the amount of money is less important than the manner in which it is spent. As of June 2003, of the reconstruction aid provided to Afghanistan only 16 per cent was disbursed through the government, while less than 10 per cent of pledges had resulted in completed projects (Goodson 2004). Even less of the money has got anywhere near benefiting ordinary Afghans. The cut taken for overheads by the International Organisation for Migration for PRT construction projects in Gardez in 2003, for example, represents one-third of the project costs.[1] Meanwhile in Kabul, resources have been swallowed up in new layers of management designed and implemented by international organizations, rather than being used for essentials such as teachers or police salaries. Funds that do reach government are often tied to elaborate arrangements that require an additional tier of consultants to manage them. Gleaming, well-equipped project 'cells' have sprung up in many a ministry in Kabul. In many cases, they make little difference to the work of the regular staff. While by no means all competent or effective, the opportunity for training would have allowed at least some of the regular staff to contribute to the process of reforms from their wealth of previous experience, and could have laid a base on which the ministries could build when the new funding disappears. Yet in many cases these people are portrayed as the 'old guard', and any knowledge and experience they might have are dismissed.

The ADB announced in December 2002 that it had resumed lending to Afghanistan. The first loan was $150 million to support capacity building in the ministries and policy revision – both likely to involve substantial contracts for external consultants; the second was another $150 million loan, this time for infrastructure rehabilitation of essential roads, power and gas supplies – 83 per cent of the funds were slated to go to foreign contractors (Carlin 2003).

Currently international assistance is filling the gap left by the lack of state revenues. There is little doubt that Afghans deserve assistance, and given the extent to which the country has suffered as a result of the wars of others, this could be seen as a form of war reparations rather than assistance. However it is characterized, this level of dependence will clearly have an effect on the administration's efforts to establish domestic legitimacy. Much has been written on the way in which the state's dependence on external revenues in the 1960s and 1970s enabled it to sidestep the building of government structures to control the country, and how this ultimately was part of its downfall (Rubin 1995). The parallels with today are clear but rarely acknowledged.

Civil service Whatever form the state takes it will not function without a professional civil service. One of the remarkable things about Afghanistan is the way some senior civil servants have remained at their posts throughout the various changes that have gone on around them, growing beards with the Taliban, shifting back to western suits with Bonn. Given the numbers of educated Afghans who sought refuge from the upheavals outside the country, many outside observers tended to assume that there was nothing left of the bureaucracy of state – even though some level of services and functions continued. For those of us who witnessed attempts by civil servants to maintain the basic, threadbare functions of state through successive regimes, it was difficult to accept the absolute notion of a failed state. It was not until November 2002, however, when a World Bank mission visited Herat as part of a study of provincial administration, that it was more widely acknowledged that some official capacity survived in the provinces.

That does not, of course, mean that there are not huge problems with the civil service, and that these will not take time to solve. Civil servants are paid next to nothing, and until this changes there is no hope of rooting out the corruption that has become endemic within the administration. The need for reform was acknowledged early on, and the establishment of a Civil Service Commission was provided for in the Bonn agreement in December 2001. Progress, however, has been slow, due both to inertia and vested interests. There are currently few incentives for professional Afghans to join public service, which in the past might have allowed them to earn a living wage while carrying a degree of status and security of employment. None of this applies to the Afghan civil service of today, which bears the legacy of having been used by successive regimes to provide official jobs for loyal supporters. Indeed, some ministers in the current administration continue to distribute posts as a form of patronage, and are therefore unlikely to push forward reforms. Although Afghan entrepreneurs often rail against the bureaucracy, a more efficient, and therefore less corruptible, civil service might not in fact serve their interests, if they are no longer able to get what they want through bribes.

In mid-2003, a system of reforms was instituted in several ministries of the Transitional Administration, allowing significant increases to be made in staff salaries, based on merit and performance. Yet while this has brought salaries up to what is a realistic level for a future government to maintain, in the overheated labour market of Afghanistan, where even NGOs can be found paying five times this amount, this has still not solved the staffing problem. At the same time, the selective nature of its implementation risks being perceived as another form of patronage.

Misplaced faith While the IMF talks of the 'strong economic recovery that has recently taken place', claiming rates of economic growth of almost 30 per cent in 2002/3 and an expected 20 per cent in 2003/4 (IMF 2003), this is somewhat misleading. As the report itself acknowledges, much of this is due to an increase in agricultural production, which was almost inevitable as the country emerged from the worst drought in living memory. What is more, in 2003 farmers in the country enjoyed the best recorded harvest for twenty-five years (WFP 2003). While this recovery is indeed good news for Afghans, much more will need to happen before we can begin to talk of real growth in agriculture. For the rest, the growth might be put down largely to expansion in the construction and service sectors, fuelled by donor money and the related property boom. Were this money going into long-term investment in infrastructure or production, this would indeed be positive, but much of it is going into real estate or showpiece projects. The Kabul to Qandahar road is typical of the latter. The importance of this road not only to trade but to reconstruction and the establishment of government authority is clear. Yet far from investing in a solid piece of engineering that would be of lasting benefit to the country, the construction of the road was rushed to meet US political deadlines, with serious consequences for the quality of the works. But while the recovery of the licit economy has not really got off the starting blocks, the illicit economy is well away, with the revenue from the narcotics industry now estimated to be equivalent to more than half that of the formal economy of the country (IMF 2003).

The liberal state has not in most parts of the world brought economic success. America is often cited as an example, but all states cannot be America, for America's wealth is built on its dominant position. The pattern of Western Europe and the USA is not the norm. In Latin America the liberal state has brought unstable and unbalanced economic growth and uneven political progress. Many countries that have tried to go the liberal route have ended up like Russia, with criminal, mafia-like clans controlling the economy, bringing in high levels of privatized violence and undermining any political development – let alone something that could be called democracy.

Economists often talk about the market economy as if it were composed simply of prices, profits and private property. But for markets to function properly they require established property rights and courts to enforce them, competition and accurate information (Stiglitz 2002). There need to be legal and regulatory frameworks and institutions of state to ensure these function. Otherwise, privatization all too easily becomes asset-stripping, and private businesses have no protection from those who do not pay their debts or deliver their dues. What then happens, as in Russia, is that criminal networks take over that space, providing the protection that the state cannot. Protection rackets are the inevitable criminalized side of the private economy in a situation where the state cannot provide a suitable regulatory environment. Afghanistan does not, as yet, have either the frameworks or the institutions to impose them; pushing ahead the privatization and liberalization agendas in this environment is dangerous.

In what could be words of warning to Afghanistan, Anatol Lieven considers the closest political analogy to Russia was the 'cacique' system of colonial Spain and much of Latin America. It was, he writes:

> a time when Spain's governments never ceased to trumpet their alle-giance to constitution, law and enlightened progress, but in which real power on the ground was held by corrupt local political chieftains, who distributed patronage and government contracts, fixed or 'made' elec-tions on behalf of their patrons in Madrid, and occasionally bumped off inconvenient political opponents, critical journalists, trade unionists and so on. (Lieven 1999: 151)

To their better-off inhabitants, who can afford some form of 'protec-tion', such systems can offer personal freedoms and opportunities; but they are not systems that will bring about development or, in the long term, a stable state. They are characterized by high levels of organized crime and personal insecurity, and by rampant bureaucracy and corrup-tion. As Lieven notes, such states are generally too weak and corrupt to enforce the law honestly and equitably, raise taxes efficiently and fairly or to protect the weaker sections of society. In extreme cases, such as Colombia, the state itself may be largely taken over by criminal forces. External finance may flow in, but what results is the development of two separate economies, only one of which benefits from the new money. Typically, wealth is concentrated in the capital and perhaps one or two other centres. Moscow's economy, for example, is estimated to have grown by 10 per cent in the mid-1990s while the rest of Russia was declining precipitously – and the city may now account for as much as 35 per cent of the country's GDP. New elites in Russia acquired their wealth by privatization of state property, with the help of massive corruption and under the banner of liberal capitalism (Lieven 1999).

If warlordism simply becomes organized crime then there is little hope for the development of a democratic system in Afghanistan – and the evidence is that, once established, organized crime is very difficult to get rid of. Nor will it be just Afghanistan that suffers. Experience shows that complete freedom from political control of capital flows creates pools of offshore wealth in which non-state, including criminal and terrorist organizations, can vanish without trace. As capital has gone global, so has crime.

The issue is not that Afghanistan should adopt some blueprint from other countries, nor that it should attempt to return to the command economy of the Soviet days. The issue is that there needs to be debate and a thorough consideration of the situation in the country, including its regional context, and how various policies would work in the light of this. Despite the view put forward by the USA and the IFIs, there are alternative ways of doing things. Even within capitalism there is not just one model; a Japanese market economy is very different from an American one. There are ways of using the market but of also having a role for government; one can recognize the need for reform but also the need for a gradual approach that puts safeguards in place.

Fundamentally it is not donor money that Afghanistan needs but a working economy. The failure of the state to bring about long-term jobs or deliver services to the poor will fundamentally undermine its legitimacy with its own people – for if the state delivers nothing why should people defend it? Many Afghans saw in the defeat of the Taliban an opportunity for long-awaited change, and will not readily forgive their rulers for betraying their hopes. Nor will they forgive those western countries that have been so clearly identified with the transition.

International failure
The United Nations

This project assumed a state-centric *terra nullis* and an open season on institutional invention. East Timor was not, however, a political no-man's land. In a sense, there is never a vacuum as long as there is a population. There is a profound difference between anarchy defined as the absence of a national executive, legislature and judiciary, and the actual breakdown of indigenous social structures. If this point appears obvious, then it was absurd and extraordinary to exclude the population from the paradigm of transitional administration. (Chopra 2002)

What is most striking about the performance of the United Nations Assistance Mission in Afghanistan (UNAMA) is how few lessons have been learned from UN experience elsewhere. For all the differences between the mission in Afghanistan and East Timor – where UNTAET represented the interim administration – much of what is quoted above also rings true for UNAMA. Despite the UN's previous assistance-related experience of working with indigenous structures, it failed to draw on this to develop an inclusive political strategy. While the volatile circumstances in which the mission was deployed certainly called for a degree of political caution, the risk-averse behaviour of the mission meant that many opportunities to build a more inclusive political process were not taken. UNAMA's mandate explicitly included the responsibility to assist in 'establishing a politically neutral environment' in which the transition could take place, yet this was interpreted in a minimalist manner by the head of the mission, the Special Representative of the UN Secretary General. The failure of the UN in Afghanistan, however, goes deeper than the approach of the individuals working for it; rather, it lies in the fact that the UN is not structurally adapted for the role it is now being called upon to play.

Establishment of the mission UNAMA was established in March 2002 for the purpose of helping to implement the Bonn agreement on the political transition in Afghanistan and to assist in the relief, recovery and reconstruction of the country. It was the first UN peace operation to be established in the shadow of the 'war on terror', and in the early stages this gave rise to an unusual unity of purpose among the main states concerned with a post-war strategy for Afghanistan. In the early months there also appeared to be a willingness on the part of donors to heed the lesson of the past that stability in Afghanistan requires sustained and unified international commitment.

UNAMA was also the first attempt by the UN to establish a fully integrated mission. The SRSG, as head of the mission, was tasked with providing 'directive coordination' to all UN programmes and agencies operating in Afghanistan. He was not, however, given any power in terms of either appointments or budget control to implement such coordination. He was further hampered by the fact that it took four months to set up the mission, by which time the individual UN agencies had long since re-established themselves in Afghanistan and staked out their territory.

Unlike in Iraq, the USA had from the beginning accepted that the UN should play a major role in Afghanistan once the first stage of the military campaign had ended. There was also early agreement among Security Council members that the UN should take a lead political role in defining a post-Taliban transition for the country. Since the brokering of the Geneva Accords in 1989, the UN had maintained successive political missions in Afghanistan, while the United Nations Office for the Co-ordination of Humanitarian Assistance for Afghanistan (UNOCHA) had overseen a significant humanitarian programme, implemented by UN agencies and others.[2] This experience should have placed the UN in a strong position to deal with the transition process, as should the appointment of the highly experienced Lakhdar Brahimi as the UN Special Representative.

If the mission had things going for it, it also faced severe constraints. The war against the Taliban was far from finished, and designing and executing a peace operation in the middle of a war deemed crucial to the national security of the USA was, to say the least, difficult. The short-term focus of the USA, and its tendency for unilateral action, more often than not worked against the processes of state building that the UN was attempting to support. While it was inevitable that UNAMA would need to deal with the interests of key member-states, its apparent unwillingness to defend the interests of the people of Afghanistan in the face of these has affected the course of the transition.

Moreover, it signalled to the Afghan population that the UN was unable to deliver what was believed to be a prerequisite to any degree of political stability, namely, security. Although the crucial importance of security was repeatedly stressed by the SRSG, his voice appeared to make little difference.

A review of UN peace operations undertaken during 2003 identified four principles as having guided the design and operation of the UNAMA mission:[3]

- *Light interventionism*: to be sustainable, institutions of good governance must be Afghan; a transitional administration run by Afghans will be 'far more credible, acceptable and legitimate' than one run by the UN or a constellation of foreigners. Afghans must be in charge and have ownership of the process.
- *Light footprint*: parachuting in a large number of internationals would be counterproductive; the large pool of skilled Afghans inside and outside the country must be fully utilized.
- *Integrated strategy*: 'reconstruction will require a clear ... subordination of the interest of individual agencies or donors to the overall agenda of peace and stability'.

- *Unitary structure*: an integrated strategy requires 'clear lines of authority and responsibility' among the donors and within the UN system, possibly including 'the creation of a single system for the delivery of flows of money'. (King's College London 2003)

All four principles, however, have proved difficult to realize on the ground. Unlike Kosovo and East Timor, the UN mission in Afghanistan was restricted to an advisory and support role, rather than having direct governance responsibilities. While this was undoubtedly appropriate for the circumstances, the notion of 'Afghan ownership' has over time been used as an excuse for the UN and other international players to abdicate their responsibility in the face of the more difficult issues of the transition. Nowhere was this more apparent than on the issue of human rights, and specifically transitional justice. Although the Bonn agreement did not specifically mention transitional justice, it did give the UN the right to investigate human rights violations. On the ground, however, the SRSG appeared to rule out retrospective investigations of abuses as 'inadvisable', and UNAMA decided that only reports of incidents after the establishment of the mission would be considered. This allowed the mission to sidestep the sensitive case of alleged massacres in the north by the Northern Alliance in late 2001, and thereby avoid implicating commanders who were then members of the administration in Kabul, not to mention the risk of raising awkward questions about the role of coalition forces present at the time as partners of the Northern Alliance. As a senior UNAMA official put it during the King's College study: 'Transitional justice only applies to post-conflict situations, and Afghanistan is not in a post-conflict phase.'

While clearly a desirable aim in the light of the scale and expense of previous UN missions, the 'light footprint' also proved difficult to realize in Afghanistan, and UN agencies with their vehicles and other infrastructure became highly visible in Kabul. The profile of the UN presented very real problems of credibility, and the question being asked by Afghans who had seen very little change in their lives was: 'Just what is everyone here to do?' While some operations did indeed expand immediately, and needed staff to manage them, many UN managers made little secret of the fact that they were hiring because they had the funds to do so, and the programmes would follow. In the case of UNAMA, bizarre UN regulations that applied to peacekeeping operations required that the mission bring in international staff to maintain vehicles and fridges. Meanwhile, Afghans who had worked with the UN in Kabul throughout the time of the *mujahideen* and the Taliban found themselves being effectively demoted as expatriates took over their responsibilities. 'I used to do more in a month than I have done in the last four,' said an experienced ex-liaison officer for the UN, who was relegated to secretarial and translation work once transferred to UNAMA. 'I'm simply pushing bits of paper around.'

While UNAMA has undeniably been successful in assisting the transition process to stick to the timetable agreed at Bonn, its goal was not simply to hold events on time, however important they may be, but to 'restore peace and stability to Afghanistan' (Brahimi 2004). Yet increasingly one is left with a sense that, as Barnet Rubin put it, 'even if formal timetables are respected, these political activities are becoming more and more devoid of the meaning that they are supposed to have' (Rubin 2003b).

The challenge of the transition is to broaden the process of political engagement and build up popular legitimacy for an emerging administration, in order to enable it to stand up to factional interests that had begun to assert themselves. Yet it was here that UNAMA failed most. The delegates who had been elected for the Emergency Loya Jirga could have formed the nucleus of this engagement; yet despite efforts by some UNAMA staff to support a continuing process of dialogue with these people, they received little support and in some cases were actually stopped from pursuing this opportunity. For a legitimate political authority to develop, UNAMA needed to guarantee some space for dissent and debate, even if this was perceived as being in opposition to the Interim Administration. However, any talk of opposition was, it seems, not to be tolerated, with the result that a number of committed and experienced staff left the mission.

UNAMA's way of working, and that of the international diplomatic community more generally, has been to talk to the leadership within the Interim and Transitional Administrations, both in Kabul and the regions, as if they represented the people. In a sense this is not surprising, for the head of the mission, Lakhdar Brahimi, is a high-ranking diplomat, used to dealing with leaders, at a remove from local politics and the social processes that lie behind it. The danger of this diplomatic approach, however, is that it risks lending legitimacy to the very factional elements that many Afghans see as totally illegitimate. While it may indeed be necessary to engage with those within the administration who have blood on their hands, this needs to be done with clear conditions. The UN's own staff in the north remarked on the tendency of colleagues to deal with Generals Dostum and Atta on everything – not just on military matters – rather than talking to the civilian authorities. The process did not just happen in formal meetings but through routine encounters. Standing one morning in 2003 in the UNAMA office, a political officer came in, excitedly recounting how he had just had breakfast with a local warlord. 'And he says he needs a seat on our plane,' he said breathlessly, as if this request should be treated with great importance, by dint of the warlord's position. It was far from a one-off incident, and illustrates the tendency of many of the younger politicos in UNAMA to be seduced by the power of men with guns. One might be forgiven for wondering whether UN missions might not need a professional cadre of experienced staff who can deal more effectively with the political responsibilities that should go with such postings.

The failure to integrate Perhaps inevitably, the UN mission failed to achieve integration. Despite the SRSG's best intentions, the management structure and funding arrangements of the UN agencies meant that he did not have any means of enforcing compliance. As with earlier attempts at common programming, heads of agencies dealt in the first instance with their headquarters rather than UNAMA, and at times seemed to be driven by the need for agency profile rather than by anything else. At a UN meeting in Islamabad before the Bonn agreement was even negotiated, heads of agencies squabbled about who would get seats on the first plane back into Kabul, at a cost of $5,000 each way.[4] When asked whether his presence did not risk legitimating the warlords who had taken possession of Kabul, one agency head responded: 'Everyone else is going – and my headquarters says we have to be seen.'

As soon as they were back inside Afghanistan, the UN was busy treating the country as if it were a blank slate upon which it could try out its ideas of how things should be. At worst, it seemed like straightforward agency positioning. A UNICEF convoy set off over the mountains from Peshawar to deliver school books to Badakhshan, even before the Taliban were driven from Kabul, taking in tow a CNN camera crew and forty print journalists. It was as if no one had ever done it before, but a small Norwegian NGO had been taking convoys over for years. The convoy was the start of UNICEF's much-publicized 'Back to School' campaign, aimed at getting between 1.5 and 1.7 million children back to school. In the rush, little attention was paid to what they would do once they got there. Three million children went back that year but, two years later, many schools still had no text books; only 22 per cent of all teachers had graduated from teacher training college, and most teachers had only grade 12 education or less. Many teachers were not receiving regular salaries, and even when they did it was a pittance. As of mid 2004, half the schools in Afghanistan did not have access to safe water and more than a third did not have adequate sanitation facilities. No one knew how many of the 3 million children who registered for school were still attending.

A member of the Constitution Drafting Commission in the north recalled:

> In Andkhoi, when they announced that pupils could once again join schools, 600 girls came in one day. And there was nothing: there were no teachers, there were no textbooks, no notebooks, no school building. They were just disappointed. And in Maimana, when we went for consultations, the director of one school came and said, 'Please, take a picture of my school.' We said, 'We are here for the constitution, we can do nothing about education.' He said, 'Please, come. Maybe you can show it to someone. Tell them, we are here, we are trying to survive.' It was a historic school, very old, and there was not one chair in the building.
>
> Afghan people may be illiterate but they are also politicians. Now, after all these years of conflict, Afghan people can analyse everything. They say: 'There is supposed to be reconstruction, and there is a tent for a school. What use is a tent? In the summer we cannot stay for the heat, and in the winter for the cold.'

The campaign did not even help to build the credibility of the Ministry of Education. While it was meant to be a joint endeavour, all the neat little children's rucksacks and the plastic carrier bags that had been imported for the purpose bore only the UNICEF logo, not that of the ministry.

There is a huge desire for education in Afghanistan, and children would have gone back to school without any campaign; but even if the campaign helped to increase numbers, this is hardly an achievement if they found almost nothing when they got to their classrooms. All the energy that went into the campaign would have been better used to develop a coherent strategy for a service all Afghans identify as an important priority.

The Ministry of Public Health was, by contrast, in much better shape, being led by experienced health professionals and with more capacity at all levels. The number of players, in terms of donors and major assistance agencies, was also smaller in health, facilitating coordination. UNICEF, which was a key player in both areas, managed early on to field an experienced team of health professionals who had a genuine commitment to capacity building for the ministry, whereas it singularly failed to find proper professional support for education until well into the second year of transition. But there was also a problem of strategy. The whole notion of universal primary education as an immediate goal is questionable in the Afghan context. Yes, of course people want it, and as a long-term goal it is undeniably important, but as the basis on which to plan for the early years of reconstruction it is leading to less, not more, education. In schools across the country there are children learning nothing – nor is there any hope of their learning anything in the foreseeable future. The country is so far from having the human resources to implement a policy of universal primary education that spreading resources thinly just means that no one gets anything. It would make more sense to concentrate on provincial and district centres first, to use the years of donor funding to establish the core of a system, to get staff trained and resolve how to pay them, and only then to spread out. But this is, of course, politically difficult for an agency that has built universal primary education into an unquestionable mantra, and it needed both more confidence and more analytical rigour than was available to reframe the goal into a workable strategy.

Nor was UNICEF the only UN agency to imagine a country that was unlikely to exist in a two-year time-frame. UNHCR similarly thought that things could get better faster than they did. Nearly one-third of Afghanistan's population fled the country during the years of war, most of them becoming refugees in Pakistan and Iran. Between September 2001 and September 2002, about 2 million of them returned home. While this seemed to suggest a vote of confidence in the transitional process, the reality was more complex. The refugees came home under what was known as 'voluntary return', which meant that UNHCR provided assistance but did not officially encourage them. The shades of meaning of UN refugee policy were, not surprisingly, lost on Afghans living in neighbouring countries. Both Pakistan and Iran had long been trying to get rid of some of the refugees and started to put pressure on Afghans to go home. Many feared that if they did not take this chance to return, when there was support, they might miss out (Turton and Marsden 2002). Media coverage of the reconstruction also encouraged return; as one returnee to the Shomali plain north of Kabul put it, 'The whole world told us they were rebuilding Afghanistan'. The fact that the UN was supporting return added to the sense that conditions were good – whatever UNHCR's official policy might have been. Yet security was still poor in some areas, and for many there were few prospects of making a living. Many were to be deeply disappointed.

There is little doubt that the repatriation effort was driven as much by political as by humanitarian considerations. The USA, a key donor to UNHCR, and the Interim Administration were keen to show the dividends of the change of regime in Kabul, even if return on this scale was neither in the interests of those returning nor of the long-term recovery of the country. 'Many returnees found themselves in a worse position after their return than before,' said the authors of a report on the issue, while 'the scale and speed of the return helped to divert yet more of the limited funds available for reconstruction into emergency assistance' (Turton and Marsden 2002). Having worked with Afghan refugee communities in Iran and Pakistan for decades, UNHCR should have known the risks of mass returns, and should have made refugees aware of the realities of what they might face in different parts of the country. Instead, they portrayed the flow as an unstoppable human tide over which they had little control, and continued to issue appeals for yet more funds.

The political transition has required operational UN agencies to change the way that they do business in Afghanistan. While they continued at first to operate largely independently of official structures, as they had in the past, the administration in Kabul soon asserted itself by insisting on a greater degree of transparency and requiring them to work in partnership with ministries. As a result, from having been an anathema to agencies at the time of the Taliban, 'capacity building' became the norm. An Afghan working with UNDP was excited to be assigned to support an emergency capacity-building initiative for the line ministries in the early days of the Interim Administration at the end of 2001. 'There is so much that needs to be done, after so long,' he said. Then he found out that his instructions were simply to procure a vehicle, a computer and a desk and chair for each minister.

While things have improved since then, the track record of the UN agencies in working with the Transitional Administration has been patchy. The performance of some UN agencies as facilitators in consultative groups serves to illustrate the extent to which they themselves might need capacity building. These sectoral groups were set up by the administration in an effort to bring some degree of coordination to the chaotic aid circus that prevailed for much of 2002. In several cases, UN agencies were appointed to provide secretariat functions for these groups, which met under the chairmanship of the respective minister. Given the limited capacity of most ministries to coordinate assistance activities, let alone plan, the UN should have had a key role in developing strategies and setting priorities for the sector. In the case of urban development, which was acknowledged in early 2002 to be a priority, UN-Habitat has still to develop a list of ongoing projects, let alone a strategy for urban rehabilitation. The urban inputs to the National Development Budget remain a wish-list, amounting to nearly $300 million for 2004/5, while the implementing partners between them were able to spend only $15 million in the previous financial year. Given this record, the Transitional Administration is perhaps justified in feeling that some UN agencies are simply not serious.

NGOs Despite all the warnings from Rwanda, Kosovo and other high-profile crises, the signing of the Bonn agreement triggered a flood of new NGOs into the country while the existing ones massively expanded their programmes, becoming badly overstretched as a result. Speaking of the early 2002 period, an experienced NGO worker noted how:

> The whole thing went berserk. It was bizarre how it shifted from one extreme to the other. Yet it was always difficult to say what the food situation was, to get a grip on things. There was no lack of food in the markets and the prices did not go up markedly. We didn't see high rates of acute malnutrition, even in Kohistan. There were high rates of child mortality, but it was not clear it was due to malnutrition – and not clear if it was any worse than before. It was interesting how much competition there was between NGOs to take on emergency food distribution. There was even fighting between them over districts. It was all politics, about visibility. And we got sucked in as well, because we know that if we don't do it someone else will in the key districts we are working in.

Her boss, interviewed in the summer of 2002, spoke of how 'It just expanded, with no attention to security. We had people running all over the north in ways that would not have been acceptable to the UN. Communications were inadequate. Until recently no one said anything about insecurity, yet there were people crouching on office floors in Gardez with bullets flying. HQs were just pushing so fast for expansion.'

By November 2002, the number of international NGOs registered with the Ministry of Planning had risen to 350, from the forty-six which had been on the books in 1999. Although field staff in established organizations argued that the basic development work they had been doing before, with a heavy reliance on Afghan staff, was often still the most appropriate, the pressure from NGO headquarters to grow was intense. Expatriates flooded into the country. Oxfam recruited sixteen, and rented four houses for them in the most expensive part of town. Their programme was, in the words of one of their Afghan staff, 'smaller than when there were just three of us'. It didn't seem to matter – money was no longer an issue. Once the NGO influx had reached a certain point it created its own momentum. Save the Children, who had long had a policy of empowering their local staff, described how, 'if you do not send an expatriate to the meeting, you become invisible'. While the rhetoric was all about 'Afghan-led' processes, this was far from the case in practice.

The influx of new NGOs, many of whose staff admitted to knowing nothing about the country, undermined the long-term approaches of established organizations to building partnerships with communities. The quality of the work almost always suffered in the endless push for quantity. Inexperience also led to problems of a lack of cultural sensitivity, and a failure to understand the conservatism of much of Afghan society. Ismael Khan held a meeting with international agencies in Herat in 2003, when he announced a ban on the consumption of alcohol and restrictions on the employment of Afghan women. While expatriates saw this as confirmation of Ismael Khan's fundamentalist tendencies, their Afghan colleagues told a different story. The drunken late-night parties, with bottles and beer cans left for all to see in the morning, were an affront, not only to the 'emir' of Herat; likewise the idea that an Afghan woman, unaccompanied by a male relative, should stay on her own in a compound with foreign men on the premises, even if she was travelling on an Australian passport. The backlash was as self-inflicted as it was inevitable, but few of the newly arrived expatriates were humble enough to see it that way.

Letting the Afghans down

Despite the opportunity that the new mission in Afghanistan seemed to represent, the United Nations can hardly be said to have served the Afghans well through their transition so far. The minimalist interpretation of the mandate that was provided to UNAMA has resulted in a consistent failure to take political risks, and rendered it unable, or unwilling, to act independently on key issues. Nowhere is this more evident than in the failure of the UN to set out clear terms under which factional leaders can legitimately occupy a seat at the transitional table. This has allowed factional, rather than national, interest to dominate the political space, at the expense of any meaningful engagement with Afghan society – on which UNAMA seems to have largely turned its back. Unless ordinary Afghans are convinced that the administration in Kabul is broadening its base beyond the familiar factional power-brokers and westernized technocrats, its legitimacy will continue to be limited. Even though the success of its mission clearly depends on the emergence of a legitimate administration in Kabul, UNAMA's vision, such as it is, seems restricted to clearing the series of political hurdles that were set up in Bonn. Having abdicated its responsibilities in creating neutral political space for the transition, UNAMA can now do little more than react to developments from the margins.

Notes

1 Personal communication with member of Gardez PRT, December 2003.

2 The United Nations Office for the Coordination of Assistance (UOCA) was succeeded by UNOCHA in 1996 which, with the merging of OCHA and UNDP representational functions in the field, was in turn renamed the United Nations Office of the Coordinator (UNOC) from 1998.

3 One of the authors was part of the team that undertook the 'snapshot' assessment of UNAMA.

4 The cost was due to high insurance premiums.

9 | Concluding thoughts

What is striking about the problems of international engagement in Afghanistan is that none of them is new. From the Balkans to East Timor, the commitments made by western leaders have run aground on a tangled heap of broken promises, incompetent organizations, muddled mandates, and local power-brokers playing to win.

Nowhere has the failure been greater than in the inability to bring security to the lives of the citizens of these countries. This was perhaps the greatest single challenge to the international community in the wake of the Taliban's removal from power in Afghanistan. Certainly it was the number one priority for Afghans. Yet security in Afghanistan is now worse than it has been for years. Most of the south and east of the country is off-bounds for government, UN and NGO staff – Afghan as well as international. Even in Kabul, many aid agencies have retreated into compounds encircled with sandbags and layers of razor wire. On the streets, ordinary Afghans are menaced by patrols of foreign mercenaries engaged by private security firms, seemingly accountable to no one but those whom they are paid to protect. Armed robbery and kidnappings abound and night-time rocketing is again the norm, demonstrating the tenuous grip that international forces have on the city.

As has been belatedly acknowledged in Iraq, the security problem is at heart a political problem. Peace cannot be bombed into existence but requires the reconstruction of political authority in the country. This will have a chance of happening only if all Afghan leaders who are prepared to renounce violence are given a seat at the table. As the USA has finally realized, this has to include the Taliban; for whether or not the western world likes their policies, they are part of the political landscape of the country and the conservative values and interests that they represent have deep roots in society. As recent events demonstrate, no number of 'search and destroy' operations will eliminate them. While they may have blood on their hands, so do many others involved in the transition.

Yet the past cannot just be ignored. Even those who renounce violence need to answer for the atrocities they have committed. Peace will not be forged in the country without some form of justice, and some formal acknowledgement of the pain so many people have lived through. The

11 *A vanished state: government officials and diplomats at a Jeshen parade in Kabul in the late 1970s. (Ministry of Information and Culture)*

Afghan Independent Human Rights Commission has taken brave steps along this dangerous path but they need support if they are to hold those responsible for grave abuses accountable, especially as many of them are today's power-brokers. Yet some of the justice now being meted out is covering up the crimes of the past, rather than exposing them. The recent covert trial of Abdullah Shah, and Hamid Karzai's subsequent order of his execution, for example, silenced someone who claimed that in committing his atrocities he had acted on the direct orders of Professor Sayyaf, a key commander and ally of President Karzai and in effective control of the judiciary. Justice has to be impartial, if it is to have any moral authority. So too with human rights, which cannot simply be picked up and put down again at the political convenience of either the West or its chosen governments. After suffering so much abuse, Afghans expect – and deserve – better than this.

Dealing with violence means not only dealing with the agents of violence but also with its underlying causes. While there are certainly those who benefit from war, there are also many who have turned to the gun for lack of an alternative. If disarmament campaigns are to have any hope of success, these men need to be convinced that there is the possibility of a secure future

There is in Afghanistan an overwhelming need to build a legitimate state with a measure of popular support, a state that once again functions and delivers some basic improvements to people's lives, a state that in the end people feel is worth defending. Building this requires far more than the series of 'events' that Afghans have so far been offered as their political transition. It demands recognition that legitimacy is not something given by the ballot box but something earned by a government that brings benefits to its citizens and is free from corruption. It means recognizing that the basis of political authority lies at the local level. It involves reconnecting the centre to its periphery, allowing for multiple and overlapping centres of power and finding ways to manage their relations. To imagine that the writ of highly centralized government can be imposed throughout the land is a delusion. The state does not have the might, and even if it did, the tactics that would be required would be unacceptable to both its people and its western backers.

Re-establishing the legitimacy of the state also means finding a way to be modern that builds on the country's strengths rather than simply relying on imported notions from the West; a way that recognizes Islam not as a set of rules but as a spiritual force in people's lives, shaping their values and giving them strength. Much has already been lost, yet opportunities still exist to tap into the will of the majority for peace.

From the many brave delegates who stood for the Emergency Loya Jirga to Malalai Joya at the Constitutional Loya Jirga, Afghans have over and over again shown themselves capable of rising to the challenge of creating a new country. It is their leaders and the international community that have failed.

Current policies of market liberalization run counter to the needs of state building on many levels. In a country that lacks both regulatory frameworks and the means to impose them, such policies fuel corruption and encourage the pursuit of political power through markets and accumulation. Meanwhile, the unseemly dash to contract everything out, in a country where market choice is meaningless in so many places, brings few benefits to its citizens. It also destroys any hope of building legitimacy, for it is UNICEF or Louis Berger that is seen to provide rather than the government of Afghanistan. Nor does the use of foreigners, be they private security firms or PRTs, to undertake tasks that should properly be the job of the state solve the problems of a government that cannot deal with its rivals. It undermines the government now, just as it has done in the past. In the end, the Afghan government must protect its own president and collect its own customs revenues.

As the key international institution tasked with supporting the transition, the UN has at best been only partially successful. Words that were written in reflection on the experience in East Timor suggest why:

> After East Timor, if there is to be any future for peace operations that are both legitimate and effective, then a much more participatory form of intervention has to be considered. The idea of 'participatory intervention' stands in contrast to the practice of state-(re)building processes of relying only on international appointees or elites self-appointed as representatives of the people. Instead, the aim would be to include direct involvement of the local population from the very beginning of an international intervention, in order to ensure justice for the parts and that new governing structures resonate with local social reality. (Chopra 2002)

If we are to move beyond merely passing the milestones of the transition – the ELJ, CLJ and even elections – the UN needs to rethink how to 'do' politics. Even if Karzai gets the required 51 per cent of the vote, and is duly elected, this will not bring peace and stability to Afghanistan. This requires a dialogue with parts of society other than those political leaders who have failed Afghanistan for so many years. Peace cannot be delivered by an agreement – although this provides a starting-point – but has to be built from the bottom up as well as the top down. It means that rather than just simply supporting a 'government', the UN has to support to a process by which the population at large can make real choices about what kind of future they wish to see in their country. Had the UN risen to these challenges from the beginning, processes such as disarmament might have made more progress, for people were then deeply tired of war and would have taken risks to bring a new Afghanistan into being.

The UN as it is today, however, is singularly ill-equipped to meet the challenges presented by a radically different political landscape. Despite attempts at reform, the vested interests of both member-states and constituent agencies continue to stand in the way of much-needed restructuring. There were assurances from the start that Afghanistan provided an opportunity for a new kind of cutting-edge UN mission, but the system proved incapable of rising to this challenge. Many staff lacked the professional skills for the jobs, or were there for only a short time and rarely moved outside Kabul. Even those who knew better were hobbled by the UN's obeisance to America's war aims.

The experience of the UN in Afghanistan suggests that there is something systemic in the failures that beset the system. If western powers are going to support regime change, whether in the name of humanitarianism, as in Kosovo, or the war on terror, as in Afghanistan, then we need a UN that is capable of effectively supporting the transition that follows. In the wake of the US invasion of Iraq, when the occupation began to prove unworkable, the UN was proposed to oversee the process towards sovereignty. Not only had the system been the prime enforcer for a decade of punishing sanctions – which damned it in the eyes of most Iraqis – but its past record suggested it was far from capable of undertaking the task needed. In any event, if the UN is to respond to the aspirations of a people, radical reform needs to takes place. This means a system that provides high-quality and impartial policy advice, that is staffed by professionals who can stay a course of duty, and in which individual agency mandates are subordinate to overarching mission goals. It's not a case of learning lessons – more studies will not help us. We know the lessons; we have difficulties implementing them because people's careers are founded on keeping things the way they are.

We also have difficulty implementing them because they run counter to the short-term interests of key member-states. The report of the Secretary-General to the UN Security Council states clearly that:

> holding elections without adequate security and political preparation ...
> can undermine, rather than facilitate, the process of building the rule of

law. Yet the international community still sometimes encourages early elections on post-conflict states in an attempt to lend legitimacy to political leaders, process and institutions. But premature elections can only bring about cosmetic democracies, at best.[1]

Yet, in Afghanistan, the UN continues to push forward elections despite the deteriorating security, the fears of ordinary people for the violence that it will inevitably spawn, and the warnings of the erstwhile SRSG. Set on this course, they find it impossible to recognize that Afghans' trust in the electoral process cannot simply be measured by a score-card of voter registration or by the number of presidential candidates, and fail to speak out about the widespread abuses of the voter registration process or to deal with a public education campaign that even UN staff consider a dismal failure.

President George W. Bush in his 2004 State of the Union address, which in effect marked the start of his bid for re-election, stated that the USA had a mission to 'lead the cause of freedom', and stated his intention of expanding the 'Bush doctrine' of pre-emptive military action to a broader goal of promoting democracy round the world, by force if necessary. It's hard to know whether this address represents real policy intent, or merely a staking out of a pre-election territory. But even if America reverts to achieving its foreign policy goals by more covert means – either because Bush counts the cost of his military adventures and considers them electorally unacceptable, or because the American people make that calculation themselves and fail to re-elect him – there has been an underlying consistency in US foreign policy goals ever since the end of the Second World War. Ultimately these centre on maintaining the 'American way of life', including a commitment to ever-increasing standards of living, and to ensuring the profitability of US companies – particularly in relation to the need for oil.

The mess in both Afghanistan and Iraq is testament to the fact that the West is nearing a point of reckoning in these policies. Since 11 September 2001, America and its close allies have tried to believe that it can have it both ways: homeland security and the pursuit of political systems elsewhere in the world that will support their interests. But the people of other countries also have a right to development. Afghanistan is one of the poorest countries in the world and its citizens have suffered nearly a quarter of a century of war. They need a future. And if that is continually denied they will produce desperate people, particularly young people, some of whom will ultimately in their despair become what America terms 'terrorists'. The term is emotive, the tactics horrible, yet what other strategy are poor people to have against the world's superpower and its allies? So far both America and the UK have tried to pretend to their own people that this danger can be met by a combination of war abroad and increasing limitations on civil liberties at home. It cannot. The war in Afghanistan has failed to defeat either al-Qa'eda or the Taliban and, despite repeated campaigns by US forces against 'remnants', they persist in their tactics of disrupting the political process, and rendering a large part of the country inaccessible to those associated with the transition, including government officials. The history of Afghanistan shows all too clearly that a military victory is impossible; nor can you seal off the 'homeland' from terrorist attacks, for those who are prepared to die for their cause will always find a way.

It has long been acknowledged that stability in Afghanistan hinges on a solution to wider regional problems. These issues relate both to formal relations between states and the activities of trans-border networks. Yet, over the past three years, the process of international engagement in Afghanistan has obscured the need for a comprehensive political strategy for the region. This will not be achieved simply by focusing on the 'war on terror'. Military incursions against the Waziri tribesmen of Pakistan enmesh the coalition forces in a game that they do not understand in a dangerous territory that has defeated others before them, even as they destabilize a nuclear power that they need on their side. Meanwhile, support for the deeply repressive regimes in Uzbekistan and Turkmenistan undermines any credibility that the West might have had as a protector of human rights – had it not already been shredded by the detention of suspects without charge, trial or legal defence in Guantanamo Bay.

There is a danger that in reaction to the difficulties and threats the West tries to beat as hasty a retreat as possible; but leaving the job unfinished will improve neither the lot of the population nor the security of the West. Rather, there is a need for a new form of international engagement with new codes of conduct to regulate that action and assign responsibilities in the aftermath of an imposed transition. Where a country has been invaded and occupied, the terms of responsibility towards the civilian population are clearly laid out in the fourth Geneva Convention. Afghanistan was not invaded, not quite, but what happened was close enough to an invasion to demand that the intervening countries have responsibilities. The old security regime was dismantled through the might of coalition bombs – for without those bombs the Northern Alliance would not have prevailed; it was an international not an internal conflict. Ordinary Afghans were not consulted in the matter, and were in no sense party to the conflict. Responsibility should therefore fall on those intervening, in the same way as if they were direct occupiers. The basic minimum standards that need to be met are that the country has a transition to a legitimate government and that it has the chance to choose the development path that best meets the needs of its people.

Moral responsibilities have never, however, lain much on the conscience of the rich world. Of more concern is the self-interest of a small elite. The justification for the war against the Taliban was that it would make the world a safer place; but without a successful political transition and sufficient development to enable the majority of Afghanistan's citizens to live free of poverty, there will be no safety.

The various international players have to leave their own agendas behind and start concentrating on Afghanistan. This may sound hopelessly idealistic, yet unless this happens little will be achieved. America needs to stop fighting its war in someone else's country and instead learn how it can play a support role. Afghans have no more wish to see al-Qa'eda on Afghanistan's soil than America has, but the way this war is being conducted is likely only to provoke a backlash. Al-Qa'eda have become the reason, or maybe the excuse, for ventures from Iraq to Sudan,[2] but opposition in Afghanistan as in Iraq is not just the work of al-Qa'eda and movements related to them but of a range of people who see themselves as having no stake in the current dispensation, no voice in government. One cannot counter these things with bombs.

As we were in the final days of finishing this book, an Afghan friend told us the words of a Kabul taxi-driver earlier in the day, talking to himself as he watched US soldiers leaning out of the window of their vehicle, guns pointing menacingly into the crowd. 'At the moment, we can do nothing, we have no real leaders. All those who have led us have looted us. But wait until we get a leader in whom we trust – then you will see, this will not happen'.

There is in Afghanistan a current of anger that remained, until recently, invisible to many outsiders. The UN and western powers are so identified with this transition that if it fails it will not just be the Afghan government's failure but also ours. We will be held responsible.

Notes

1 *The Rule of Law and Transitional Justice in Conflict and Post-Conflict Societies*, July 2004, United Nations.

2 'US Forces hunt down al-Qu'eda in Sudan', *Sunday Telegraph*, 1 August 2004.

Who's who

Abdullah Abdullah Tajik. Minster of Foreign Affairs in the Interim and Transitional Administrations. With Fahim and Qanooni, one of the powerful triumvirate of Shura e Nizar ministers in the post-Bonn agreement political landscape.

Amir Abdur Rahman Known as the 'Iron Emir'. Ruled Afghanistan between 1880 and 1901 when he consolidated the territory now known as Afghanistan into a nation-state.

Hafizullah Amin Deputy Prime Minister from April 1978, before becoming Prime Minister in April 1979 and President in September 1979, after he had Taraki killed. Killed by KGB, December 1979.

Lakhdar Brahimi Ex-Foreign Minister of Algeria. Personal Representative of the UN Secretary General in Afghanistan between 1997 and 1999, when he attempted to broker peace between the Taliban and Afghan factions. Returned as UN Special Representative in September 2001 and appointed head of UNAMA after its establishment in 2002. Ended his assignment in Afghanistan at the end of 2003.

Mohammad Daoud Cousin and brother-in-law of Zahir Shah, Prime Minister 1953–63. Overthrew Zahir Shah in 1973 to become President of Afghanistan until 1978 when killed in coup d'etat.

Abdul Rashid Dostum Uzbek from Jowzjan. Union leader whose Jumbesh-e-Milli militia supported Najibullah's government. Mutinied in January 1992 and allied himself with Ahmad Shah Massoud to take control of Kabul, while consolidating his control of northern Afghanistan from bases in Shebergan and Mazar i Sharif. Changed sides in 1994 to fight with Hekmatyar in Kabul against Massoud. By 1996, he was realigned with the Rabbani government after the takeover of Kabul and Herat by the Taliban. Driven out of Mazar in May 1997, returned in September, driven out again in 1998. Deputy Minister of Defence in the Interim Administration. Candidate in 2004 presidential elections.

Mohammed Fahim Tajik from Panjshir. Deputy to Massoud and head of intelligence in Kabul during the Islamic State of Afghanistan between

1992–96. Succeeded Massoud as head of Shura e Nizar and became Minister of Defence in the Interim and Transitional Administrations, when he took the rank of marshal. Vice President of the Transitional Administration.

Ashraf Ghani Pashstun. Worked for the World Bank before returning from the USA to head the Afghan Assistance Coordination Authority. Minister of Finance and one of the key technocrats in the Transitional Administration.

Gulbuddin Hekmatyar Pashtun from Baghlan. Involved in Islamic activism while a student at Kabul University. In 1972 founded Hizbe Islami, which received the bulk of military aid provided by the USA and others through the Pakistan ISI (military intelligence) during the *jihad* against the Soviets. Having been forced into exile in Iran by the Taliban, Hekmatyar is now loosely allied with those, including the Taliban, opposed to the administration in Kabul.

Ali Ahmad Jalali Pashtun. Involved in military planning for the Afghan resistance, he reported on Afghanistan for VOA until returning from exile in the USA in 2003 to become Minister of Interior in the Transitional Administration.

Babrak Karmal Founder of PDPA and leader of Parcham faction. Deputy Prime Minister of Democratic Republic of Afghanistan between April and July 1978, when he was exiled. Returned with Soviet troops and served as Secretary General of the People's Democratic Party of Afghanistan and President of the Revolutionary Council between 1980 and 1986, when he was exiled to the USSR, where he died in 1996.

Hamid Karzai Pashtun from Qandahar. Chairman of the Interim Administration and current [July 2004] President of the Transitional Administration of Afghanistan.

Karim Khalili Hazara. In 1998 succeeded Abdul Ali Mazari as leader of Hizbe Wahdat after his assassination by the Taliban. Vice President in the Afghan Transitional Administration.

Ismael Khan Tajik from Farah. Staff officer in the Herat garrison and co-leader of the Herat mutiny in March 1979 against pro-Soviet military leadership. Member of Jamiat-i Islami and important commander in resistance to Soviet occupation. Served as leader of the Herat *shura* between April 1992 and September 1995. Fled to Iran when the Taliban took Herat. Captured by the Taliban during an offensive in western

Afghanistan and imprisoned for several years in Qandahar, before escaping. Currently self-styled emir of Herat, and vocal critic of the Kabul administration.

General Abdul Malik (Palawan) Uzbek commander, formerly loyal to Dostum. Took control of the northern capital of Mazar-i Sharif in May 1997, in league with the Taliban, but was driven out in September of the same year, after again changing sides.

Ahmad Shah Massoud Tajik. Perhaps the most famous *mujahideen* commander. Led the resistance in the Panjshir valley. Founded Shura-ya Nizar (Supervisory Council of North), a grouping of Jamiat commanders in north-east Afghanistan, in 1985. First Defence Minister in the administration of the Islamic State of Afghanistan. Assassinated in the Panjshir valley, September 2001.

Sibghatullah Mojaddedi Spiritual leader of Naqshbandi Sufi order. Exiled after 1973, he founded the Afghan National Liberation Front (ANLF) in 1979. Selected head of the exiled Interim Islamic State of Afghanistan in 1989. Served as the acting President of the Islamic State of Afghanistan between April and June 1992.

Sayed Mansour Naderi Spiritual leader of the Ismaili community in north-eastern Afghanistan. His sons controlled militias in support of Najibullah's government, and defected to the *mujahideen* in 1992.

Dr Najibullah Student leader of Parcham faction at Kabul University before serving as Director-General of KhAD (secret police) between 1980 and 1985. President of Republic of Afghanistan between 1987 and 1992, when he resigned and took refuge in UN offices in Kabul. Killed by Taliban troops when they entered Kabul in September 1996.

Mullah Mohammed Omar Pashtun from Uruzgan. Taliban leader of the Taliban movement, and self-styled 'Amirul Momineen' (leader of the faithful), based in Qandahar. Now believed to be in southern Afghanistan or western Pakistan.

Yunous Qanooni Tajik from Panjshir. Key aide to Massoud during the *jihad* and Islamic State of Afghanistan. Minister of Interior in the Interim Administration during 2002, and currently Minster of Education in the Transitional Administration. Candidate in 2004 presidential elections.

Professor Burhanuddin Rabbani Tajik from Badakhshan. Appointed Professor of Islamic Studies at Kabul University in 1963. In 1972 selected as head of Jamiat-i Islami (JIA) and in 1974 fled to Pakistan. Acting

President of the Islamic State of Afghanistan between June 1992 and March 1993, after which he repeatedly extended his term until forced from Kabul upon the arrival of the Taliban in September 1996.

Professor Abdur Rab Rasool Sayyaf Pashtun from Paghman in Kabul Province. Lecturer at Kabul University where he was involved in the Islamic movement during the early 1970s. Imprisoned in Kabul between 1974 and 1980. Leader of Ittihad-i Islami, a group which participated in the exiled Islamic Government of Afghanistan, of which Sayyaf was 'Prime Minister' during 1989. A key conservative in the post-Bonn political order.

Nur Muhammad Taraki Founder of PDPA and leader of the Khalq faction. President of Revolutionary Council and Prime Minister of the Democratic Republic of Afghanistan from April 1978 until his assassination in September 1979.

Zahir Shah Pashtun, educated in France. King of Afghanistan 1933–73, after which he lived in exile in Rome before returning to Kabul in early 2002.

Parties

Hizbe Islami (Islamic Party) Led by Gulbuddin Hekmatyar, this is one of the seven major *mujahideen* parties based in Peshawar during the 1980s. It enjoyed the bulk of military support provided through the Pakistani ISI until 1994, when assistance began to be provided to the Taliban movement. Opposed to the Transitional Administration in Kabul, although there are reports of a rapprochement between elements within Hizbe Islami and President Karzai.

Hizbe Wahdat (Unity Party) The major Shi'a party, formed in 1989 when Iran put pressure on the various Shi'a factions to unite into a single organization. Split between groups loyal to Khalili and Akbari respectively after the Taliban took Hazarajat in 1998, but since reunited.

Ittihad-i Islami (Islamic Union) A conservative party led by Sayyaf, which enjoyed significant support from Saudi Arabia through the 1980s.

Jamiat-i Islami (Islamic Society) A *mujahideen* party that has long been led by Burhanuddin Rabbani, Jamiat draws most of its support from Tajiks in the north and west of Afghanistan. Its most famous commanders were Massoud and Ismael Khan.

Jumbesh-e-Milli e Islami (National Islamic Movement) Uzbek militia force led by General Dostum, who supported Najibullah before allying with the *mujahideen*.

People's Democratic Party of Afghanistan (PDPA) Communist party, formed in 1965 and spilt into two factions, Parcham (flag) and Khalq (people). Ruled Afghanistan from 1978 to 1992.

Taliban (religious students) Formed from some former *mujahideen* and religious teachers and students from the *madrasas* of Pakistan, the Taliban took Qandahar in 1994 and went on to control 90 per cent of Afghanistan. They are led by Mullah Omar. Now in opposition to the current government they operate organizationally out of Pakistan, although they still have supporters within the country.

An Afghan chronology

1839–42   First Anglo-Afghan War

1878–80   Second Anglo-Afghan War

1881–1901   Consolidation of the state under Amir Abdur Rahman

1901   Habibullah succeeds his father

1919   Habibullah assassinated; Amanullah takes throne. Third Anglo-Afghan War

1921   First constitution of Afghanistan

1928   Rebellions against Amanullah; Bacha i Saqao proclaimed Amir

1929   Nadir Khan takes Kabul; beginning of Durrani dynasty

1933   Nadir Khan assassinated; his son Muhammed Zahir Shah succeeds him

1949–52   'Liberal Parliament'

1964–73   'New Democracy' years

1973   Ex-Prime Minister Daoud stages coup

1978   Saur Revolution; PDPA takes power

1979   Soviets send in troops

1980   Karmal installed as President of Afghanistan

1985   Gorbachev takes power in USSR; Soviet policy towards Afghanistan begins to change

1986   Karmal goes into exile in USSR

1987   Najibullah installed as President of Afghanistan

1988   Beginning of Soviet withdrawal

1989   Last of Soviet troops leave Aghanistan

1991   UN tries but fails to get political settlement

1992   *Mujahideen* take Kabul. Under the Peshawar Accords, signed 26 April, Mojaddedi becomes President, followed by Rabbani. Fierce fighting in Kabul

1993   Fighting in Kabul continues; a new international effort leads in March to the Islamabad Accords

1994	Taliban rescue Pakistani convoy and move on to take Qandahar
1995	Taliban take Herat
1996	Taliban take Kabul; Najibullah executed
1998	Taliban take Mazar, the last major city Afghanistan to be in Northern Alliance control. USA attacks suspected Osama bin Laden training camps in Afghanistan with Cruise missiles
1999	The UN brings in sanctions against Afghanistan
2000	Further round of UN sanctions agreed. Drought continues
2001	Massoud killed by suicide bombers. USA attacks Afghanistan in retaliation for 11 September to remove Taliban from power. Northern Alliance forces walk into Kabul. Signing of Bonn agreement
2002	ELJ held in June in Kabul
2003	CLJ

Further reading

Cooley, J. K. (2000) *Unholy Wars: Afghanistan, America and International Terrorism* (London: Pluto Press).

Dupree, L. (1980) *Afghanistan* (Princeton, NJ: Princeton University Press).

Hopkirk, P. (1991) *The Great Game* (Oxford: Oxford University Press).

Levi, P. (1972) *The Light Garden of the Angel King* (London: Collins).

Maley, W. (2002) *The Afghanistan Wars* (London: Palgrave).

— (ed.) (1998) *Fundamentalism Reborn? Afghanistan and the Taliban* (London: C. Hurst).

Marsden, P. (1998) *The Taliban: War, Religion and the New Order in Afghanistan* (London: Zed Books).

Rashid, A. (2000) *Taliban: Islam, Oil and the New Great Game in Central Asia* (London: I.B. Tauris).

Roy, O. (1986) *Islam and Resistance in Afghanistan* (Cambridge: Cambridge University Press).

Rubin, B. R. (2002) *The Fragmentation of Afghanistan* [1995] (New Haven, CT: Yale University Press).

References

ACF (1999) *Food Security, Nutrition and Health Assessment, Sharistan and Dai Kundi* (Kabul: Action contre le Faim).

Anderson, B. (1991) *Imagined Communities: Reflections on the Origins and Spread of Nationalism,* rev. edn (London and New York: Verso).

Anderson, M. (1996) *Do No Harm: Supporting Local Capacities for Peace through Aid* (Cambridge, MA: Collaborative for Development Action).

Asia Watch (1991) *Human Rights in Areas of Afghanistan under the Control of the Republic of Afghanistan* (Washington, DC: Asia Watch).

ATA (2004) *Securing Afghanistan's Future–Technical Annex: Counter Narcotics.* <http://www.afghanistangov.org/recosting/index.html>

Baitenmann, H. (1990) 'NGOs and the Afghan War', *Third World Quarterly,* vol. 12, no. 1: 62.

Bearak, B. (2002) 'Unknown toll in the fog of war', *New York Times,* 10 February 2002.

Berry, J. de, A. Fazli, S. Farhad, F. Nasiry, S. Hashemi and M. Hakimi (2003) *The Children of Kabul: Discussions with Afghan Families* (Westport, CT: Save the Children Federation, Inc.).

Brahimi, L.(2004) 'Statement of Mr Lakhdar Brahimi, Former Special Representative of the Secretary-General for Afghanistan on the situation in Afghanistan, UN Security Council, New York, 15 January 2004'.

Brill Olcott, M. (2002), *Preventing New Afghanistans: A Regional Strategy for Reconstruction* (Washington, DC: Carnegie Endowment for Peace).

CARE (2003) *Policy Brief: Secure a Lasting Peace in Afghanistan* (Kabul: CARE International in Afghanistan).

Carlin, A. (2003) *Rush to Reengagement in Afghanistan: The IFI's Post-Conflict Agenda* (Washington, DC: Bank Information Center).

Chabal, P. and J.-P. Daloz (1999) *Disorder as a Political Instrument* (Oxford: James Currey).

Chopra, J. (2002) 'Building State Failure in East Timor', *Development and Change,* vol. 33, no. 5: 979–1000.

Chossudovsky, M. (2002) *Hidden Agenda behind the 'War on Terrorism': US Bombing of Afghanistan Restores US Trade in Narcotics* (Montreal: Centre for Research on Globalization).

Constable, P. (2004a) 'Afghan election process "alarmingly" slow', *Washington Post,* 16 February 2004.

— (2004b) 'Projects put strain on Afghan province', Washington Post, 24 May 2004.

Cooley, J. K. (2000) *Unholy Wars: Afghanistan, America and International Terrorism* (London: Pluto Press).

Cordovez, D. and S. S. Harrison (1994) *Out of Afghanistan: The Inside Story of the Soviet Withdrawal* (New York: Oxford University Press).

CPI (Center for Public Integrity) (2003) *Windfalls of War: US Contractors in Iraq and Afghanistan* (Washington, DC: CPI).

Cramer, C. and J. Goodhand (2003) ' "Try again, fail again, fail better?" War, the State and the Post-conflict Challenge in Afghanistan', *Development and Change*, vol. 33, no. 5: 911–33.

Curtis, M. (2003) *Web of Deceit* (London: Vintage).

Duffield, M. (2001a) 'Governing the Borderlands: Decoding the Power of Aid'. Paper presented at Commonwealth Institute seminar, London, 1 February 2001. <www.odi.org.uk/hpg/confpapers/Duffield.pdf>

— (2001b) *Global Governance and the New Wars* (London: Zed Books).

Dupree, N. (1984) 'Revolutionary Rhetoric and Afghan Women', in M. Shahrani and R. Canfield (eds), *Revolutions and Rebellions in Afghanistan: Anthropological Perspectives* (Berkeley, CA: University of California Press).

— (1998) *The Women of Afghanistan* (Islamabad: UNOCHA).

Durch, W. (2003) *Peace and Stability Operations in Afghanistan: Requirements and Force Options* (Washington, DC: Stimson Center).

Edwards, D. (2002) *Before Taliban: Genealogies of the Afghan Jihad* (Berkeley, CA: University of California Press).

Elklit, J. and P. Svensson (1997) 'What Makes Elections Free and Fair?', *Journal of Democracy*, vol. 8, no. 3.

Elphinstone, M. (1815) *Kingdom of Caubul* (Karachi: Indus).

Ermacora, F. (1990) *Report to the UN General Assembly* (New York: UN).

Fielden, M. and S. Azerbaijani-Moghadam (2001) *Female Employment in Afghanistan: A Study of Decree No. 8* (Islamabad: Inter-agency Taliban Edict Task Force).

Fry, M. (1974) *The Afghan Economy: Money, Finance and Critical Constraints to Economic Development* (Leyden: E. J. Brill).

Goodhand, J. and P. Bergne (2003) *Evaluation of the Conflict Prevention Pools* (Bradford: Bradford University, Channel Research Ltd, PARC).

Goodson, L. (2004) *US Strategy in Afghanistan* (Washington, DC: Center for American Progress).

Gossman, P. (1990) *The Forgotten War* (Washington, DC: Asia Watch).

Gray, J. (2003) *Al-Qa'eda and What It Means to be Modern* (London: Faber).

Griffiths, P. (2003) *The Economist's Tale: A Consultant Encounters Hunger and the World Bank* (London: Zed Books).

Hohe, T. (2002) 'The Clash of Paradigms: International Administration and Local Political Legitimacy in East Timor', *Contemporary Southeast Asia: A Journal of International and Strategic Affairs*, vol. 24, no. 3.

Human Rights Watch (1998) *The Massacre in Mazar i Sharif*, vol. 10, no. 7.

— (2002) *Fatally Flawed: Cluster Bombs and Their Use by the United States in Afghanistan*, vol. 14, no. 7.

IMF (2003) *Islamic State of Afghanistan: Rebuilding a Macroeconomic Framework for Reconstruction and Growth*, Country Report 03 / 299 (Washington, DC: IMF).

Johnson, C. (2000) *Hazarajat Baseline Study* (Islamabad: UNOCHA).

Johnson, C., W. Maley, A. Thier and A. Wardak (2003) *Afghanistan's Political and Constitutional Development* (London: ODI).

Kakar, H. (1978) 'The Fall of the Afghan Monarchy in 1973', *Journal of Middle East Studies*, vol. 9: 195–214.

Kaplan, J. (2003) 'Privatising Iraqi Health', *Prospect*, November.

King's College London (2003) *A Case for Change: A Review of Peace Operations* (London: Conflict, Security and Development Group, King's College).

Kleveman, L. (2003) *The New Great Game: Blood and Oil in Central Asia* (London: Atlantic Books).

Kolhatkar, S. (2003) Foreign Policy in Focus, 3 October 2003 (Znet) <http://www.fpif.org/commentary/2003/0310afghan.html>

Krugman, P. (2003) *The Great Unravelling: From Boom to Bust in Three Scandalous Years* (London: Allen Lane).

Kumar, K. and M. Ottaway (1998) 'General Conclusions and Priorities for Policy Research', in K. Kumar (ed.), *Postconflict Elections, Democratization and International Assistance* (Boulder, CO: Lynne Rienner).

Leader, N. (2000) *Report of Consultancy on Capacity-Building Strategies* (Islamabad: UNDP).

Lieven, A. (1999) *Chechnya: Tombstone of Russian Power* (New Haven, CT, and London: Yale University Press).

Macrae, J. and N. Leader (2000) *Shifting Sands: The Search for 'Coherence' Between Political and Humanitarian Responses to Complex Emergencies*, HPG Report no. 8 (London: Overseas Development Institute).

McSmith, A. and P. Reeves (2003) 'Afghanistan regains its title as world's biggest heroin producer', *Independent*, 22 June 2003.

Maley, W. (2002) *The Afghanistan Wars* (London: Palgrave).

Malikyar, H. and B. Rubin (2002) *Center–Periphery Relations in the Afghan State: Current Practices, Future Prospects* (New York: Center for International Cooperation, New York University).

Manuel, A. and P. W. Singer (2002) 'A New Model Afghan Army', *Foreign Affairs*, July/August: 44–59.

Niland, N. (2003) *Humanitarian Action: Protecting Civilians – Feedback from Afghanistan* (New York: United Nations, OCHA).

Ospina, S. and T. Hohe (2001) *Traditional Power Structures and the Community Empowerment and Local Governance Project* (Dili: World Bank).

Ottaway, M. and A. Lieven (2002) *Rebuilding Afghanistan: Fantasy versus Reality* (Washington, DC: Carnegie Endowment for International Peace).

Physicians for Human Rights (2001) *Women's Health and Human Rights in Afghanistan* (Washington, DC, and Boston, MA: PHR).

Rashid, A. (2000) *Taliban: Islam, Oil and the New Great Game in Central Asia* (London: I.B. Tauris).

Reno, W. (1999) *Warlord Politics and African States* (Boulder, CO: Lynne Rienner).

Roy, O. (1986) *Islam and Resistance in Afghanistan* (Cambridge: Cambridge University Press).

— (2003) 'Afghanistan: Internal Politics and Socio-economic Dynamics and Groupings' 2003. WriteNet.

Rubin, B. (1995) *From Buffer State to Failed State: The Fragmentation of Afghanistan* (New Haven, CT: Yale University Press).

— (1997) *Muslim Politics Report No 11.*

— (2003a) *Disarmament, Demobilisation and Reintegration* (New York: New York University Press).

— (2003b) Edited Transcript of 'Remarks Delivered at Seminar Sponsored by the Swedish Committee for Afghanistan'.

Rubin, B., H. Hamidzada and A. Stoddard (2003)*Through the Fog of Peacebuilding: Evaluating the Reconstruction of Afghanistan* (New York: Center for International Cooperation, New York University).

Said, E. (1978) *Orientalism* (New York: Vintage Books).

— (1997) *Covering Islam*, rev. edn (New York: Vintage Books).

Sedra, M. (ed.) (2003) *Confronting Afghanistan's Security Dilemma. Reforming the Security Sector* (Bonn: BICC).

Shahrani, M. N. (1998) 'The State and Comunity Governance', in W. Maley (ed.), *Fundamentalism Reborn? Afghanistan and the Taliban* (London: C. Hurst).

Snyder, J. (2000) *From Voting to Violence: Democratization and Nationalist Conflict* (New York: W.W. Norton).

Stapleton, B. (2003) *Security Developments in Afghanistan* (London and Kabul: British Agencies Afghanistan Group).

Starr, F. (2003) 'Karzai's Fiscal Foes and How to Beat Them', in M. Sedra (ed.), *Confronting Afghanistan's Security Dilemma. Reforming the Security Sector* (Bonn: BICC).

Stiglitz, J. (2002) *Globalization and Its Discontents* (London: Penguin).

Suleman, M. and S. Williams (2000) *Strategies and Structures in Preventing Conflict and Resisting Pressure: A Study of Jaghori District, Afghanistan, under Taliban Control* (Cambridge, MA: CDA).

Thrupkaew, N. (2002) 'What do Afghan women want?', *American Prospect*, 5 August.

Transitional Government of Afghanistan (2002) *Plan and Budget for 1381–1382 National Development Pogramme* (Kabul: Transitional Government of Afghanistan).

Turton, D. and P. Marsden (2002) *Taking Refugees for a Ride? The Politics of Refugee Return to Afghanistan*, Issue Paper Series (Kabul: Afghanistan Research and Evaluation Unit).

UN (United Nations) (1998a) *Memorandum of Understanding Between the Islamic Emirate of Afghanistan and the United Nations* (Kabul: United Nations).

— (1998b) *Strategic Framework for Afghanistan: Towards a Principled Approach to Peace and Reconstruction* (Islamabad: United Nations).

— (2002a) *Civil and Political Rights Including the Question of Disappearances and Summary Execution* (New York: United Nations).

— (2002b) Press Release SC/7429.

— (2003a) *Report of the Secretary-general to the Security Council*, S/2003/1212 (New York: United Nations).

— (2003b) S/2203/1212, UN.

— (2003c) S/2003/754, UN.

UNDCP (2000) *Annual Opium Survey 2000* (Islamabad: UNDCP).

UNOCHA (1998) *Strategic Framework for Afghanistan* (Islamabad: UNOCHA).

UNODC (2003a) *Afghanistan Opium Survey 2003* (UNODC/Government of Afghanistan).

— (2003b) *The Opium Economy in Afghanistan: An International Problem* (New York: United Nations).

— (2004) *Afhanistan Farmers' Intention Survey 2003/4* (Vienna: UNODC).

US Department of Energy (2001) *A National Report on America's Energy Crisis* (Washington, DC: US Department of Energy).

WFP (2003) *WFP Afghanistan Quarterly Report: July–September 2003* (Kabul: World Food Programme).

Woodward, B. (2003) *Bush at War* (New York: Simon and Schuster).

World Bank (2003) *Afghanistan: Transitional Support Strategy* (Washington, DC: World Bank).

Index

Rice, Condoleeza, 92
Richardson, Bill, 10
rights: ideology of, 74, 76; principles of, 69; universality of, 96 see also women's rights
Riyadh Agreement, 6
Rubin, Barnet, 201
Russia, 10, 88, 138, 139, 185, 186–7, 195–6; interest in drugs trade, 121
Russian mafia, 116, 192

Salma, a singer, 171
sanctions, 93
Saqao, Bacha i, 80, 138, 139
Saud, House of, 92
Saudi Arabia, 3, 10, 90–1, 92
Saur Revolution (1978), 141, 155
Save the Children organization, 66, 67, 207
Sayyaf, a warlord, 163
Sayyeds, position of, 52–4
seclusion of women, 80
security, as political problem, 209
segregation of sexes, at universities, 78
sexual aggression, 23
shabnama, 1, 6
Shah, Abdullah, 211
Shamali, 77; scorched earth tactics in, 70
Shari'a law, 77, 88, 91, 117, 124, 171
Sherzai, Gul Agha, 50, 51
Sherzai clan, 50
Shi'a Islam, 5, 28, 52, 97, 168; jurisprudence, 168
Shura e Nazar, 51, 61, 144, 158, 160, 163, 166, 176, 177
shura, 37, 41–2, 47, 48–9, 145; female participation in, 42
smuggling, 75; of drugs, 122
soap, use of, 79
South Africa, 108, 149
Spain, 196
Standard Chartered bank, 187
Starr, Frederick, 192
state, 135–54; failure of, 170–4; notion of, 65; re-establishing legitimacy of, 211; rentier, 192–4; strong, 159–63; tribalization of, 140

Stimson Centre, 159
Strategic Framework for Afghanistan (SFA), 69–73, 95, 150–2
Sudan, 216
Sunni Islam, 28, 52, 65, 124
Supervisory Council of the North see Shura e Nazar
Supreme Court, 163, 168
Suraya, Queen, 80
Swedish Committee for Afghanistan, 148
Syria, 86

Tajikistan, 121, 131
Tajiks, 52, 53–4, 61, 70, 135, 154
Taliban, 4, 7, 8, 9, 10, 11, 12, 13, 14, 35, 47, 48, 49, 56, 62, 65, 66, 67, 70, 72, 75, 82, 83, 87, 89, 96, 104, 167, 215, 216; ban on poppy growing, 113, 114, 116, 127–8; confrontation with, 66–9; demonizing of, 82; edicts forgotten, 75; isolating of, 93; portrayal of, in the West, 84; pressure on NGOs, 68–9; recognition of, 209; state structure of, 145–8 see also US, policy towards Taliban
tanzeems, 45
Taraki, Nur Muhammad, 138
terrorism, 10, 15, 101, 108, 129, 197, 214
Thailand, 100
Transitional Administration, 17, 19, 161, 164, 166, 173, 176, 178, 194, 201, 205
Trotskyism, 39
Turkey, 88, 122, 129, 133
Turkmenistan, 122, 215

ulema, 28, 40, 146
uluswal, 44, 162
Union of Soviet Socialist Republics (USSR), 3–4, 12, 14, 28, 57, 63–4, 97, 141, 153, 159; invasion of Afghanistan, 110–11, 141–2, 148, 180; occupation of Afghanistan, 39, 45, 47, 53, 113, 197; resistance to, 97; withdrawal from Afghanistan, 3, 61, 65, 177

Printed in the United States
35008LVS00003B/61-1008